A Passion

for the Land

John F. Seiberling and
the Environmental Movement

❧

Daniel Nelson

The Kent State University Press

KENT, OHIO

© 2009 by The Kent State University Press, Kent, Ohio 44242
ALL RIGHTS RESERVED
Library of Congress Catalog Card Number 2009016414
ISBN 978-1-60635-036-2
Manufactured in the United States of America

LIBRARY OF CONGRESS CATALOGING-IN-PUBLICATION DATA
Nelson, Daniel, 1941–
A passion for the land : John F. Seiberling and the environmental movement /
Daniel Nelson.
p.   cm.
Includes bibliographical references and index.
ISBN 978-1-60635-036-2 (hardcover : alk. paper) ∞
1. Seiberling, John F. 2. Seiberling, John F.—Political and social views.
3. Legislators—United States—Biography. 4. Environmentalists—United States—
Biography. 5. United States. Congress. House—Biography.
6. Environmentalism—Ohio—History—20th century. 7. Cuyahoga Valley
National Park (Ohio)—History. 8. Ohio—Environmental conditions.
9. Ohio—Politics and government—1951–   I. Title.
E840.8S44N45 2009
328.73'092—dc22
[B]
2009016414

British Library Cataloging-in-Publication data are available.

13 12 11 10 09   5 4 3 2 1

Contents

Foreword

Mark Udall, U.S. Senator, Colorado

I am impressed with the wisdom and balanced approach of this book and the excellent view that it gives us of the record of John F. Seiberling of Ohio.

While I did not have the opportunity to serve with John, I knew of his distinguished career and especially of his being a longtime friend and colleague of my father, Morris K. (Mo) Udall, both during and after his own service in the House of Representatives. John and my father not only served at the same time, they worked closely together on many measures that came before what was then the House Committee on Interior and Insular Affairs—now known as the House Natural Resources Committee. My father chaired the full committee and for ten years John chaired, sequentially, several of its subcommittees.

Examples of their accomplishments include legislation dealing with the strip-mining of coal, the Surface Mining Control and Reclamation Act, finally signed into law by President Carter after President Ford had vetoed earlier versions; the Alaska National Interest Lands Conservation Act, ANILCA (also known as the Alaska Lands Act), which was signed into law on December 2, 1980; and numerous acts for the designation of millions of acres of wilderness throughout the country.

Also, for many years John Seiberling was the voice of historic preservation in the Congress. He authored the legislation that created the Historic Preservation Fund and the 1980 Amendments to the National Historic Preservation Act, and he helped win passage of the first federal tax credits to preserve historic buildings.

Indeed, both as a private citizen and a public leader, John inspired and elevated the stewardship of our nation's land and its natural and cultural heritage. At home, he was a leader in saving the historic heritage of Ohio, including his birthplace, Stan Hywet Hall in Akron. And while he was the shepherd in Congress of more than sixty national park-related bills, he took special pride in writing and achieving the enactment of the act to protect the Cuyahoga Valley between Akron and Cleveland as a national recreation area, now a national park.

As his hometown paper, the *Akron Beacon Journal,* put it on August 5, 2008:

> John F. Seiberling often explained that in preserving land, we preserve something of ourselves. One generation sends an enduring message to its successors about what it holds dear. Who has forgotten the wisdom of Theodore Roosevelt and others advancing the cause of national parks? In that same way, Mr. Seiberling long will be remembered . . . for his vision in seeking to preserve 33,000 acres in Northeast Ohio, a vast urban parkland between Akron and Cleveland, and then having the political skills to turn the dream into reality.

The same editorial also noted an important point about John's character and why he was so effective here in Congress and back home:

> Almost anyone who spent time with Mr. Seiberling soon encountered his intelligence and wit. What his legislative colleagues and others appreciated was his modesty and civility, He listened to opposing views. Perhaps that stemmed from his own story, the scion of the family that founded Goodyear becoming a liberal Democrat. His calm, informed and reasoned approach proved most effective in aiding his causes. It meant that when he got his back up (say, his snapping "Who the hell are you?" at James Goldsmith, the corporate pirate seeking to consume Goodyear), his passion proved all the more persuasive.

Most telling, John knew who he was and didn't pretend otherwise. With his devoted wife Betty at his side, he cut a national profile conserving public lands while at the same time he understood his leading role in representing the city of Akron and its surroundings. He brought federal backing to the Akron-Canton Airport, the Goodyear Technical

Center, and other projects critical to the community. He didn't duck confrontations. He felt comfortable in his own skin and at ease in the face of opposition.

John led an admirable life. He might have been content to become the fine attorney and avid amateur photographer that he was. Instead, he jumped into the political fray and in doing so provided an example of what it means to pursue the highest standards of public life. That is something very much worth remembering and preserving.

This book builds on the legacy of John F. Seiberling and lets us know why he was a man whose principled legacy was so sound and so in the foreground.

Preface

This project originated nearly twenty years ago, shortly after John Seiberling's retirement from Congress. Loretta Neumann, a member of his subcommittee staff and a personal friend, began to collect material from Seiberling's sixteen-year congressional career and to interview individuals who had worked closely with him. Her goal was a biography. As the materials kept accumulating and she became involved in more pressing assignments, that goal gradually receded into the future. By the early years of this century she had a treasure trove of materials but still not enough free time to do the subject justice. I entered the picture in 2006, largely because of my familiarity with Seiberling's role in crafting the Alaska National Interest Lands Conservation Act, which had been the focus of my *Northern Landscapes*, published in 2004. As a professional historian I was also accustomed to working with the archival materials that were essential to this study. Although I am solely responsible for the research, organization, writing, and interpretative judgments that emerge from this account, I have been the beneficiary of Loretta's diligence and generosity. Her materials, together with Seiberling's private papers and the two major collections of his office files, have made possible this story of his contributions to environmental politics and environmental legislation.

John Seiberling was a legendary figure in Ohio politics and an indisputably significant contributor to the campaign to make the U.S. government more environmentally aware and responsible. He is worthy of a full-scale biography, one that examines in depth his personal life, beliefs, motivations, and interests. I have touched on all these topics, but only to the degree necessary to explain his involvement in the environmental movement of the last third of the twentieth century and his lasting impact on the nation's public lands.

I am indebted to Loretta Neumann, who gave me unrestricted access to her extensive collections, introduced me to many of her colleagues from Seiberling's staff, and read a draft of the manuscript. My colleagues George W. Knepper and Jerome Mushkat also read the entire manuscript and provided many valuable suggestions for improvements. David E. Kyvig read the section on the Nixon impeachment and was similarly helpful. Peg Bobel and Elaine Marsh, longtime activists in northeast Ohio, read the chapters on the Cuyahoga Valley National Recreation Area and offered valuable suggestions based on their recollections. Andrew Wiessner, Seiberling's staff expert on wilderness, likewise applied his judicious and critical eye to the chapters on wilderness legislation. My wife, Lorraine, as usual, did most of the initial typing and proofreading, saving me from a variety of errors.

I am thankful to all of these people and, most of all, to John F. Seiberling, who set a high standard for public service in the 1970s and 1980s, continued to be a keen observer of environmental politics in the years after his retirement, and was unfailingly helpful in the preparation of this book. Seiberling was able to read the early chapters. After his death on August 2, 2008, Betty Seiberling, his wife, with the help of several friends, read the rest of the manuscript. I am indebted to them for their openness, encouragement, and attention to detail.

DN

September 9, 2008

Abbreviations

AA	Alcoholics Anonymous
ACS	Alaska Conservation Society
AFL-CIO	American Federation of Labor–Congress of Industrial Organizations
ANCSA	Alaska Native Claims Settlement Act
ANILCA	Alaska National Interest Lands Conservation Act
BLM	Bureau of Land Management
BOR	Bureau of Outdoor Recreation
CVA	Cuyahoga Valley Association
CVNRA	Cuyahoga Valley National Recreation Area
FLPMA	Federal Land Policy and Management Act
FWS	Fish and Wildlife Service
GAO	Government Accountability Office
LWCF	Land and Water Conservation Fund
MSLF	Mountain States Legal Foundation
NEPA	National Environmental Policy Act
NIA	National Inholders Association
NPS	National Park Service
NRA	National Recreation Area
OSM	Office of Surface Mining
PVHA	Peninsula Valley Heritage Association
RARE	Roadless Area Review and Evaluation
SMCRA	Surface Mining Control and Reclamation Act
URW	United Rubber Workers

❧ 1 ❧

John F. Seiberling and His Times

Just before noon on Monday, June 22, 1969, an oil slick near the mouth of the Cuyahoga River, a quarter mile from Lake Erie and from Cleveland's Public Square, caught fire. Over the years there had been at least ten fires along the heavily polluted waterway, but this one proved to be larger and infinitely more influential than any of its predecessors. Alerted at 11:56 A.M., the fire department dispatched units from three fire battalions and a fireboat and had the blaze under control by 12:20 P.M. In the meantime the flames had shot up forty feet and had largely destroyed the Norfolk and Western trestle across the river and badly damaged a second railroad bridge. Downtown Cleveland office workers were treated to an unexpected but all too familiar show.

The burning of the Cuyahoga on that June day soon became a cause célèbre, a vivid report on the accumulated problems of midcentury urban America. The *Cleveland Plain Dealer* interpreted it as one more embarrassment for a tired and beleaguered city. "Cleveland, eh? Isn't that the place where the river is so polluted, it's a fire hazard? Yuk, yuk, yuk." Complaining that the river had given the city "a bad name for years," the editors called for more stringent regulations. "We are tired of Cleveland being the butt of a joke that isn't a joke."[1] A month later, in a widely noted article, *Time* magazine described the plight of American rivers generally, using the Cuyahoga as a lurid example. The article featured photos of the Cuyahoga fire and of Cleveland's mayor surveying the scene and bemoaning the blow to the city's image. A caption read: "If you fall in, you don't drown—you decay away."[2]

Unhappily for the residents of Cleveland, the Cuyahoga River conflagration became an enduring symbol of the problems that all cities, indeed virtually all communities, faced in the late twentieth century. The growing sensitivity to those problems, such as water pollution, had far-reaching results. Like racial segregation, poverty, and other contemporary concerns that evoked similar responses, pollution was most effectively addressed through national legislation, with uniform restrictions and an overarching regulatory authority. A series of congressional acts, notably the Clean Air Act of 1970 and the Clean Water Act of 1972, attracted bipartisan support and comparatively little opposition. President Richard M. Nixon's contribution, the Environmental Protection Agency, created in 1970 by a reorganization act that consolidated the staffs and duties of several existing agencies, was also widely greeted as evidence of a new determination to ameliorate the social costs of postwar prosperity.[3]

But the infamous Cuyahoga River had a second symbolic role, arguably as important as its association with pollution. For nearly a decade local activists had argued that the river valley—the area between the southern Cleveland suburbs and Akron, Ohio, approximately thirty miles to the south—was the last large natural area in an increasingly urban region and deserved to be preserved as a public park. The polluted river was an obstacle, but not an insurmountable one, as the waterway itself was too small, irregular, and unpredictable to permit more than occasional recreational activities. It was the broad and surprisingly pristine valley, the "green shrouded miracle," in the words of a later National Park Service author, bounded by steep hills on the east and west, that made the area appealing.[4] The river's periodic floods had discouraged farming in the nineteenth century and housing developments in the twentieth. An early canal, a later rail line, and a handful of farms and villages suggested, however, that the valley's relatively pristine condition was not assured and that the encroaching suburbs were a harbinger of the Valley's future. By the 1960s the campaign for a Valley park had enlisted public authorities in Cleveland and Akron; a variety of environmental, recreational, and historical groups; and many interested citizens. The most influential member of that diverse group was John F. Seiberling, a local attorney with a well-known name and a strong personal interest in the Valley and its possibilities. If revulsion against the burning of the Cuyahoga represented one major thrust of an emerging environmental movement, the campaign to preserve the Valley represented another, complementary expression of concern about the fate of nature in an urban-industrial world. Together, they accounted for the far-reaching changes in public policies toward the use and misuse of air, water, chemicals, and other dangerous substances and toward national parks and public lands generally that characterized the 1960s and 1970s.

Seiberling was well suited to this role. His family had arrived in northeast Ohio in the early nineteenth century, had flourished, and had become closely identified with the area's industrial growth. His grandfather and great-grandfather had, for brief periods, been among the richest individuals in the region, and even in the nation, but their fortunes had waned, and Seiberling inherited little apart from his name and the memory of living in the family's great estate at the north edge of Akron, overlooking the Valley. After a distinguished military career and a legal apprenticeship in New York, he had returned to Akron to work for Goodyear Tire and Rubber, the company his grandfather had founded at the turn of the century. In the late 1950s he and his wife had begun to buy land in the Valley, and in 1960 they had built a home on a steep hill in Bath Township, north of Akron, with a magnificent view of the surrounding forest and ravines. This move was suggestive of other changes in Seiberling's life: a growing civic role, notably in the burgeoning movement to preserve the Valley and in the larger environmental community; an association with the local Democratic Party (which made him something of a black sheep among the Seiberlings); and a more active interest in organizations devoted to world peace and, after 1965, opposition to the Vietnam War.

The antiwar movement prompted Seiberling's decision, at the age of fifty-one, to run for Congress, but his link to the Cuyahoga Valley was a better predictor of his political career and the mark he would leave, quite literally, on the American landscape. In part because of an abiding interest in land use, and in part because of the narrow jurisdictions of congressional committees, Seiberling would play a leading role in the wholesale reorganization of public lands that began in the 1960s and peaked during his congressional career. Together with a handful of other political leaders and a much larger group of political activists, scientists, and enthusiasts outside government, he would help redefine the role of public lands for a burgeoning urban and suburban population and an environmental movement that increasingly viewed the ecosystem as the basic landscape unit.

None of this would have been possible without the groundswell of public interest in protecting and preserving the natural environment that became the basis for a wide-ranging political movement. Earlier efforts to conserve wildlife, special landscapes, and other natural resources had had lasting impacts on public policy, especially in the form of parks and wildlife refuges. But the post–World War II growth of the U.S. and world economies and the proliferation of new technologies demanded more vigorous and complex compensatory measures. The emerging environmental movement was both more holistic in perspective and more varied in its organizations and goals. Seiberling, for example, worked closely with the Sierra Club, Wilderness Society, National Audubon Society, and other groups that had a strong presence in Washington, D.C., by the 1970s. Yet he also had frequent contacts with the Cuyahoga Valley Association, the many groups that fought strip-mining abuses in Appalachia, and the wilderness coalitions that appeared in most states with substantial national forest lands after 1977. The organized environmental community proved to be as protean as the problems it addressed.

As a member of the House, and a practical politician, Seiberling quickly gravitated to the northern "liberal" bloc that dominated the House of Representatives and to a lesser degree the Congress in the 1960s and 1970s. Although he scorned labels and insisted on his independence, he shared many values with other representatives of urban districts in the Northeast and Midwest. As a student he had become an enthusiastic supporter of President Franklin D. Roosevelt's New Deal and, contrary to family tradition, a Democrat. Like most Roosevelt partisans, he believed that government had a responsibility to set and enforce appropriate standards for economic behavior. The Seiberling enterprises had been based on private entrepreneurship and a strong sense of social responsibility, but they were exceptions. As Seiberling explained to an executive friend in 1975:

> I believe strongly in the free enterprise system, but I also believe that it must be subject to regulation where experience has shown the need to protect the public, and the system itself, from abuses. . . . I am old enough to remember the beginnings of the New Deal and to have heard at first-hand many dire predictions and complaints about the disastrous effect all the new regulatory agencies were going to have on business. However, as it turned out, the period since those days has seen the greatest material progress and the greatest prosperity and growth of business in our nation's history. . . . So

when I hear sweeping denunciations of government regulation, I am inclined to take them with a "grain of salt."[5]

He was more concerned about unregulated or poorly regulated economic activity. Appalachia was the best (or worst) example. Seiberling was alternately appalled and fascinated by that vast and beautiful region, where government seemed oblivious to the surface (or strip-) mining of coal and the devastating impact it had on both the natural environment and the region's citizens. The plight of Appalachia became a powerful argument for restrictions on natural resource industries in other regions, notably the West and Alaska. But the problem was even more complicated and challenging than the absence of adequate regulations. During the second half of Seiberling's congressional career he devoted most of his attention to publicly owned lands and the professional public agencies that managed or, according to the many watchdog environmental groups that monitored their behavior, mismanaged them. Even capable public officials could become captive to the powerful groups they dealt with on a daily basis.

These were challenging assignments, but nothing that would have surprised a student of contemporary public policy. What Seiberling did not anticipate and found himself largely powerless to influence was the economic turmoil that beset Akron and most other midwestern communities from the early 1970s to the mid-1980s, virtually his entire political career. The rubber industry, which had been so closely identified with Akron's growth and his family's fortunes, underwent a series of upheavals that made the city's future more uncertain than at any time in the previous century. Like most elected officials, Seiberling worked to ameliorate the effects of these changes (including the application of pollution standards to the city's industries). Yet, for all his flexibility, he remained independent and impossible to take for granted. He refused to cooperate, for example, when his union allies demanded protectionist measures to preserve jobs and traditional opportunities.

Seiberling's opposition to protectionism was an indication of an underlying distrust of politicians and government that was another theme of his career. One reason for going to Washington had been to make government more transparent and accountable. He and like-minded colleagues enjoyed some successes in the 1970s, but the challenge remained nearly as formidable in 1987 as it had been in 1970. He made even less progress in curbing

the Pentagon and its allies in the Congress. His frustration was evident in
a letter to one of his staunchly Republican uncles: "Obviously, even the
government of the United States cannot afford to go on indefinitely running
a deficit year after year. A great many so-called 'liberals' have held this
feeling for a long time, even if, unlike 'conservatives,' they did not make
it their battle cry. What do you think I have been talking about the last
6 years when I constantly proclaimed that our national priorities needed
some basic changes? How many times have I pointed out that waste in
government, particularly in the Defense Department, was slowly wreck-
ing our economy?"[6] In the meantime, his battles for parks and wilderness
provided more evidence that "nothing happens in Congress just because
it's right."[7] The only possible resolution of this dilemma, of flawed and
highly corruptible public agencies performing important, indeed indispensable services, required the presence of an alert and public-spirited
citizenry and enough honest, independent elected officials to maintain the
integrity of the system. He summarized this perspective in 1977 when he
told a Denver audience that he was often appalled by the "crassness" of
Washington. He preferred to "come out and listen to the ordinary people
who are approaching something not from the standpoint of selfish profit
but of what is in the public interest."[8]

Although Seiberling was involved in virtually all of the major political
controversies of his time, his greatest interest and his greatest achievements
were in the design and execution of public land policy. Casting himself
as a representative of all the people, he attempted to chart a course that
addressed the needs of a more congested and urbanized country, more
sensitive to the natural environment. That meant creating new national
parks, particularly parks near urban centers, such as the Cuyahoga Valley National Recreation Area; redefining the functions of the federal land
agencies, the Forest Service and Bureau of Land Management in particular; and limiting the managerial authority of the agencies by setting aside
public lands notable for their scenery, wildlife, unusual characteristics or
resources, potential for watershed protection or other distinctive qualities
as official wilderness, where commercial activities were forbidden and
government would tread lightly. Taking advantage of the public attention
that events like the Cuyahoga River fire had generated, he was among
those most responsible for the initiatives that resulted in a quintupling
of federal "acres managed for conservation" between the mid-1960s and
the mid-1990s, and for the new order in public land management that
accompanied and occasionally inspired that expansion.[9]

Seiberling's career is best seen, then, as an expression of the growing environmental consciousness of the second half of the twentieth century, a consciousness that took myriad forms and was shaped and given permanent character by a relative handful of individuals in and out of government. In the right place at the right time, Seiberling brought a refined ethical sense, a keen intelligence, and infinite patience to that task. Two decades later, the significance of that contribution is more apparent than ever.

❦ 2 ❧

Origins

"I am deeply disgusted with the way the world is rushing headlong into world war no. 3," John Frederick Seiberling Jr. wrote to an uncle on April 21, 1946. Three years of military service in Western Europe had made him aware of the "demoralization and disintegration that has been taking place in the democratic nations." During a brief interlude at home before enrolling at Columbia University's School of Law, he joined several concerned friends in founding the Akron United Nations Council. Meeting at the Akron Public Library on April 2, they had elected officers and formed committees; Seiberling agreed to serve as secretary. Their goal, he explained, was to "start the people as a whole to thinking creatively and in terms of basic principles again."[1]

Nearly a quarter century later, when Seiberling first ran for public office, he expressed similar sentiments. He was disillusioned with government, anxious about the future of the country and the world in the face of uncontrolled militarism and destructive military technologies, and yet hopeful of the people's ability to think "creatively in terms of basic principles." No less concerned about war—at this time, the Vietnam War—he was also alarmed by the accelerating assault on nature, the profligate use of natural resources, and an all too common tendency to disregard the environmental costs of economic activity. Immediate challenges drove Seiberling to seek political office just as they had led him to help form the United Nations Council. But they are only a partial explanation of his actions. A half century of experience as a student,

8

soldier, attorney, and member of one of the Midwest's most prominent families also contributed to his political awakening.

Family

The Seiberling family arrived in Summit County, Ohio, in 1831, when John's great-great-grandfather Nathan Seiberling, a Pennsylvanian, acquired land in the southern part of the county. Nathan speculated in agricultural land, prospered with the community that grew up around him, and fathered a total of fifteen children, eleven of whom survived to adulthood. The oldest son, John Franklin, inherited his father's business acumen. Sensing his neighbors' increasing interest in labor-saving agricultural machinery, he became an inventor and manufacturer. By 1861 he had a factory in nearby Doylestown, Ohio, where he made mower-reapers, the most important of the midwestern farmer's labor-saving devices. The Civil War was a great spur to business, as hundreds of thousands of Ohio farmers and farm laborers served in the army. Machines such as Seiberling's mower-reaper enabled Ohio's farms to provide an ever-increasing bounty despite the loss of so much of its labor force. In 1865 Seiberling moved his operation north to Akron, the largest town in the area, with good canal and rail service, and continued to prosper. He also became involved in a host of other enterprises in the growing community, including a flour mill and a theater. By 1890 Seiberling had become the richest man in Akron and Summit County: one of the region's handful of millionaires.[2]

Like his father before him, Seiberling had eleven surviving children, ensuring, among other things, that the Seiberlings of later years would be related by marriage to almost every member of the Akron elite. Two sons, Frank Augustus (1859–1955) and Charles W. (1863–1946), had particularly notable careers as business partners and entrepreneurs. Charles was genial and outgoing, often cited in the 1920s and 1930s as Akron's most beloved citizen. Frank was more energetic and creative. Restless, imaginative, adventurous, generous, unfailingly loyal to family members, he was also combative, outspoken, secretive, and remarkably irresponsible in money matters. He delegated most day-to-day responsibilities to subordinates and became involved in an ever-lengthening list of businesses. By his late twenties he was secretary and treasurer of his father's

farm machinery company, and treasurer, president, or vice-president of a
half-dozen other firms, including fire insurance and streetcar enterprises.
In 1895 he and other partners formed one of the nation's first interurban
train companies.

The overcommitted Frank was partially responsible for the overextended finances of the farm machinery company and its collapse during
the severe depression of the 1890s. Yet this proved to be only a temporary setback, as the ever-alert and curious young man concluded that
farm machinery had, in fact, little future in Akron, but that a relatively
new industry, rubber tires, had great potential. Taking his cue from the
fast-growing B. F. Goodrich Company, a manufacturer of hoses, tires,
and other products, and Akron's largest firm by the mid-1890s, Frank,
together with his father and brother Charles, had formed a small rubber
products company, which they sold to Goodrich in 1896.[3]

Now, with much of the rest of their empire in disarray, Frank recon-
sidered. In 1898 he began to sell stock in a new firm he called Goodyear
Tire and Rubber after the inventor of rubber vulcanization. His hunch
about the future of rubber was correct, as was his decision to emphasize
tires. With the advent of the automobile, the market for pneumatic tires
burgeoned, and Goodyear grew at a frenzied pace. In the mid-1910s it
overtook Goodrich and U.S. Rubber, the big New England manufacturer of rubber products, and by the late 1910s employed thirty thousand workers at its Akron complex, the largest in the world. During
those years Frank Seiberling earned more than $3 million per year, or
about $54 million in 2008 dollars.[4] Not only were the family's fortunes
refurbished, but also Frank was able to resume his career as a business
adventurer. He became a major real estate developer in the Akron area
and had other properties in Florida and Montana; was part-owner of
an Akron railroad and owner of the Midland Continental, in North
Dakota; and was involved in numerous other schemes. The finances of
all these enterprises were thoroughly intertwined.

At first Frank and Charles and their families lived modestly, in spite
of their wealth. Frank and his wife, Gertrude Penfield, daughter of a
prosperous Willoughby, Ohio, family who had attended Buchtel College
(the University of Akron after 1913) and was known as an accomplished
singer, had four boys and two girls. They lived first on Fir Hill and then
on East Market Street, the neighborhoods favored by Akron's well-to-do
families. Their East Market Street home was next to Frank's parents (his
father died in 1903, his mother in 1911). Their one extravagance was a

summer home on one of the Les Cheneaux islands off Hessel, Michigan, on the south shore of the Upper Peninsula. Frank's sister Grace and her husband, William Chase, the family's physician, had vacationed on the island in 1899 and highly recommended it. Frank negotiated with the owner, finally purchasing the mile-long island in 1900 for $640.[5] The Chases took the eastern half, the Seiberlings the west. Frank and Gertrude built a rustic, rambling house that he called Cedar Lodge; together with several other buildings, including a boathouse, the Seiberling compound could accommodate as many as thirty people. Gertrude hired local women to cook and clean and presided over what became a substantial resort as the Seiberling children grew up, married, and brought their families for several weeks each summer.[6]

Back in Akron, the Seiberlings remained on East Market Street, mostly to please Frank's elderly mother. However, by 1907, with Frank's fortunes improving, Gertrude's horizons as a leader of Akron society widening, and the house straining under the burdens of a large and active family, they began to plan something more appropriate for an affluent family. Together with his real estate speculations, Frank began to buy land for himself, choosing not the familiar but increasingly congested East Market neighborhood but a remote, undeveloped area in northwest Akron six miles away. By the mid-1910s he had purchased more than one thousand acres. Charles built a large but unpretentious home on West Market Street, a neighborhood that came to be dominated by the homes of the Firestones, their business rivals. In time Charles and his family spent most of their time at a large farm north of Akron.

With the death of old Mrs. Seiberling in 1911, planning for the new home accelerated. In 1912, Frank, Gertrude, and their selected architect, Charles S. Schneider, went to England to inspect historic homes. In view of the family's close association with the newest technology and manufacturing methods, one might assume that they would favor an avant-garde architect and a modern design. But on the contrary, they remained wedded to the aesthetic of Akron's conservative bourgeoisie. Their home would be a grand Tudor revival mansion, based on the fifteenth- and sixteenth-century English homes they visited. The timing was also critical. By 1907 or 1908, Frank had recouped his position as the community's most energetic entrepreneur but was no wealthier than he had been fifteen years before. By 1912 it was clear that the rubber tire industry had a far greater potential than farm machinery and that Goodyear, as the largest of the dozen or more Akron firms that now made tires, was positioned to exploit that opportunity. Frank's vision was already paying off on a scale unimaginable in the 1890s. He had originally planned to spend about $150,000 on his new mansion. But the English trip, the architect's prodding, Gertrude's ambitions, and above all, the vast wealth generated by the tire plants, made that plan seem grossly inadequate. By 1915, when it was completed, Stan Hywet, or "stone quarry" in Old English, after the property's most notable feature at the time the Seiberlings purchased it, had cost $2 million.[7]

This enormous undertaking taxed Frank's organizational ability as well as his bank account. The house had 65 rooms, 23 fireplaces, 469 windows, an indoor swimming pool, a gymnasium, a large music room complete with stage, and extensive servants' quarters. There was also a gatehouse, with living quarters for the estate superintendent; a large greenhouse with rooms for the head gardener; a garage and stable with rooms for the groom, chauffeur, and butler; and a house for the poultry superintendent.

The grounds were designed with no less attention and care. Warren H. Manning, a distinguished Boston landscape architect, worked closely with Schneider to enhance the external appearance of the house and the views from the mansion's windows. A London plane tree allée and a birch allée both extended for more than five hundred feet from the house. A variety of gardens, an apple orchard, a croquet court, a bowling green, tennis courts, a small golf course, and ten miles of bridle paths through the forests and rugged hillsides at the north end of the estate provided for every taste and hobby.

The Seiberlings became the employers of a large corps of domestic workers. The house required a dozen maids, cooks, and maintenance workers. Twice as many gardeners and laborers attended to the grounds, at least in the early years.[8] The annual cost of maintaining the buildings and grounds and paying the employees' salaries proved to be a huge and nearly insupportable burden as Frank's economic fortunes waned in later years.

Moreover, by the time Stan Hywet was completed, the family's need for such a large and diverse estate had considerably lessened. By mid-1917 most of the children were in boarding schools or college: John Frederick, known as Fred, the oldest son, went to Cornell; Willard, Penfield, and Frank Jr. to Princeton; and Virginia and Irene to finishing schools. They were only present during summer vacations, and then often at Cedar

Lodge, not Stan Hywet. Gertrude remained a major force in the local arts community and often served as the city's unofficial hostess to prominent visitors, but those activities only occasionally required a setting like Stan Hywet. In practice, the estate was an exercise in self-indulgence and pretentiousness and, after 1920, when Frank's fortunes crashed once again, a white elephant. It did serve one vital function, however. It was a home away from home for the entire family as long as Frank and Gertrude lived, a tangible symbol of family cohesion that persisted despite intramural disputes and physical separation, and a sanctuary for those like Fred Seiberling and his son, John Jr., who loved the property. When Frank finally died, at the age of ninety-five in 1955, the children agreed that it should not be sold. None of them was wealthy enough to live there, but they insisted that, if possible, the house and furnishings should be preserved as an educational or cultural institution.

Fred Seiberling personified the challenges that the Seiberlings would face after 1920. Born in 1888, he attended Lawrenceville Academy in New Jersey and Cornell for several years before leaving because of ill health. He went to Southern California to work on an uncle's ranch, and then to Montana, where the family owned a mine. In 1912 he and his brother Willard spent the summer in France. Returning to Akron he became involved in another of his father's enterprises, the Lehigh Rubber Company of New Castle, Pennsylvania. Fred, however, had little aptitude for business. He loved the outdoors, devoted much time to hunting and fishing, and became an accomplished amateur naturalist. In a revealing letter written at Thanksgiving 1917 cataloging the things he was thankful for, he listed, together with health, family, and American citizenship, his home. But, he hastened to add, "not only my Akron home but that equally splendid summer home in Michigan where I gained so much health and self-reliance and love for the great outdoors."[9] Had he been a few years younger, Fred might have found a satisfying career in the U.S. Forest Service, which became a haven for wealthy young men with Ivy League educations and a love of the outdoors. If he thought of such a career he left no record of it. More likely, he assumed that he would find a place at Goodyear or another of the Seiberling enterprises that would allow him ample opportunities for hunting, fishing, and similar endeavors.

In the meantime, Fred, who had a lifelong interest in guns and military strategy, joined the Ohio National Guard. In 1916 his unit was one of those President Wilson activated for service on the Mexican border, and Fred spent more than a year at Fort Bliss near El Paso, Texas. His service was neither significant nor satisfying; when the United States entered World War I, he badgered his father to use his friendship with Newton D. Baker, the Clevelander who was secretary of war, to obtain a commission in the regular army so he could escape the National Guard. That effort failed, but Fred was admitted to officer candidate school in the fall of 1917. He later went to France with his army unit but contracted amoebic dysentery and was sent home before he reached the trenches.[10]

Although his military career proved a disappointment, Fred's stay in Texas became a turning point in his life. Responding to the suggestion of one of his sister's friends, he met and was subsequently attracted to Henrietta Buckler, the daughter of a prominent local judge. Henrietta was a Vassar graduate who had majored in music—bright, attractive, and one of the most eligible young women in El Paso. Fred later boasted that she had had many suitors but had rejected them all in favor of him. By the summer of 1917 he confessed, "I'm completely in *love* with *Henrietta,* have been for some time" and planned to marry her, hopefully before he left for France.[11] Henrietta's parents were wary of the relationship and at first refused to consent to the marriage. Frank Seiberling asked, with characteristic shrewdness, "Are her parents opposed to your engagement, or merely to the early marriage?"[12] Fred assured him that they were only worried about the timing and the possibility that Henrietta might soon be a widow. A visit to Akron lessened their concerns. After all, the Seiberlings were not only extraordinarily rich but also gracious hosts and affectionate parents. They liked Henrietta and approved of the match. Presumably they also agreed to support her if Fred were injured or killed. On October 11, 1917, Henrietta and Fred were married in the music room at Stan Hywet. Frank gave the couple a Cadillac automobile, a building lot near Stan Hywet, and partial or complete forgiveness of a substantial debt that Fred owed him.

An exchange of letters between Henrietta and Frank in late 1917 hinted at some of the issues that would soon surface. She wrote, "I took Fred to vote yesterday for *suffrage* and prohibition—was that right? I am not ardent [Gertrude and Irene were active in the campaign for woman suffrage] but feel that there are often critical issues" that demand "the good brain and the unerring instinct of woman for Right. Fred let me have my way—so long as I am careful not to cramp his style—that 'style' never seems to bother us—in fact I most quite adore it."[13] Frank responded that Fred has "a rather hot-tempered, rash disposition, inclined to fight at the drop of the hat and to take ... desperate chances on results." He was thinking specifically of his possible behavior on the battlefield, but his observation can also be read as a comment on Fred's "style."[14]

The immediate problem facing the couple was the war and the long separations and anxieties it produced. Henrietta lived in Montgomery, Alabama, while he was stationed nearby and moved to Stan Hywet when he went overseas. She was pregnant by December, and on September 8, 1918, before Fred had returned, gave birth to their first child, a son, in the tower room, which had been outfitted as a nursery. The boy was named John Frederick Jr. The photos from that era show a happy, proud, and above all self-confident family, with Fred, having returned from Europe, still in uniform, and John dressed in the flowing gowns characteristic of the era.

At about that time Frank Seiberling made the greatest miscalculation of his long career, one that would prove irredeemable and force drastic changes on every member of the family. He had criticized Fred for tak-ing "desperate chances on results," but it was he who needlessly risked everything he had achieved. By 1919, Frank, now sixty years old, headed one of the world's largest, most technically progressive and benevolent corporations, was a pillar of the community, and was the proprietor of a vast showplace estate that required at least $50,000 in annual ex-penditures. He could have retired to devote himself to philanthropy or community service. At that time, Akron, by some measures the great-est boomtown of the 1910s, was increasingly chaotic and in desperate need of shrewd and efficient leadership. Or, if that was too radical a departure for Frank, he might at least have followed the example of his closest competitor, Harvey S. Firestone, and bought an annuity to cover his living expenses regardless of his business fortunes.

Frank, however, was unable to resist his gambler's instincts. The au-tomobile and tire industries had boomed in the previous years because of the automobile's appeal to people who had never yet owned a car and because of the rapid, inflationary growth of the economy in general. Now, with peace secured and millions of wage earners released from military service, the auto and tire industries would expand at an even more rapid pace. Seiberling bet on it, ordering vast quantities of rubber and other raw materials at the dramatically inflated prices of 1919. Given his role as Goodyear's largest stockholder and the many interconnections between his Goodyear and other investments, he was in effect betting his personal fortune. If Gertrude, or more likely, his brother Charles, protested at this unnecessary gamble, no record of the complaint has survived.

For more than a year, until the summer of 1920, the gamble seemed to pay off. Goodyear sales continued to rise; retail prices rose, making the high cost of raw materials seem more reasonable; and Seiberling's income and wealth increased. In the meantime, Congress slashed the military budget and scrapped many of the war-related programs that had appeared in 1917–18. With less fanfare, the Federal Reserve, anxious about the accelerating inflationary spiral, raised interest rates. The combination reduced total spending and made it more expensive for firms and individuals to borrow. By the summer of 1920 many manufacturers discovered, to their surprise, that sales had leveled or were even falling. They became more cautious. By the autumn they were forced to cut production and lay off workers. The winter of 1920–21 would be the most difficult since the mid-1890s, characterized by thousands, then millions of laid-off workers; collapsing prices; and many firms and individuals who had overextended themselves during the prosperous, inflationary years, facing disaster.[15]

By the end of 1920, Goodyear was on the brink of insolvency. As sales and prices collapsed, it suffered enormous losses. Tens of thousands of workers lost their jobs, but that did not suffice; because of the raw materials contracts Frank had agreed to, the company could not make money under any circumstances. Frank could have sought bankruptcy protection while he renegotiated his contracts and waited for the economy to improve, but he resisted that solution, supposedly because it would bankrupt many of his creditors, including relatives and family friends. (In contrast, about two-thirds of Goodyear factory workers lost their jobs, devastating whole neighborhoods in east Akron.)[16] Instead, he opted for a financial bailout. The Wall Street firm of Dillon, Read and Company provided additional capital in return for a large share of the company's profits for several years. It also installed one of its own executives as president and turned over day-to-day operations to George Stadelman and Paul W. Litchfield, Seiberling's key lieutenants. Stadelman died shortly thereafter, and Litchfield, the factory manager, would guide and dominate the company for more than thirty years. In May 1921, Frank found himself out of work, saddled with huge personal debts and temporarily worthless Goodyear stock. It was the 1890s all over again, and for the same reasons.

Frank reacted as he had at that earlier time. He rallied his local friends and business associates, bought a small tire plant in Barberton, Ohio, a suburb of Akron, and created the Seiberling Rubber Company. Charles became vice-president; Frank's son Willard and two of Charles's sons also joined the firm; Penfield, who Frank had been grooming for an executive position at Goodyear, arrived several years later, rose rapidly, and ultimately succeeded Frank as president. Between 1922 and the 1960s, Seiberling Rubber served as a professional haven for the male members of the Seiberling family.[17]

Yet the recovery was not complete. The auto industry had matured by the mid-1920s and was increasingly dominated by the largest firms. Tire quality and durability also improved rapidly, forcing the manufacturers to embrace technological changes that reduced the number of tires they could sell. Intense price competition increasingly became the hallmark of the industry. The Seiberling Company, which sold through dealers in the replacement market, grew slowly. It had a .7 percent market share in 1922 and 1.5 percent in 1928. Profitable by the mid-1920s, it never was more than a minor participant in the industry.[18] Frank's fortunes improved somewhat in this period, as his new company became established and his Goodyear stock began to pay dividends again, and he even tried to arrange a merger with Goodyear or U.S. Rubber. But the coming of the Great Depression shattered any hope of a return to prominence and wealth. Sales and earnings collapsed between 1930 and 1933, and the company skirted bankruptcy until 1938. Even in that year sales were only two-thirds of the 1928 figure. During this difficult period the elderly industrialist became best known as a spokesman for the small and precarious producers in an industry dominated by giant firms.[19] Despite vastly changed conditions, Frank's financial affairs remained as tangled as in earlier days. Penfield would later write that "he seemed to delight in operating on a 'rob Peter to pay Paul' basis—settling nothing, putting off the day of reckoning to some unknown future date, and then meeting with the reckoning at the time it arrived, as best possible." Nevertheless, Penfield acknowledged that "he had met with more than passing success, as somehow, some way, since the date he left Goodyear, he has managed to hold things together fairly well and work out of what seemed like inextricable position[s]."[20]

Troubled Years

If the Goodyear collapse was a setback for the Seiberling family that was only partially reversed in the following years, it was an even more serious blow to Fred. He had not yet settled on a career, and his accustomed financial cushion had largely disappeared. At the same time, his obligations were growing rapidly. John Jr. was followed by Mary Gertrude in 1920 and Dorothy in 1922. In early 1921, Fred and Henrietta planned to remodel a house on nearby Garman Road for their growing family, but the Goodyear debacle made that impossible. A December 1921 letter from Frank captures their situation: "It behooves both of us," he lectured, "to cut our expenses to the minimum and make no unnecessary purchases until our business gets on its feet. . . . I realize that with all the expense you are now being subjected to, it is going to be very close figuring for you."[21] Soon thereafter Fred and Henrietta moved into the gatehouse, Gate Lodge, which became available as the Seiberlings cut back their staff. It was small for a family of five, but for many years they lived there rent-free. Henrietta remained until 1944 and spent her summers at Gate Lodge until 1952.

In the meantime, Fred struggled to make a living. The Lehigh Rubber Company merged into the Seiberling Rubber Company in 1922, and his position disappeared. Sometime later he opened an automobile dealership on East Market Street, a half-mile east of his grandparents' old house in what had become a commercial neighborhood. Fred sold Star and Durant automobiles, manufactured by the Durant Motor Company, a firm created by William C. Durant, the founder of General Motors (GM) and one of Frank Seiberling's friends, after he had been forced out of GM. Like other Durant dealers, Fred struggled; the Durant cars were unappealing, and the company was unable to afford the advertising and other marketing techniques that GM was perfecting at the expense of the rest of the industry. It is doubtful if Fred ever made more than a modest income. By 1929 the Durant Company had collapsed, and its dealers closed their doors.[22] In the 1930 Akron directory, Fred is listed as secretary and treasurer of the Tandem Wheel Company, a manufacturer of truck wheels. That venture also failed, and Fred was unemployed for an extended period.

Fred Seiberling and his family were no worse off than many of their neighbors in the early 1930s. Like most industrial cities, Akron experienced waves of business failures and layoffs. The leading manufacturers

remained profitable, or at least solvent, by slashing production and lay-
ing off workers. By the end of 1932 employment in the rubber industry
had declined by nearly 50 percent. Many employees were reduced to
part-time work; though not destitute, they could barely afford necessities
and worried constantly about the future. Their anxiety was palpable.
For the less fortunate who were unable to find even part-time work,
the community offered little assistance. The traditional charitable agencies were overwhelmed, and there were only sporadic attempts to find
useful alternatives until the Roosevelt administration introduced state-
administered relief in mid-1933 and a work relief program several months
later. With that development and the beginning of a modest recovery,
the city's mood changed from resignation to rebellion. An explosion of
industrial unrest accompanied the revival. In the ensuing years Akron
would become as famous for strikes and class conflict as it was for tires
and rubber products.[23]

Despite their economic plight, the Seiberlings were effectively insulated
from the more general distress that characterized Akron in the early
1930s. In the first place, they, or at least Henrietta and the children, were
physically isolated. During the previous two decades, Stan Hywet had
served as a magnet for the city's upper class. By the late 1920s, most of
Akron's affluent families had moved to the city's northwest quadrant.
Frank Seiberling had accelerated this process with several real estate
speculations, including a large area east of Stan Hywet that he sold to
Paul Litchfield, his chief lieutenant at Goodyear. As Litchfield's star
rose, he built his own mansion on Merriman Road and sold lots to other
Goodyear executives. By the 1930s Charles Seiberling's home on West
Market and Stan Hywet, two miles away, roughly bounded the elite
neighborhood. In that area there was no evident distress, even in the
depths of the Depression.

Fred and Henrietta had other advantages as well. Their home was
rent-free, and as they exhausted their savings, they were able to turn to
a humiliating but effective private relief plan. In 1931, Frank Seiberling
began paying their bills with the understanding that they adhere to a
strict budget. Except for food and medical bills, and a $30 per month
auto allowance, they had to have prior approval for any purchases. Penfield, who was assigned to administer the arrangement, was sympathetic
but businesslike in dealing with his older brother. When an unexpected
invoice arrived, he explained, "While this item is small, they could
very well pile up into fifty, seventy-five or a hundred dollars on various

items without any knowledge on our part."[24] On another occasion he reprimanded Henrietta for buying flowers without permission. On yet another, he assured the clerk who was in charge of the account that he had investigated and found that the bicarbonate of soda Henrietta had purchased was indeed $1.19 "in the large size bottles." "There is no foundation to our suspicion" that she had padded the bill.[25] With each of these conflicts the tension between Henrietta and Penfield, and indirectly Henrietta and Fred, grew. Unlike most Akron housewives, Henrietta was accustomed to a life of middle-class comforts and had come to Akron with the assumption that her material world would expand, not contract. By late 1933 the clerk who had to deal with her on a day-to-day basis was fed up. "During this period I have been called every name speakable and still smiled and said nothing," he explained. "At times we failed to authorize certain purchases and later were obligated to pay the same, making you or I a liar . . . all of this being part of the game we played." He refused to continue, returning the checkbook, bank statements, and unpaid bills, including a tuition bill from Old Trail School, the local preparatory school that John attended.[26]

Hard times brought other problems to a head. Fred and Henrietta's marriage was marked by growing tensions. Fred was, in his brother's words, "a natural born naturalist." A friend later recalled receiving an eight-page letter devoted to the flowers and wildlife at Cedar Lodge. "Fred loved the woods and lakes and, best of all . . . he loved the vastness of the prairie." A trip to the Dakotas made him ecstatic. "This is it: here there is no limit—here is freedom," he had said.[27] He tried to get away for hunting and fishing whenever possible, seemingly oblivious to other obligations. Henrietta was disappointed and increasingly exasperated by her husband's self-absorption and seeming immaturity. These differences exposed deeper conflicts. As John Seiberling recalled, his father had "some dark sides." He "grew up feeling he couldn't match [his parents'] achievements." Fred was also impatient and headstrong, with a hair-trigger temper, qualities that his business failures accentuated. His small stature (he was 5'5"; Henrietta was 5'8") had not mattered in 1917, but it now contributed to his sense of insecurity.[28] By all accounts Henrietta was outgoing, friendly, and generous. But she had little understanding of the larger economic circumstances that had defeated her husband, accentuated his "dark sides," and made her life so unexpectedly difficult.

Their mutual frustrations led to heated arguments and occasions when Henrietta locked Fred out of the house. In 1932 he became a commission salesman for Seiberling Rubber and spent much of his time on the road. In 1935 he moved out of Gate Lodge and into the tower at Stan Hywet, where he lived until the last year of his life. He would stop to see the children whenever he was in town, and his relations with Henrietta improved somewhat.

The Seiberling children were well aware of these problems, but they, unlike the majority of children whose parents were poor, unemployed, or on the verge of divorce, had the benefit of a large and affluent extended family. The wealth of their grandparents, the comfortable neighborhood in which they lived, and the vast estate that lay at their doorstep, with its myriad gardens, forests, and space for games and sports, reminded them that the world was indeed a place of excitement and beauty, regardless of what might happen at home. Seventy years later, John Seiberling would recall:

> We looked on Stan Hywet as a wonderful playground. . . . There were secret passages to explore, trees and cliffs to climb, haylofts to romp in. We played games and put on plays in the Dell and the Japanese Garden. We fished for bass and bluegill in the Lagoon. . . . Our choice of sports included croquet, tennis, and golf. . . . In the winter we went sledding on the gentle slope of the great lawn. The more daring among us tried sledding on a steep slope north of the Lagoon. . . . We also skated on the Lagoon . . . and sometimes had a wild game of ice hockey.[29]

Most of the estate's land remained undeveloped in the 1920s and 1930s. Except for the area immediately surrounding the mansion, it was heavily wooded with mature oaks, maples, and cherries; there were steep ravines to the north and west and several streams. Apart from providing an outlet for youthful energies, the estate was also a place where the children could learn from their naturalist father. Here he was comfortable and informed. John recalled a 1926 outing with his father and sister Mary. "It was a perfect spring morning," he reported. Fred "told us the names of the different kinds of plants and trees as we went along, showed us skunk cabbage, dogwoods in blossom, violets, trillium, and other wildflowers. . . . It was a magical, eye-opening experience. It left me with a new, conscious love of nature."[30] The following year John contracted pneumonia and, his doctor suspected, tuberculosis, at that time a potentially fatal affliction. To aid his recuperation, his parents took him to El Paso to live with the Bucklers for what proved to be nine months. He became homesick, not just for his immediate family and friends, but for "green landscapes."[31]

The contrast between the opportunities available to the Seiberling children and those available to other Akron children, including some of their neighbors and school friends, was striking. The city had nearly tripled in size in the 1910s. To meet the need for housing, builders had put up block after block, mile after mile, of large, nearly identical, poorly built houses on small lots. East and south Akron, the working-class neighborhoods, were notable for their congestion, grim appearances, and lack of amenities. (The exceptions were Goodyear Heights, adjacent to the Goodyear complex, which Frank Seiberling had developed as a model workers' community, and Firestone Park, which Harvey Firestone had introduced in emulation of Seiberling. Impressive though they were, these developments housed only a handful of workers, mostly supervisors and highly skilled, long-term employees.) The distribution of community resources, notably schools and playgrounds, became the most heated local political issue of the 1920s and a harbinger of the intense conflicts that would characterize the 1930s. To most Akron families, Stan Hywet was a reminder of the chasm between the industrial elite and the rest of society. To John Seiberling, looking back forty years later as a member of Congress, it had a somewhat different function, a reminder of the need to preserve public open spaces near congested urban centers so that city residents of modest means could share the opportunities he had known as a child.

While Stan Hywet served as a private sanctuary for a fortunate few, it also became a catalyst in a larger movement of the 1920s, an effort to blunt the rough edges of city life and preserve some remnants of the natural world. Gertrude Seiberling was a founder of the Akron Garden Club (1924) and of the larger organization that coordinated the efforts of local groups across the country. The revival of the family's fortunes in the late 1920s permitted her to update the estate's formal gardens. Warren Manning returned for an extended period in 1928, and noted garden designer Ellen Biddle Shipman recast the English garden, creating an impressive setting for the gardeners' gatherings. Frank Seiberling embraced a larger vision. He was an early member of the Akron park board and remained an influential member of that group until he was unceremoniously removed in 1934 as the city's political balance shifted away from the traditional elite.[32]

During the years he served on the park board, Frank was responsible for two major initiatives. In 1925 he persuaded the board to employ the firm of Frederick Law Olmsted Jr., the noted landscape architect, to create a master plan for the entire community. This was a bold gesture, especially as the board had no money for land acquisition. The Olmsted plan, prepared in part by Harold S. Wagner, who stayed on to become the park system's longtime superintendent and a friend of the Seiberlings, emphasized the potential of the Cuyahoga River Valley just to the north of Stan Hywet. In 1929 Frank made the first substantial gift to the park system, the steep hillsides that marked the northern edge of his property and Sand Run Creek, which flowed into the Cuyahoga. It became and remains the most picturesque of the area's parks as well as the first step toward the creation of a metropolitan park system.[33]

New Directions

As the relationship between Fred and Henrietta deteriorated, and it became apparent that their differences were irreconcilable, Henrietta became increasingly anxious. Should she leave Fred and attempt to support herself and her children, perhaps in some other city? She would probably be dependent on Frank Seiberling for whatever support she received, and her prospects for meaningful employment were even poorer than Fred's. Given the grim economic conditions of the early 1930s, it made more sense to preserve the outward appearance of conventional family life and take advantage of the benefits that the Seiberling properties and name conferred. The emotional costs were nevertheless high and help to explain her behavior during the following years as she adopted a new, more assertive and independent role within the Akron community.

During the 1920s, a small, vigorous movement of spiritual reform had emerged in the Protestant churches of western Europe and the United States. Led by a charismatic clergyman named Frank N. D. Buchman, who had at first attempted to proselytize at American Ivy League universities and then at Oxford and Cambridge (hence the name Oxford Group), its American center by the early 1930s was Calvary Episcopal Church in New York City. The Oxford Group reflected the prevailing postwar disillusionment with society and its institutions. Buchman, unlike many of his contemporaries, rejected the hedonism of the postwar era. He called for a new kind of simplified Christianity, freed from dogma and bureaucracy with an emphasis on ethical behavior. He called for "absolute honesty, absolute purity, absolute unselfishness and absolute love." His followers thereby hoped to recapture the character of the original Christian movement. Their message struck a responsive chord in establishment circles, and Buchman was highly successful in recruiting wealthy and influential supporters. By the late 1920s, Calvary Church was hosting large gatherings of bankers and brokers from the city's financial community. By 1931 that group included Russell Firestone, the alcoholic son of Harvey Firestone. Russell subsequently experienced a religious awakening, became aware of his shortcomings, and, above all, stopped drinking.[34]

By 1933 Harvey Firestone was so impressed with Russell's recovery that he agreed to finance a large undertaking in Akron. Buchman and a number of his prominent and colorful European converts would preside at public meetings, and Firestone's minister, Walter Tunks of St. Paul's Episcopal Church, would ensure that Akron area churches cooperated. The Buchman contingent arrived in mid-January 1933, was welcomed at a dinner for 130 of Akron's leading citizens, and began the elaborate preparations that preceded the public meetings. On Friday, January 20, more than 1,800 people attended three separate meetings. A reporter noted that "evening gowns and tuxedos were in evidence, but did not predominate."[35] On Saturday there were sessions for business and professional men, business and professional women, and a grand rally in the Mayflower hotel ballroom, the city's most elegant public meeting place. On Sunday, Oxford Group representatives spoke at many of the city's churches, and Reverend Tunks hosted a final Sunday night meeting. Buchman and his wife and perhaps others among the foreign notables stayed at Stan Hywet.

The timing of the Buchman crusade was a revealing commentary on Akron society. The winter of 1932–33 was the trough of the Depression. Mass unemployment was the city's most notable problem. Poverty and deprivation were evident everywhere. Private relief efforts had collapsed, and local and state government were seemingly paralyzed, and yet Akron's most elaborate, best-financed community effort of that winter focused on the private behavior of the city's affluent citizens.[36] Oxford Group meetings featured personal testimony by Russell Firestone, his wife, Dorothy, or others such as George Hall Smith, an investment banker who explained how drinking and wild living had threatened his marriage and career, and how he had discovered the Oxford Group. Newspaper accounts of the events cite only one reference to the Depression, which Miss Ella Lee, a British guest, attributed to "impotent" Christians.[37] Although most ministers of affluent churches endorsed the Oxford Group, others were more skeptical. J. C. Fulton of the Goodyear Heights Presbyterian Church, whose congregation included many former or part-time Goodyear employees, reflected cynically that "the novelty of men in dinner jackets and women in expensive evening gowns attracts the attention of folks who'd nod through a sermon."[38]

Among the city's increasingly isolated elite, however, the Oxford Group meetings had a substantial, occasionally profound impact. After Buchman and his cohorts departed, local groups continued, usually in the form of house parties at private homes. One of these groups met at the home of T. Henry Williams on Palisades Drive in west Akron. Among the most enthusiastic members was Henrietta Seiberling.

Henrietta had been raised in a conventional Protestant household. One source reported that she was not an "avid churchgoer" but was an "avid student of the Bible."[39] The Seiberlings were members of Trinity Lutheran Church near their old East Market Street home but rarely attended; Henrietta was not a member. Like her friends and in-laws she attended the Oxford Group gatherings, in at least one case with John. The effect was immediate. The Group's message of unselfish love seemed tailor-made for her situation. Her daughter Mary recalled that she "became intensely interested in the teachings and story of Jesus."[40] She read the Oxford Group literature and began to attend the meetings at the Williams' home. She wrote in her Bible: "What does it matter if external circumstances are hard? If we give way to self pity . . . we banish God's riches from our lives and hinder others from entering in His provision. No sin is worse than self-pity."[41] She and the children joined the new Westminster Presbyterian Church in west Akron, because the minister was active in the Oxford Group.

Among those with whom she became acquainted at the Oxford Group meetings were Anne and Bob Smith. Smith was a west Akron physician whose behavior had become a source of concern. By early 1935 several members of the Group were convinced that he was an alcoholic. Acting on the principle of "absolute honesty," Henrietta organized a meeting at the Williams' home to call attention to his behavior. "Come prepared to mean business," she told his wife. "There is going to be no pussyfooting around." After much soul searching and prayer, Smith confessed that in fact he was a "secret drinker" and asked for help. That night a voice—Henrietta considered it the voice of God—told her that Smith "mustn't touch one drop of alcohol." When she told Smith of this "guidance," he was disappointed, expecting something more elaborate and compelling.[42]

Several days later Smith's confession took on a larger significance when a New York broker named Bill Wilson appeared at Gate Lodge. Wilson had made a fortune in the 1920s, lost most of his money in the 1929 crash, and began to drink heavily as he attempted to revive his career. Hospitalized for alcoholism in the early 1930s, he became involved in the Oxford Group at Calvary Church and resolved to help other recovering alcoholics. In early May he came to Akron on business. Disappointed with the results, he thought about drinking but instead called Reverend Tunks, who referred him to several local men, who in turn urged him to call Henrietta. "I'm from the Oxford Group and I'm a Rum Hound," he told her. "This is really manna from Heaven," she thought. She asked him to dinner, took him to church the next day to meet Smith, and invited the two men to meet at Gate Lodge.[43] The men talked for six hours, trading recollections and pondering how they might help others. Wilson was so excited that he decided to remain in Akron to perfect their plans. With Henrietta's help, Wilson arranged to stay at the Portage Country Club, the community's most exclusive club, for several weeks and then moved to the Smiths' home. She called or visited almost daily.[44] Out of their collaboration emerged Alcoholics Anonymous (AA), a self-help organization that spread rapidly and became and remained a major force in combating alcohol abuse. Henrietta attributed the remarkable events of May 1935 to divine intervention.

Henrietta remained active in the Oxford Group and especially its local "alcohol squad" for the rest of the decade. Eventually she became disillusioned with both the Oxford Group and AA. She was particularly unhappy with their increasingly secular appeals. As Mary recalled, "She clung to the inspiring version of First Century Christianity as it paralleled Christ's own methods. . . . She advised Bill [Wilson] against seeking Big Money contributions from foundations, etc. because she felt—and I remember her saying it—that if it was right and meant to be, God would see that the necessary funding would be forthcoming."[45] Her perspectives may have seemed naïve to the organization builders who succeeded Wilson and Smith, but they had an enduring impact on Henrietta's teenage children.

Making a Career

John Seiberling, fourteen years old at the time of his mother's spiritual awakening, was profoundly affected. He attended some of the Oxford Group meetings but was most influenced by the change in his mother's attitude and outlook. Her role in the founding of AA seemingly demonstrated the fruitfulness of the Oxford Group approach and the new life she had begun. By the mid-1930s she had regained a sense of purpose and a new, more focused religious faith. Her approach would inform John's religious perspective for several decades and his emphasis on honesty, humility, and consistency, regardless of external circumstances, throughout his life.

By 1933, when he left Akron for what proved to be more than two decades, John had had a number of formative experiences. From his father he had gained an appreciation for the natural world and the infinite complexity and interrelatedness of nature. He had also acquired something of the rich man's nonchalance toward money and position and, at the same time, a distaste for the scheming that was so much a part of his grandfather's character. From his mother's experience he had developed a strong ethical sense and an appreciation of high culture. He was well versed in classical music and poetry. He recalls that his mother insisted that they go to a Cleveland dentist, which required long auto trips. "Once to pass the time I brought a copy of Grays' 'Elegy Written in a Country Churchyard' with me, and I read it through several times and memorized the whole poem."[46] Yet he knew almost nothing of the community where he lived, not to mention the world around him.

That exposure would come quickly and profoundly in the following decade. He left Stan Hywet and Akron in the fall of 1933 and, apart from a few summer vacations when he worked on the Stan Hywet garden crew, and holidays, did not return until 1954. He grew to be over six feet tall, reflecting the Buckler side of his family, and towered over his father and other male Seiberling relatives, who tended to be short and heavyset. His earnest manner and interest in literature, history, and the arts also set him apart. Still, he remained close to his parents and to his myriad uncles, aunts, and cousins, even though he spent little time with them. In the meantime he compiled a record of conspicuous success that marked him as a young man on the rise.

These developments began with an inauspicious start at Buchtel High School, the west side school that served the children of Akron's well-to-do families, in 1932–33. Whether the problem was the tension and conflict that increasingly marked his parents' relationship, the stresses of adolescence, or some combination is not clear, but his academic performance was sufficiently troubling to call for remedial action. One of the Seiberling Rubber executives had a son at Staunton Military Academy in Staunton, Virginia, and was doing well. After extended discussions, and assurances of financial assistance from Frank and Gertrude, Fred and Henrietta decided that John should go to Staunton as well. He was agreeable and entered in the fall of 1933.

Staunton was a type of preparatory school that flourished in the pre-Vietnam era. Uniforms, military discipline, and an all-male atmosphere were thought to reduce the undesirable temptations of the high school milieu and to inculcate self-discipline and seriousness. Because the tuition was beyond the means of most American families, the students were drawn from the upper class. Many came from troubled situations or families that were living outside the United States or had seemed susceptible to antisocial influences. The school did not try to create professional soldiers; it sought to ensure that spirited, often rambunctious and occasionally reckless youths stayed out of trouble and continued their education at respectable universities.

The Staunton school dated from the nineteenth century, developed a wide reputation in the early twentieth century, and reached its apogee in the years after World War I. A majestic campus in the Blue Ridge foothills, a rigorous academic program, and a variety of approved extracurricular activities made it irresistible to many affluent parents. The school's best-known alumnus of that period was Barry Goldwater, the Arizona senator and 1964 presidential candidate, but many others who achieved distinction in professions or business counted themselves among its alumni. Like many of his contemporaries, Seiberling responded positively to this environment. The uniforms and marching did not interest him, but the personal freedom, the camaraderie of the boys, and, very likely, the relief from the Gate Lodge atmosphere proved exhilarating; his grades improved and he graduated as an honor student.[47]

Staunton thus provided detachment from his family without replacing it. Apart from ties that were renewed during vacations, a steady stream of letters kept him up-to-date on family affairs and, especially, Henrietta's Oxford Group activities. In September 1936, at the beginning of John's senior year, she wrote, for example, that "there is not much news," but then added that she had had "8 alcoholics and wives" at Gate Lodge on Sunday, and would have Clifton Slusser, Goodyear's powerful vice-president and a notorious alcoholic, at the next meeting. Henrietta and her associates had "prayed for a guided way to get at Slusser for some time." His decision to attend was a coup for her group, though the session apparently proved less inspiring to Slusser, who continued on his disastrous course. She was more interested, however, in John's new role as the head of a YMCA group at the school.

> I got a guided vision and am sure of the tremendous possibilities you have there. You may start with just a handful of maybe pious boys who are religiously inclined but devoid of power. Now you can get them to find the Way. They are at least *seeking*. If you can get them to see that . . . they are really *changed*, their lives will radiate something that will make the whole school want to be like them. . . .
>
> I would suggest that . . . you open your meeting with the customary prayer and a time of quiet . . . when every man tries not only to ask God what his plan is for him and how he would like him changed, but that each one write down the thoughts. . . . Give them the idea of 2 way prayer and listening as well as asking. Then take the Quiet Hours 5c/ pamphlet [an Oxford Group publication] to study together about God's guidance — there are Bible references to look up and your YMCA work, emphasize, is not routine organization — It must be all "organism" not just organization — working to build bridges from 1 human to another, class to class, from race to another race, nation to nation —
> It must not be an institution
> Nor a point of view
> It must start a spiritual revolution by
> Starting one in you.[48]

Although there is no evidence that the eighteen-year-old Seiberling shared his mother's proselytizing zeal, the fact that she wrote in such a vein, with confidence that he would take her lectures seriously, was illuminating. He had grown into a serious, studious young man, an intellectual, and to some degree an idealist, who subscribed to his mother's faith in the improvability if not the perfectibility of humankind. He recalled that the Oxford Group "made a big difference in my life. . . . It helped me get through military school because it gave me the perspectives I might not otherwise have had, as well as [a commitment] to really try to see that my parents and grandparents . . . got their money's worth."[49] It had no less significance for his future. "The worst sin of all," Henrietta was fond of saying, "is a sin against the spirit of the truth. Christ had no use for hypocrites. It's important not only being right but the appearance of being right. How you are inside is the most important thing."[50]

Seiberling's father and uncles had all attended Ivy League schools, and with the promise of Frank's continuing financial support, there was no reason for John not to follow in their footsteps. (Mary and Dorothy both followed their mother's example and enrolled at Vassar.) Three of his uncles were Princeton alumni, but Frank Jr., the youngest uncle and by virtue of his youth and broad cultural interests, a major influence on John at this stage, told him that he was "too serious a student to want to go to Princeton." He recommended Harvard or the University of Chicago.[51] John applied to Harvard and, to the surprise of some who recalled his experience at Buchtel, was admitted.

In Cambridge, John joined a talented but diverse group of young men, many of whom would become household names over the next quarter century. Journalist Theodore H. White, a senior during Seiberling's freshman year, recalled that the Harvard student body consisted of three distinct factions. There were "white men," prep school grandees who lived comfortably and fashionably, with automobiles, luxurious apartments, and elegant clothes. They devoted themselves to debutante balls, country club parties, and other social events as they completed their preparation for careers in family banks or law firms. Next were the "gray men," bright public high school graduates of more limited resources who studied hard, sustained the university's extracurricular organizations and athletic teams, and generally prepared to make their way in the world. Finally, there were the "meatballs," the scholarship students of modest means, many of Italian or Jewish origins, who were separated from the others by virtue of their limited resources and humble backgrounds.[52] Seiberling had some claim to "white man" status, a well-known name and a prep school education, but lacked the financial resources necessary to join in his classmates' activities. During his junior year he won a scholarship, but it was an honorary distinction, recognition of his superior academic record. In other respects, he was a prototypical gray man.

Like many of his classmates, Seiberling found the Harvard atmosphere exhilarating. He was drawn to history, one of the most demanding majors with a distinguished faculty, in White's terms, "a colony of storytellers."

Roger Bigelow Merriman, a spellbinding classroom performer, taught an introductory course in European history that persuaded a generation of social science–oriented students, including Seiberling, to opt for history over political science. Frederick Merk mesmerized students with his accounts of the role of the West in American history. And Michael Karpovich, a Russian émigré and classicist who became Seiberling's junior year tutor, was popular among the students for his exotic background and command of early European history.[53]

Although most of these professors dealt with the distant past, their courses helped reorient Seiberling's perception of contemporary politics. His family, like most wealthy families of the time, had been economically conservative and Republican. Even the turmoil that had engulfed his immediate family had not shaken his parents' political orientation. But among young people coming of voting age after 1933, there was a wholesale shift, and Seiberling was no exception. His study of history and government provided a new perspective and convinced him of the potential of activist government. By 1940 he had become an enthusiastic New Dealer.

Like most of President Roosevelt's supporters, he believed that laissez-faire capitalism concentrated excessive power and wealth in the hands of a small minority and led to debacles like the Depression. Government regulation would curb the excesses, preserve competition, and strike a balance between private and public spheres. Government was also the only institution that could provide an effective safety net for the elderly, the handicapped, and the unemployed. More dramatic was his conversion to the administration's foreign policy. Like most midwesterners and most outspoken college students of his generation, Seiberling had been an isolationist. But the German invasion of Poland, the "phony war," and the collapse of France, all during his junior year, posed serious challenges for traditional isolationists. The intense national debate between America First and the Roosevelt administration's allies, which culminated in the spring and summer of 1941, as he was preparing to graduate, forced him to reexamine his position. The magnitude of the threat represented by Nazi Germany and the moderation of the president's calls for aid to Britain and other opponents of Germany were ultimately persuasive. He graduated an interventionist, ready, if necessary, to serve in the armed forces.[54]

Seiberling's new political consciousness must have surprised and disappointed his relatives and Akron acquaintances, who undoubtedly attributed his apostasy to the malignant influence of his Harvard professors.[55] The Harvard faculty, and the history faculty in particular, were largely left-of-center in political orientation and probably had some influence, as did Seiberling's exposure to the world beyond Akron and rural Virginia. But there were other factors as well. Frank Seiberling's devotion to the Akron park system underlined the need for a broader perspective on society's needs. Fred's interest in the outdoors could be interpreted as a critique of the assumption that natural resources were mere raw materials for industry. Henrietta emphasized the individual's potential for improvement. In combination, these perspectives help to explain Seiberling's conversion to activist government and the directions he took afterward.

A New Era

Seiberling graduated from college in June 1941, with the United States already involved in an undeclared naval war with Germany and engaged in tense negotiations with Japan over the future of Southeast Asia and China. It would be hard to imagine a more challenging time to embark on a career. Yet there were also opportunities associated with military service and with a transformed and rapidly growing postwar economy. A supporter of Roosevelt's foreign policy, Seiberling was preoccupied with the crisis at hand. Yet unlike his father a quarter century before, he found that military duty opened doors and pointed him toward a new career that he might not have otherwise considered.

He was better prepared for military service than most men of his generation. His prep school background had given him a taste of military life, and his political awakening, at a time when a majority of Americans remained wary of the conflict, made this war seem justified, even necessary. His university degree placed him in the small circle of men of his age with obvious leadership potential. Returning to Akron after graduation, he worked at Goodyear as a management trainee through the Pearl Harbor crisis and, encouraged by a high draft number and the prospect of officer candidate school, enlisted in the army in March 1942. Assigned to the Quartermaster Corps, he took basic training at Camp Lee, Virginia, and was sent to officer candidate school in Mississippi. After graduating in September, he was assigned to the 131st Q. M. Truck Battalion, possibly, or so he believed, because he was assumed to know something about tires and trucks. The battalion had already been ordered to England. In October, Seiberling and other members of the battalion traveled to Fort Dix, New Jersey, where he served as liaison with the port authorities in New York. In December the battalion sailed aboard the Queen Mary.[56]

In Europe, Seiberling moved up rapidly, rising from second lieutenant to major in the Transportation Corps, which became a separate administrative entity in 1943. After months in Cheltenham, the battalion was ordered to London where Seiberling and his fellow officers were assigned to help plan the Normandy invasion. He was supposed to determine "what kind of trucks and what kind of truck organizations we were going to need to take the invasion through the first 90 days." On receiving his orders, he remarked to the commanding officer: "Gosh Colonel, I don't know anything about this." The colonel replied: "Neither does anyone else. You went to Harvard, didn't you?"[57] What Seiberling soon discovered, to his discomfort, was that the Pentagon paid little attention to his analyses. On the eve of the invasion the transport planners had less than 1 percent of the heavy-duty trucks they had ordered. They had little choice but to improvise and hope for the best.

Seiberling landed on Utah Beach in Normandy in late July, six weeks after the initial invasion. He had bittersweet recollections of that day: "It was towards evening. We had spent the day unloading the freighter, lowering tanks and trucks and gear onto landing craft that took them onto the shore. As we finished that and finally pulled up to the shore—it was a beautiful evening. . . . And as we landed I looked up and I happened to see far above us in the sky a V-formation of wild geese flying. It immediately took me back to my boyhood days in the Upper Peninsula of Michigan . . . and just gave me a tremendous lift of Spirit."[58]

This was one of the few moments of reflection he was able to enjoy during his first hectic months in France. The biggest problem he and his colleagues faced was a severe shortage of trucks and drivers. During the first weeks of the invasion, when the battlefield was confined to a small area in Normandy, they could improvise. But by late July, after the St. Lo breakout, when Allied soldiers began to move rapidly inland, the Transportation Corps began a "desperate effort to keep pace with the advancing armies."[59] Seiberling spent his first month in France racing from depot to depot, trying to make the overextended system work.

In late summer he was ordered to Paris to organize an office devoted to emergency situations. The timing was auspicious. Two months later the German counteroffensive known as the Battle of the Bulge became a major test of the army's ability to mobilize additional troops and equipment. Seiberling's office was responsible for assembling the hundreds of trucks that rushed troops and supplies to the front. When the German offensive had been blunted and the Allied advance into Germany resumed, the problems of military transport became even more formidable. Gen. Franklin S. Ross, the chief of transportation, faced "an acute motor transport equipment shortage."[60] Finally, he ordered his staff to find someone "who doesn't know anything about" the mess, "so he won't get bogged down in details."[61] They picked Seiberling, who suddenly found himself in charge of a staff of eighty, with several men who outranked him, and with far-reaching responsibilities and powers. Two hectic months followed, but by March 1945 the crisis had passed. The army historians note prosaically that "the dislocations in the transportation system were rapidly corrected."[62]

More bottlenecks emerged after the German surrender, when the overworked French rail system approached paralysis. Seiberling was a member of the team of American officers who investigated. They discovered that the French authorities were giving precedence to the return of refugees and concentration camp inmates. The scenes of these people, gathered at railway stations, were a chilling reminder of the brutality of the struggle.

At the end of the war, General Ross singled out the Motor Transport Service for special praise. Its work was characterized, in the words of the army historians, by "improvisation, overwork, inadequate maintenance and communications and rough operating conditions."[63] Shortly after returning to the United States, Ross happened to meet Fred Seiberling in Washington, where Fred was managing Seiberling Rubber's government contracts. Ross noted that John had done "a magnificent job" in France. The general "never ceased to be amazed how one who talks so slowly and moves so slowly could think so fast and accurately, and decide so wisely, and then effect the execution of his decisions so splendidly."[64] For his efforts Seiberling received the Bronze Star, Legion of Merit, and other decorations from the French and Belgian governments.

During the more relaxed months of summer and fall 1945, Seiberling was at last able to enjoy his European sojourn. He visited the Riviera and many of the cultural attractions of Paris. The high point, however, came in late summer when he received an unexpected phone call: "This is Betty Behr. I'm a friend of your sister Dotty." Elizabeth "Betty" Behr, a 1943 Vassar graduate, had worked for the Office of Strategic Services in London and, after the war, in Wiesbaden, Germany. Seiberling thought to himself, "Well, I ought to be nice to my sister's friend and invited her to have dinner with me at our officers' mess." Afterward they went to the Lido nightclub. A month later, Seiberling was in Germany and stopped in Wiesbaden to say hello. As he was leaving, his driver turned to him: "That's marrying stuff, Major."[65] After their return to the United States they continued to meet occasionally, as Betty's family lived in Brooklyn and Seiberling's mother and sisters now lived in Manhattan.

Seiberling would soon join them. Demobilized in late 1945, he joined the throng of soldiers who were deciding what to do with their lives. Three years in Europe and the war experiences had had an effect comparable to his earlier exposure to the Harvard liberals. The contrast between the cultural richness of Europe and the destruction and loss of life caused by the war left an indelible impression. The challenge of preserving peace in a highly militarized world, and the threat of new wars, even nuclear war, would remain major concerns. The immediate outlook was not good, but he did not despair. His role in the formation of Akron's United Nations Council in the spring of 1946 was the first of many such associations with the goals of promoting disarmament and international dialogue.

He also abandoned any thought of returning to the Goodyear training program and a career in corporate management. (Within the Seiberling clan, his high-mindedness was viewed with ill-disguised scorn. At the time he was active in the UN Council, the Seiberling Rubber workers went on strike and occupied the plant. Frank Seiberling supposedly quipped that "if there's another strike at the factory, we'll just send John down to talk about world federalism, and when they're all asleep, we take back the factory.")[66] His grandfather Buckler's career as a lawyer and judge had always interested him. He soon decided on the law as an alternative career that would be compatible with his new interests. He applied to the Harvard University and Columbia University law schools, with Columbia as his first choice. Taking advantage of the G.I. Bill, he enrolled there in the fall of 1946.

Seiberling attended Columbia from 1946 to 1949. Henrietta reported in March 1947: "John has one week's vacation which he plans not to take but we are plotting to get him here [their Manhattan apartment] and make him rest a little. He looks like a war wraith. He studies night and day and [sister] Mary G. was shocked to see him last night. He takes 2 hours off once a week to eat with us. . . . John has his first case to try tomorrow and he will not let one little line of printed matter slip by. His capacity to work is far beyond physical endurance."[67] His hard work and attention to detail paid off, and he graduated with honors. Shortly afterward he began his legal career at the New York law firm of Donovan, Leisure, Newton, Zimbard and Irvine, at that time one of the leaders of the Wall Street legal community.

Despite his long hours in the library, Seiberling had also found time to continue his courtship of Betty Behr, then working in Washington, D.C. Betty was well acquainted with his sisters and mother and during the summer of 1947 joined Dorothy and other family members at the Seiberlings' Michigan retreat for several weeks. In the meantime Seiberling "woke up one morning thinking Betty Behr is the nicest girl I know. I realized I was in love with her." When she returned to New York in the summer of 1948, they went to dinner several times and spent a day at the beach. Before Betty returned to Washington, Seiberling proposed. Her reply was "I'll think about it." Several months later, having concluded that he was serious, she accepted.[68] They were married on June 4, 1949, shortly after his graduation.

By all accounts it proved to be a highly successful union, based on mutual devotion, shared values, and common interests. Outwardly, they were indistinguishable from their upper-middle-class friends and neighbors. John devoted most of his time to his career and, after the mid-1960s, to the political initiatives that ultimately made him an attractive congressional candidate. Betty managed their home and growing family, which included three sons by the mid-1950s. She was also interested in a variety of community activities, though she seldom appears in the letters and reports that document John's political rise. Still, they made major decisions together, and she was one of his most enthusiastic political supporters, even when his actions were unpopular among members of their extended family and created financial strains for their immediate family.

Seiberling was soon immersed in his new career. His salary at Donovan, Leisure was high by the standards of that era, and the exposure to the commercial life of New York at a time of renewed prosperity, rising optimism, and the city's unquestioned leadership in domestic and international finance was invaluable. Yet he was not satisfied. He disliked New York, the crush of people, absence of green space, and difficulty of getting away to the country. "I hated living in New York," he recalled. "We had to travel miles to get away from the concrete streets."[69] The Seiberlings had two sons by 1954 (a third would be born in 1956), and he could not imagine raising a family there unless they moved to a distant suburb and he undertook a long daily commute. Despite the presence of his mother and Betty's family in New York, it did not seem like a suitable home. In late 1953 he learned of an opening in the legal department at Goodyear. Contacting the general counsel, he arranged an interview and was offered a position as a staff attorney. He eagerly accepted. He began his new Goodyear career in January 1954. He and Betty bought a comfortable home on Wiltshire Road in west Akron, not far from Stan Hywet.

In the following years, devoted largely to his career and family responsibilities, Seiberling did find sufficient time for two hobbies, photography—another expression of a family interest in art—and downhill skiing. He soon realized that they could complement each other. A trip to Yosemite and the Sierra Nevada in 1967 marked the beginning of what was to be a passionate interest in mountain scenery and nature photography. It also anticipated features of his political career—his attraction to visually impressive scenery and his use of photographs to sell his proposals and bills to colleagues. Subsequent vacations in the Rockies and in California reinforced these interests and sustained a lifelong devotion to outdoor activities.

In short, Seiberling had returned to his roots, but under radically different conditions. He knew more of the world and its problems than most of his friends and neighbors, and while he was soon drawn back into family affairs, he retained the broadened perspective he had acquired in the years since 1933.

The Akron that Seiberling returned to in 1954 was largely unchanged from that of the mid-1930s. It was still an industrial city, still dominated by the same three large tire firms that had emerged in the 1910s and the half-dozen smaller rubber companies—such as Seiberling Rubber—that had survived a brutal competitive environment. The executives of those firms and their families dominated the city's social and civic life. The two most obvious differences in the intervening years were the return of prosperity, most evident in the growth of suburbs around the city's periphery, and the advent of industrial peace. Union officials were now routinely included in civic organizations and activities. Day-to-day industrial relations remained contentious, and contract negotiations often led to strikes, but an atmosphere of peaceful coexistence prevailed in factory and community. The price of peace, however, was a gradual shift of investment and jobs to other communities, notably in the South, where union power was almost nonexistent. As a result, after the World

War II boom added thousands of new, often temporary, residents, Akron settled down to a stagnant maturity. The population in 1950 and in 1960 was only slightly larger than that in 1930.[70]

If the city was at least superficially unchanged, the Seiberling family was now in disarray. Gertrude and Charles Seiberling had both died in 1946, ending an era. Frank lived on at Stan Hywet with a nurse and housekeeper, increasingly infirm and irascible as friends disappeared and his influence waned. Both of his daughters, John's aunts Ginny and Irene, became financial burdens because of their husbands' ill-considered business activities. After a few good years during and after World War II, Seiberling Rubber also began a new and ultimately fatal decline. In the mid-1950s Penfield Seiberling's conservative stewardship sparked a stockholders' revolt. Looming over everything was Stan Hywet, a costly monument to a bygone era that remained an emotional anchor for family members, regardless of where they lived or their financial well-being. Penfield wrote in 1947 that "when my father and mother departed this life, the heavens were going to open and the deluge descend. . . . [Now even before Father] has departed, the storm clouds have gathered and the troubles have started."[71]

The estate posed intractable problems. Even without many social events, it cost nearly $50,000 per year to maintain. Frank's salary as chairman of Seiberling Rubber was $36,000 per year, which paid his personal expenses and income tax. To sustain Stan Hywet, he had to devote the bulk of his earnings from the Midland Continental Railroad, his most important remaining outside investment.[72] This meant that there was little or no surplus, that the pleas of his penurious children could not be satisfied, and that a family that was still wealthy by most standards was increasingly embarrassed. The Firestone heirs sold off their West Market Street estate to developers in the late 1950s, seemingly anticipating the fate of Stan Hywet. But if Seiberling's sons and daughters could agree on anything, it was that the estate ought to be preserved as a cultural or educational institution even at considerable personal financial sacrifice to themselves. But how to proceed? Penfield recalled that "such meetings as we have had in the past have been highly unorganized and have resulted in an endless variety of opinions, beliefs, distortions of fact, etc.—all of which have been conducive to producing more heat than light . . . everything being discussed and nothing handled."[73]

In fact, the solution proved to be relatively simple. Even before Frank's death on August 11, 1955, Fred and Irene had talked to various civic groups about their plans to create a public foundation that would preserve Stan Hywet and sponsor educational programs in antiques, landscape architecture, and gardening. In September 1955 the heirs convened a meeting of community leaders to elicit support. That group authorized a study, which concluded that an endowment of at least $1 million would be needed. Spurred by women who had been active in the cultural organizations long associated with the estate, the Stan Hywet Foundation gradually raised about $400,000, enough to preserve the house.[74] John Seiberling did much of the legal work for the new foundation and remained involved in its operations for many years. He would look back with "a great sense of personal gratification" at the success of the foundation in increasing its endowment and recruiting an able staff. It had done "an absolutely first-rate job of preserving the house and, as far as possible, the atmosphere it had when it was a family home."[75] The surprisingly positive end to the saga of Stan Hywet had larger implications as well. Seiberling became a powerful advocate for publicly supported historic preservation and was personally responsible for the legislation that made it possible for many notable buildings to avoid the wrecker's ball.

In the meantime he was pursuing a generally satisfying career as a corporate attorney. He specialized in antitrust law in the United States and abroad and was deeply involved in Goodyear's overseas expansion in the 1950s and 1960s. Typically, when the company acquired a foreign firm he would accompany the operating executives to work out the legal details. These trips were stressful because of the complexity of the negotiations. In the midst of one prolonged, exhausting episode, he contrasted his sons' "fresh innocent minds" with the "rather cynical, unidealistic" men he had to deal with. "I really want to get out of this international work and break into other things. . . . Otherwise I think I will seriously consider leaving Goodyear."[76] Yet there were compensations. His European trips permitted him to gauge the changes that had occurred in Europe since 1945 and to enjoy aspects of European life that had been inaccessible or invisible a decade and a half earlier. He was pleased to report "the absence of any expression of animosity" between the French and Germans, who had "acquired a new sense of their common values and do not want to emphasize the old divisions."[77] On another occasion he wrote a long, enthusiastic account of a visit to the cathedral at Chartres. "It is almost too wonderful, too overpowering," he wrote. When he encountered one of his colleagues at the hotel and recounted his experience, the other man replied that cathedrals "left him cold" and that "Oak Ridge [the wartime atomic bomb facility] had done more for the human race than Chartres." Seiberling replied acerbically that "if what was exemplified at Oak Ridge did not destroy the human race, it would only be because men are still moved in their hearts by what is exemplified at Chartres."[78]

While he found his work intellectually stimulating and fulfilling—he complained about the wear and tear of corporate travel, not the role of big business in society or the international economy—he disliked its narrow, technical focus. In partial compensation he became increasingly involved in activities that drew on his legal background but addressed broader and more interesting issues. In 1970, when he decided to run for Congress, the precipitating factor was the Vietnam War, but in retrospect his decision was the culminating step in a long process that might have led to a career change even in absence of the Vietnam crisis.

During these years, two elements from his past helped shape his approach to these extracurricular interests. The first was the doctrines of the Oxford Group, at least as interpreted by Henrietta. She emphasized private meditation and prayer, a conscious effort to understand God's will for each individual, with Jesus as a model, and the gradual conversion of others (to ethical behavior) through positive examples. Seiberling wrote in 1961:

I think the idea that we can, by quietly praying and listening for God's word, receive his special guidance is sound . . . although people must be extremely careful to sift out thoughts which are merely human impulses, and must apply any "guidance" in terms of common sense and ethical standards. Nevertheless, I know from experience that by attempting to understand spiritual truth, by prayer and making one's mind a "tabula rasa," one can draw on sources of truth and wisdom and strength which surely come deep in our better nature or from outside ourselves. . . . In my own case, I often tend to let the day to day problem crowd out the prayer and meditation from my life and to make me work-centered and family-centered and, maybe, even self-centered. But I do try to retain humility and to follow Jesus's teachings in my conscious dealings with others. I have not always done a good job of it, but I can say that my whole attitude toward human relationships has definitely been affected for the better.[79]

The second element was an interest in the land and land use, an extension of his youthful experiences at Stan Hywet and Cedar Lodge, together with a growing awareness that development on the urban periphery was altering the fabric of society. By 1957 he was thinking of a new home for his family. His first plan was to buy land at the north edge of Stan Hywet that the foundation planned to sell off. "If I could get a good slice of the old peach orchard and a piece of that hillside above it," he explained to his mother, he could sell part of it to a friend and "still have nice views and plenty of space." He confessed, "I would love to live in the country, but I have too much regard for my wife and children to put them in a position where schools, medicine, sitters, friendly neighbors and other amenities so important to raising up small children are either remote or non-existent. When the children are old enough to go away to school, that is a different matter."[80] He was unable to obtain the Stan Hywet land but in 1958 purchased two acres on Martin Road in Bath Township, about four miles farther north, a place where the family had occasionally picnicked. The property was on a steep hillside with a stunning view of the Cuyahoga River Valley. The surrounding area included deep ravines, a small stream, and mature forests. The Seiberlings had an architect friend plan an elegant modern home—Seiberling himself designed the fireplace—and moved in October 1960. In 1964 they bought an adjoining five and a half acres "to keep our view from being spoiled in that direction."[81] By the end of the decade they owned eighteen acres.

The point, however, was that living "in the country" no longer meant foregoing "schools, medicine, sitters" and other amenities. All around the Seiberlings, farmland was being subdivided and transformed into suburban neighborhoods. Stores and service businesses followed. This meant not only that it was not necessary to wait until the children went away to school to have an agreeable country home but also that undesirable developments likely to "spoil the view" or in other ways compromise the character of country living were almost inevitable. Suburbanization thus threatened to turn the urban periphery into an area of chaotic property use and misuse. The answer, to those like Seiberling who recalled the New Deal, was systematic land-use planning by public authorities. By 1963 Seiberling had become active in the local Democratic Party and worked on several campaigns. He requested an appointment to the Tri-County Regional Planning Commission, an advisory group that helped local governments in Summit County and the surrounding area obtain federal grants. The Tri-County Commission had little authority and little or no ability to affect the pace of urban sprawl, but it gathered data and permitted those, like Seiberling, who actually bothered to read its reports, to understand what was happening.

One other immediate and perhaps unexpected benefit of moving to Martin Road was the presence of many "friendly neighbors." Of special importance were James, or Jim, and Margot Jackson, whose home on nearby Ira Road also overlooked the valley. Jim had had a distinguished career as a labor reporter for the *Akron Beacon Journal* during the years when Seiberling was away and by the 1960s was the paper's chief editorial writer, and Margot was a community activist. Together they knew nearly everyone and everything about the Akron area. At the time the Seiberlings moved into their Martin Road home and became part of the Bath community, the Jacksons were becoming involved in an effort to save the entire Cuyahoga Valley from the kind of problems that had persuaded the Seiberlings to buy out their neighbors. They soon introduced the Seiberlings to the preservationist cause. It proved to be an auspicious combination. The grassroots effort to preserve the Valley ensured that, long before the Cuyahoga River burned or the environment became a fashionable cause, John Seiberling would be deeply involved in the effort to save the land that had become so important to him.

✥{ 3 }✥

A Political Career

In the fall of 1968 John Seiberling was fifty years old, reasonably happy with his job, devoted to his family, including sons John, David, and Stephen, now seventeen, fourteen, and eleven, and increasingly involved in a promising effort to preserve parts of the nearby Cuyahoga Valley. A year later he decided to abandon his career, run for Congress, and, if successful, live apart from his family for long periods and give up most of his local associations. That was a gauge of the polarizing impact of the Vietnam War and the determination of antiwar groups to force an end to the conflict. Yet Seiberling's motivation was more complex. The escalation of the war under President Richard M. Nixon flew in the face of everything he believed about the proper role of the United States in the world community, but it was also a symbol of other, deeper problems in American political life, of confused priorities, half-hearted reforms, and an underlying cynicism about the voters' interests and intelligence. The situation was not hopeless, but it demanded immediate, determined action. Seiberling explained his decision to enter politics in characteristically understated language: "I talked to my wife . . . and she suggested that since we weren't getting any younger that we try to do something meaningful while we had the chance. I decided to take the plunge."[1]

He later cited three specific goals in running for Congress: ending the war, redirecting public resources to domestic problems, and reforming the Congress. By 1970 each of these goals seemed attainable. The antiwar movement had spread from college campuses to the larger society, and Nixon was on the defensive. The escalating war had necessitated—or

43

provided a convenient excuse for—cutbacks in domestic antipoverty and environmental programs. Ending the war would make resources available for those efforts. Finally, many protestors and reformers had concluded that Congress was almost as much to blame as the president for the nation's problems. The seniority system had made it possible for representatives and senators from "safe" districts to dominate and, in many cases, paralyze the Congress. After embracing the landmark civil rights and antipoverty legislation of the mid-1960s, Congress had reverted to its accustomed routines; reform was not dead, but it had been pushed to the sidelines in favor of more familiar and comfortable activities. That too could change, provided the right people were elected.

Seiberling was more than a protest candidate, however. At least by Ohio standards, he was a different kind of personality, more intense and more devoted to issues. As a local union paper reported, he was the "complete opposite" of the conventional politician. "No backslapping, no braggadocio. Not one word about himself."[2] If he had little interest in glad-handing and small talk, he was prepared to speak honestly, bluntly, and at length about the need for change. As he explained at his victory celebration early in the morning of November 4, 1970: "I wasn't in this campaign to beat an individual, but to try to create a new direction for the people of this district and for this country, a direction that's oriented toward human needs and not to some abstraction such as prestige, military power or the other things that seem dear to Richard Nixon's heart."[3]

Cuyahoga Valley: Phase I

Before 1969, Seiberling's political energies had been largely devoted to preserving the Cuyahoga River Valley between Cleveland and Akron. The Valley campaign was an example of a type of confrontation that became common in the 1960s and 1970s, as developers clashed with citizens' groups concerned about congestion, the loss of natural areas, and environmental degradation. A coalition of local groups sought to ward off industrial and residential projects and expand recreational opportunities in the long-neglected Valley. But this effort, which would have made as much sense in the 1920s as the 1960s, was politically attractive in the latter period because of developments that had occurred since World War II. These included a growing sensitivity to the effects of postwar economic growth; a prosperous economy that made resources available for altruistic plans; a more activist federal government, personified by Stewart Udall, the secretary of the interior, 1961–69; the creation, in 1964, of the federal Land and Water Conservation Fund (LWCF), which provided money for government units to purchase park land; and finally, the appearance of a new type of park, the urban national park, starting with the Cape Cod National Seashore in 1961.

By the early 1960s the thirty-mile valley that separated Cleveland and Akron was attracting more attention than it had since the heyday of the Ohio & Erie Canal, which had paralleled the river and opened the area to commercial agriculture and large-scale manufacturing in the middle decades of the nineteenth century. Indeed, one of the first preservation efforts arose from a state plan in 1962 to sell off the derelict canal and the adjacent state-owned lands. Apart from preserving parts of the canal, "some form of public ownership . . . that will keep the [Valley] walls forested permanently to stop erosion is also a basic requirement," concluded one local newspaper.[4] Yet relatively few people paid attention. The Ohio Turnpike had bisected the Valley in the 1950s, and a new interstate highway followed a decade later.

The development that first sparked organized opposition was, ironically, far less noteworthy. In 1962 the Episcopal Church agreed to give its tiny, picturesque chapel in Peninsula, the largest of the Valley villages, to the Western Reserve Historical Society for its Hale Farm pioneer village, which it was assembling a few miles south, near the Seiberlings' new home. The offer angered several longtime Peninsula residents, who saw it as an affront to their declining community and enlisted the aid of Robert L. Hunker, a newly arrived architect and designer. Hunker had moved there for its central location and inexpensive real estate and knew nothing of the village or its history as a nineteenth-century canal town. But he soon made their cause his own and launched a campaign to preserve "Peninsula's historic and natural features."[5] He appealed to a number of prominent local people as well as to several well-to-do Akron families that had farms or summer retreats in the Valley. Hunker and his allies called their new organization the Peninsula Valley Heritage Association (PVHA) and stressed that their interests included the "entire Valley," not just Peninsula. Jim and Margot Jackson were among those who joined that summer. When the PVHA began to recruit officers in September, it sought an attorney to serve on its board of trustees. Two names were suggested: Tress Pittenger, an up-and-coming executive at the General Tire Company in Akron, and John Seiberling. Pittenger agreed to serve, so Seiberling was relegated to a list of potential board members.[6]

Seiberling became actively involved in the PVHA in 1965 when the organization faced a potentially disastrous threat, a plan by the Ohio Edison Company to build a high-tension utility line along the river, eviscerating the Valley from Akron to the Cleveland suburbs. Seiberling, Pittenger, and another attorney who was active in the PVHA agreed to take the lead in fighting the plan. PVHA launched a fund-raising campaign to pay for a lawsuit, but Seiberling decided that more direct action was also necessary. He appealed to the Ohio Edison stockholders to renounce the transmission line and waged a two-year campaign to elect Henry Saalfield, PVHA president and Akron industrialist, to the company's board of directors. These tactics were not immediately successful though they ultimately helped persuade Ohio Edison to reroute its line. PVHA failed in its larger objective, however, which was to persuade the Summit County commissioners to make the Valley a conservancy district. The Valley remained unprotected.[7]

In the meantime, Seiberling had become a member and then president of the Tri-County Regional Planning Commission, a position that enabled him to view the threats to the Valley in a larger context. The removal of the church, the spread of utility lines, and the encroachment of an interstate highway, which for a time seemed likely to obliterate Brandywine Falls, the area's most scenic waterfall, were not isolated phenomena; they were typical of the problems that accompanied the urban sprawl of the post–World War II years and would continue until the Valley was incorporated into suburbia or some larger order had been imposed on the area. Seiberling made no secret of his goal. Working through the planning commission, he had promoted the idea of a conservancy district; when that failed, he was among the first and most dedicated proponents of a park.

Seiberling's emergence as an environmentalist paralleled the experiences of many contemporaries. His memories of growing up at Stan Hywet and accompanying his father on hikes there and elsewhere provided a foundation. An interest in the outdoors and nature led to the Martin Road home, which in turn brought him in touch with neighbors like the Jacksons and other members of the PVHA and familiarity with the plight of the Cuyahoga and the threat to the Valley. But Seiberling was not content, as the majority of his neighbors were, to focus narrowly on their immediate situation, even on the Valley. Its fate was part of a larger, seamless challenge that embraced the pollution of the Cuyahoga and Lake Erie, the sprawl that became more evident with each passing year, and the cavalier behavior of much of industry toward resources such as the Valley. And the environmental challenges so apparent in northeast Ohio were not unique; the entire country, indeed the world, faced similar problems. Where to begin? Publicity and public education would be essential in mobilizing a constituency for change and in converting the critics of Cuyahoga River pollution and urban sprawl into broad-gauged activists. Seiberling's role in the planning commission and his election to the executive committee of the new northeast Ohio group of the Sierra Club were indicators of his new perspective and the antecedents of a new career.

The preservationist campaign drew on the work of three organizations. The first was the PVHA. The second was the Tri-County Regional Planning Commission, which provided opportunities for investigation and publicity. The third organization was the Cleveland-based Lake Erie Watershed Conservation Foundation, headed by George H. Watkins, the executive director. By the 1960s Watkins perceived the severely polluted Cuyahoga River as the region's single greatest problem and began to use the foundation's funds to promote a park as one way to restore the river.[8]

The park idea dated from the Olmsted study of 1925. In the following years the Akron Metropolitan Park District had acquired large tracts of land from the Brush and Kendall families. The Boy Scouts and Girl Scouts of America had established camps in the Valley by the 1940s, and several golf courses added to a parklike environment. In 1964 the Akron Park District announced another substantial addition at the south end of the Valley, what would become the Hampton Hills Metropolitan Park. Even more significant was the acquisition by the Cleveland Musical Arts Association, parent of the Cleveland Orchestra, of more than a thousand acres of land as the setting for a summer concert center, which opened as the Blossom Center in 1968. Park proponents could argue that half of the approximately 25,000-acre Valley had already been preserved by institutions with compatible objectives.

Given these favorable developments, there were three options for establishing a Valley park. The first was to enlist the aid of the state in creating an Ohio park. The second was to win congressional authorization for a national park. A third possibility was to obtain grants from the state or federal governments that would enable the Akron or Cleveland park systems to purchase additional land and consolidate their holdings in the Valley. There were pros and cons to each of these options. The debate over the next decade was never over the desirability of a park. With the exception of a small group of Valley residents who opposed any action, local public support was broad and impressive. The critical issues were the type of park, the source of funds, and the appropriate administrative agency.

Park proponents turned first to the state. In late August 1965, at the time of the battle over the Ohio Edison transmission line, Seiberling and the officers of the PVHA met Fred Morr, the director of the Ohio Department of Natural Resources, and his staff. Morr was "very enthusiastic" about a park "for use of the people in the Cleveland-Akron area" but had no funds for land acquisitions.[9] Saalfield, Seiberling, and state senator Edward Garrigan, who represented much of the area, then went to see E. J. "Eddie" Thomas, the retired president of Goodyear and current chair of the Akron park board. They asked him to help arrange a meeting with Governor James A. Rhodes. "The objective would be to get the governor to support a State Park for the Valley." At one point Seiberling said that "it would be a shame to let this beautiful Valley go down the drain." Thomas replied, "Yes, and it was a shame we let the drain go down the Valley," a reference to Akron's sewage treatment system. Thomas then suggested that *Akron Beacon Journal* senior editor Ben Maidenburg contact the governor and arrange a meeting. Maidenburg agreed to cooperate and asked Seiberling to draft a letter for him to sign.[10]

Thomas, Garrigan, Saalfield, Seiberling, and the directors of the Akron and Cleveland park systems met the governor in Columbus in late December. Thomas explained their interest in a state park. Seiberling had had the Planning Commission staff prepare a map of Ohio showing population centers and state parks; the parks were mostly in the southern counties, far from the majority of the state's population. Rhodes asked Morr, also present, to explain. "Well," he replied, "the land is cheaper in Southern Ohio." Rhodes reluctantly authorized a feasibility study.[11]

Before Morr had begun that study a second opportunity arose. In mid-1966, U.S. Representative Charles A. Vanik, whose district included the northern part of the Valley, prevailed upon Interior Secretary Udall to visit the area and to consider the Valley as a possible national park. Udall spoke in Peninsula and encouraged the PVHA campaign; though he made no commitment, his positive statements raised the hopes of park advocates.[12] Udall subsequently asked the National Park Service (NPS) and the Bureau of Outdoor Recreation (BOR), the agency created to administer the LWCF grant program, to send a team to investigate. After a brief tour the experts concluded that the river was "excessively polluted" and that the area was unlikely to attract visitors from beyond the immediate region. In the following years both agencies made additional feasibility studies of Ohio sites but did not recommend the Cuyahoga Valley, partly because of the likely costs of cleaning up the river. Indeed, the BOR listed five other Ohio locations as better choices for national recreation areas.[13] Congress actually authorized thirty-four new NPS units between 1964 and 1966. Most were historical sites, but several, including the Delaware Water Gap National Recreation Area (1965) and the Indiana Dunes National Lakeshore (1966), bore some similarities to the Valley.

This setback might have proven fatal, as Morr had suspended his study in favor of the federal effort. Another letter from Maidenburg was necessary to persuade the governor to again authorize Morr to hire Rosenstock Holland Associates, a Cuyahoga Falls, Ohio, consulting firm, to make the feasibility study.[14] To make sure that Rosenstock was not unduly influenced by the Akron and Cleveland people, Morr indicated that the state could only provide matching funds for a park managed by the Cleveland and Akron park districts.[15] In the meantime the Rosenstock group worked closely with the Tri-County Planning Commission. When the consultants had finished, in the spring of 1968, they allowed Seiberling to review the report before sending it to Morr. He spent the night scribbling changes in the margins, most of which Rosenstock accepted.[16] The final report called for the purchase of nine thousand additional acres to go along with the twelve thousand owned by local parks and cultural organizations, conservation easements to protect the hills on either side of the Valley, and joint management by the Cleveland and Akron parks.

The report was officially presented to the public on May 21 at a meeting in Peninsula chaired by Seiberling. He called for immediate efforts to save threatened areas, such as the land adjacent to the new Blossom Center, and the creation of a "steering organization" to "put the heat on the legislature."[17] During the following days he and his allies emphasized the critical nature of the job that lay ahead. The director of the

Akron Park District issued a dire warning that "time is running out." Seiberling estimated that in two or three years it would be impossible to preserve the area.[18]

A month later the Cleveland and Akron park boards appointed a joint committee to consider ways of raising money. Seiberling, now the de facto leader of the park movement, called for the local park districts to provide 25 percent of the total, with the rest coming from the state and federal governments.[19] Responding to his plea, Representative Vanik again took the initiative. In early 1969, just before Udall left office, Vanik arranged for him to meet Saalfield, Seiberling, and the Cleveland park director. After listening to their appeals, the sympathetic Udall offered $210,000 in LWCF money, which, with an eventual state match, would purchase 510 acres adjacent to Virginia Kendall Park, the largest of the Valley parks.[20]

In April, Seiberling, Thomas, and the directors of the Akron and Cleveland park systems went to see Rhodes again to ask for funds to match the LWCF grant and for additional money to buy more land. That meeting was not fruitful, and a second meeting a month later produced only the promise of a small share of a recent state parks bond issue. Informally they learned that tensions between the Cleveland and Akron park districts and uncertainty over who would run a Valley park had made the governor and his aides wary.[21] An anguished Robert Hunker, who had earlier written Rhodes that an immediate $5 million was "imperative," blamed the delegation for allowing Seiberling, a Democrat, to represent the group to the highly partisan governor.[22] In reply, *Akron Beacon Journal* publisher John S. Knight insisted that Hunker "overemphasize[d] the political aspects." Knight believed there were enough prominent Republicans on the two park boards to ensure "continuing progress" but did concede that Seiberling was "an abrasive young man who seems to have little idea of how to deal politically."[23]

Thus, at the end of the decade, the fate of the Valley was as uncertain as it had been in 1964. There was broad public support but no obvious way to bring the campaign to fruition. In the meantime new threats were emerging, and the political environments in both Washington and Columbus were in flux. In the absence of decisive action, most of the land was almost certain to become part of the sprawl that was increasingly evident on all sides of the Valley.

Akron Politics and the Vietnam War

At this juncture, national and international events converged with the park campaign to abruptly alter Seiberling's political role and career. He had long been committed to world peace, which in his mind was inseparable from the campaign to preserve the natural world. Nuclear warfare, the ultimate form of war, would also be the ultimate assault on nature. Apart from support for the United Nations, he had been active in United World Federalists and the Akron Bar Association's World Peace through Law Committee. The Vietnam War posed new challenges. Seiberling was a founder of the Summit County Committee for Peace in Vietnam and a public critic of the Johnson administration's policies. But it was the willingness of the Nixon administration to continue and even widen the war that made more immediate action seem imperative.[24]

One other factor proved to be critical. The heavily Democratic Fourteenth Ohio Congressional District, which embraced Akron and its environs, had long had a Republican incumbent, William H. Ayres. Ayres was an anomaly. Although several Ohio cities had liberal Republican representatives whose voting records were largely indistinguishable from their Democratic counterparts, Ayres was a party stalwart. He played down his party affiliation but voted the party line. He had opposed civil rights and domestic spending bills and was a consistent supporter of the military. At home he emphasized constituent services with special emphasis on veterans' benefits. By the late 1960s he had become the senior Republican on the Veterans Affairs Committee. This record of service, coupled with a familiar face and a genial manner, enabled him to defeat a number of highly qualified Democrats. His margins in 1964, 1966, and 1968 remained steady at about 55 percent.

By 1969, however, Ayres faced new challenges. As a supporter of the Nixon administration, he was now more closely associated with the continuing war. As one of a handful of Republicans who represented an overwhelmingly Democratic district, he was a prime target of the national Democratic Party. His ties to the district also began to fray. He had been in Washington for twenty years and considered it, rather than Akron, his home. An enthusiastic participant in the capital's active social life, he appeared to many constituents, including Seiberling, as little more than a middle-aged playboy. Ayres privately acknowledged a drinking problem.[25] None of these obstacles was necessarily fatal, but together with his voting record and public statements that often gave the impression of an inattentive lightweight, he was obviously vulnerable.

The challenge for any Democratic candidate was to neutralize Ayres's appeal among blue-collar Democrats in the working-class neighborhoods of east and south Akron. There were two obvious hurdles to overcome. The first was the ambivalent position of the city's unions, given Ayres's record of favors and services. Several of the more conservative organizations, including the carpenters, endorsed Ayres; others routinely backed the Democratic candidate but provided little actual support. The second obstacle was the *Akron Beacon Journal,* the only newspaper that served the entire district. Publisher John S. Knight was an influential community figure and a pragmatic Republican. His endorsement of Ayres suggested to many nominal Democrats that Ayres was more than a party hack. And many Democrats supported a Republican or two just to show the party bosses that they could not be taken for granted. Knight, however, was an opponent of the war and, increasingly, of Nixon and his policies. By 1970 his support for Ayres could no longer be taken for granted.

A total of five Democrats ran in the May 1970 primary for the opportunity to challenge Ayres. A former state representative, a sheriff's deputy, and an activist black minister had little money or support and little chance of success. Yet their total vote would be enough to affect the outcome, and the Reverend Billy Robinson actually won in the Fourth Ward, a largely African American neighborhood on Akron's near west side. The fourth candidate was William Nye, a thirty-six-year-old state senator who had won by a large margin in 1968. Attractive and articulate, Nye was an obvious choice, favored by most of the party organization. In March 1970, at the beginning of the primary campaign, he would have won easily, probably with more than 50 percent of the vote.[26] But Nye may have been too attractive for his electoral health. He was courted by Democratic leaders for the state attorney general or auditor's race, which, given voter unrest after a long period of Republican dominance, would probably be relatively easy to win. He preferred the congressional race but knew that it might be a long shot; as a result he stalled. When he formally entered the primary in late January he still had not made up his mind what to do.

Seiberling had no intention of running for any office until the fall of 1969. Still, he had become well known among local environmental and antiwar activists who were eager to defeat Ayres and dissatisfied with the district's Democratic leadership. One of the activists, Marvin

Shapiro, headed an informal campaign to persuade Seiberling to run for Congress. When asked point-blank, Seiberling demurred, though he promised to think about it and agreed with Shapiro that a strong antiwar candidate was a priority. Seiberling then called Nye and urged him to run. Nye was noncommittal. Several other calls produced the same result. In the meantime, Shapiro and others kept pressuring Seiberling. By mid-January, with the very real prospect of no meaningful challenger to Ayres, Seiberling made up his mind. Having been involved in previous campaigns he thought he "saw how to do it."[27] At a dinner attended by personal friends and veterans of the Valley campaigns, he announced that he would take a leave of absence from Goodyear and run, provided they supported him. The response was uniformly positive. Betty Seiberling wrote at the time: "John decided to run for Congress! We'd been thinking of it for almost 2 months, had decided not to do it if Bill Nye ran . . . but Bill did not announce in December, did not announce January 1st as we expected, so finally John decided to take the plunge. We feel rather grimly determined, knowing it will be hard, physically strenuous, hard on family relations, really one big unknown as far as our role in politics go. But now is the time, if we're ever going to make such a big change."[28] Ten days later Nye declared his tentative candidacy. He later called Seiberling and asked him to withdraw. "It's too late for me to withdraw," Seiberling replied. "I've burned my bridges behind me at Goodyear just by announcing I was running. So I am going to go all out."[29]

Although Seiberling's name recognition among Democrats generally was low, he had two decisive advantages. He was able to enlist the antiwar activists who ordinarily would have become involved, if at all, only in the general election campaign, and he was able to raise a substantial war chest by appealing to peace and environmental groups. Jim Dougherty, a liberal activist and business agent of the Meatcutters Union, became his campaign manager. Two able members of the Firestone marketing department, Harry H. Hollingsworth and Thomas McGowan, volunteered as pollsters and provided weekly reports. Many of his friends and business acquaintances (including his uncle Penfield, a longtime Ayres supporter) became donors. At one point he went to see the Goodyear vice-president in charge of advertising. "I'm trying to sell a new product," he explained, "namely me." He was told to find out what the voters wanted and address that desire. Using Hollingsworth and McGowan's polling data, Seiberling and his advisors came up with a simple, straightforward slogan: "John Seiberling, the Democrat who can beat Ayres." They also agreed to disregard their primary opponents and focus exclusively on Ayres.[30] All together the Seiberling primary campaign spent $18,000, a large sum for a local race, mostly for newspaper and radio ads and billboards.[31]

From the beginning Seiberling's campaign attracted attention. His announcement on January 15 was reported on page two of the *Beacon Journal,* together with his photograph; Nye's ambivalent statement ten days later was buried in a story about local politics. Seiberling's full statement, which was circulated widely among supporters, attacked the war for making "Johnson's Great Society a myth. It has given the extreme right, the anti-labor, anti-Negro and anti-humanist forces a weapon of spurious patriotism." He also attacked the military-industrial complex and the Congress and called for the replacement of "deadwood" congressmen.[32] In late February the *Beacon Journal* endorsed him over Nye in the Democratic primary.[33]

One of Seiberling's novel campaign tactics was the "hike-in." Together with allies from the local Sierra Club, he would walk from a suburban location to downtown Akron, picking up litter along the way. The first hike-in, on April 18, was part of the local Earth Day program and attracted university and high school students carrying signs that read "Clean Air," "Pure Water," and "Let's Clean the District." A week later he and about twenty hikers collected fifteen bags of trash on their way from Portage Lakes in south Akron to the University of Akron campus. "He may not be the youngest candidate," Alice Harpley, a participant, noted, "but I'm sure none of the others can claim to be in the condition he's in."[34]

Seiberling's poll numbers rose rapidly after early March. By mid-April he was within five percentage points of Nye and passed him at the end of the month, a week before the primary. The election itself was anticlimactic. Seiberling won with 38 percent of the vote to Nye's 30 percent and took 62 percent of the precincts to Nye's 25 percent and Robinson's 10 percent. In predominantly African American precincts, Seiberling either won or finished second to Robinson. He also did well in Akron's Eighth Ward, the silk-stocking west side neighborhood, and in suburban Cuyahoga Falls, another Republican stronghold. He won all of the affluent northern suburbs but lost several of the blue-collar suburbs in the south and east.[35] All of his primary opponents except the deputy sheriff immediately endorsed him over Ayres.

During the last days of the primary campaign, President Nixon's invasion of Cambodia, which widened the war and produced a violent domestic backlash, created new challenges for Seiberling. The invasion (May 1) and the protests that led to the closing of many college campuses around the country had special meaning in Ohio. They came at the climactic moment of a bitter Republican senatorial primary between Governor Rhodes and Robert Taft, the namesake son of the senator and presidential candidate of the 1940s and 1950s. In response to riots and the destruction of an ROTC building at Kent State University, fifteen miles east of Akron, Governor Rhodes dispatched the National Guard. On May 4, in reaction to continued disturbances, the troops fired on a crowd of students, killing four and wounding many others. The incident polarized the state, with the majority blaming student radicals for the tragedy. On May 5, Taft won the primary but by a smaller margin than polls had predicted. In the following weeks the incident hardened opposition to both the war and the unruly students who were the vanguard of the antiwar movement.

On the afternoon of May 6 a large group of University of Akron students and faculty held an outdoor meeting to protest the Kent State killings. As the rally was getting underway, Seiberling and a volunteer driver passed the crowd on their way to the nearby Goodyear complex to greet workers at the shift change. Seiberling asked the driver to stop. Invited to speak, he told the crowd, "Twenty-five years ago I never thought that a peace candidate could win in a Congressional election in this district, even a primary election. . . . I disregarded the advice of some of the professionals in the Democratic party who said, 'Take it easy on the peace issue. . . . ' But you know, sometimes the people are way ahead of the professionals, and the events of yesterday [the primary] certainly proved that in this community." He attacked Nixon and then Ayres, who "personifies everything that is wrong with our government policy of the last 20 years." Citing Mahatma Gandhi's use of nonviolence to achieve political goals, he pledged "to use the system, to use the means that we have" to stop the war.[36] At the end of the speech he raised his hands with the "V for victory" sign. A photographer from the *Buchtelite*, the student newspaper, took his picture flanked by several long-haired male students. That picture would be Ayres's principal weapon against him in the following months.[37]

During the following weeks Seiberling's advisors planned a vigorous campaign. They drew up a budget of $68,000, an unprecedented amount and more than three times Ayres's expenditures in 1968. To raise money they held a number of fund-raising rallies featuring national Democratic leaders, such as Morris and Stewart Udall and Sargent Shriver. Other events emphasized local talent, including a group of artists who donated their work for an auction attended by Seiberling's sister Dorothy Steinberg, the art editor of *Life Magazine*.[38] Seiberling's pollsters scheduled telephone surveys for June, August, and October. They also planned an additional survey of selected blue-collar precincts for the week before the election. To attract volunteers they created a variety of organizations such as Independents for Seiberling, Republicans for Seiberling, and even Skiers for Seiberling.

The all-important interest group, however, was organized labor. Nye had attacked Seiberling for supposedly crossing a rubber workers picket line when he worked at Goodyear, a charge that was false but suggested his vulnerability in blue-collar neighborhoods. Rank-and-file union members, moreover, were among the most outspoken critics of student activism and campus unrest. To overcome these problems, Dougherty arranged numerous meetings with union leaders, where Seiberling spoke about inflation and economic problems. In late June, Dougherty organized a session with forty union officers and won the backing of the president of the county labor council. Several weeks later Seiberling went to Washington to seek the endorsement of the American Federation of Labor and Congress of Industrial Organizations (AFL-CIO) and the United Auto Workers.[39] By the end of the summer he had secured the active support of virtually all Summit County unions, including the large United Rubber Workers (URW) locals. He was also the beneficiary of an Ayres blunder. During a national strike by postal workers, Ayres arranged to be photographed getting off a plane carrying a mailbag, supposedly to underline his sympathy for the victimized public. His stunt backfired, enraging local unionists.[40] Blue-collar voters remained a problem for Seiberling, but unions were ultimately the most generous contributors to his campaign.

Seiberling's message to these and other voters was unambiguous. "We can no longer afford the old-style, out-of-date, out-of-touch politics so playfully practiced by our present congressman," he wrote in the *Beacon Journal*. "In this crisis, can we continue to coast with the kind of inept representation Ayres has given us?" He went on to castigate Ayres as a "rubber stamp" for the military and to attack the "antiquated system of seniority and rules." In the original draft of his statement he had added that a congressman should be "a leader, not just a jovial errand boy."[41] Still, Seiberling's efforts had little impact during the summer and early fall. His own polls showed Ayres with a steady 2 to 1 lead. R. W. Apple, who covered the race for the *New York Times,* reported in late August that Seiberling was a "fresh face" whose campaign "appears to be underfinanced and poorly organized."[42] When Ayres ran a campaign ad featuring the photo of Seiberling and the student protestors, Seiberling formally complained to the Fair Campaign Practices Committee. Ayres would make the photo the centerpiece of his campaign in the following weeks.[43]

The situation began to change in September. Seiberling received an important assist from Environmental Action, a Washington-based environmental group that included Ayres in a "dirty dozen" list of representatives who opposed environmental legislation. Ayres responded that the group promoted "candidates sympathetic to campus rioters, do-gooders, and ultra-liberal causes." He added that "the guys aren't going to take that from a bunch of long haired, hippie kids" and suggested reprisals against an Environmental Action subsidiary that had received government grants.[44] Later in September Seiberling hired James Goff as his full-time campaign coordinator. An experienced political organizer who had worked for Hubert Humphrey in 1968, Goff brought additional organizational expertise to the campaign.

The turning point came on October 10, when the *Beacon Journal* endorsed Seiberling. The "problems of 1970 are more complex," and Ayres faced an "unusual opponent" who had "broad intellectual capacity, the personal integrity and the independence" needed in Congress.[45] Several weeks later John Knight was asked about the endorsement at a public meeting. "When Mr. Ayres wrote down what he felt the main issues were," he replied, "what they amounted to was tenure. And when we look at the mess the country's in today, what's so great about seniority?"[46] The Seiberling campaign was pleasantly surprised. According to their polls, Ayres's support largely collapsed in early October.

Ayres was aware of his perilous position. His Republican allies were disheartened, and he was running low on funds. Increasingly desperate, he changed the focus of his campaign. Rather than emphasizing his own qualifications, he increasingly attacked Seiberling. He told one reporter that he thought he had "turned the corner" with the photo of Seiberling at the campus rally.[47] This assertion shocked his campaign managers. The former chairman later told Seiberling that "there was something about you or your approach that really got to Bill Ayres. He got the bit in his teeth; and he was determined to do all these things, and we tried to talk him out of it. . . . But he was insistent on doing it."[48] The attacks helped to publicize Seiberling's campaign and erode Ayres's principal advantage, his name recognition.

Although Seiberling was at first outraged at Ayres's tactic, he and his advisors soon realized that Ayres was doing their job for them. By publicizing Seiberling's actual statements, and the refusal of university president Norman Auburn to criticize Seiberling's behavior at the rally, they were able to neutralize the impact; indeed, many people came to Seiberling's defense.

Ayres's other charges proved to be equally misguided. He persuaded several of Seiberling's cousins to repudiate his candidacy publicly and claimed that he could easily organize a Seiberlings-for-Ayres committee. But a stinging rebuke by Frank Seiberling Jr., John's uncle, made it clear that the family was divided, like the rest of the electorate.[49] Similarly, a statement by a University of Akron political science professor emphasizing Seiberling's "naiveté" brought a flood of pro-Seiberling statements and letters to the editor from other faculty members.[50] Ayres distributed a pamphlet published by a "Citizens Ad Hoc Committee to Defeat John Seiberling," which was soon exposed as a front group for the extremist John Birch Society.[51] Ayres's most embarrassing faux pas, based apparently on reports that Seiberling had refused to discuss his religious beliefs, was that he was not a believer or a church member—an effort to appeal to the area's large Protestant evangelical population. This brought a widely publicized rejoinder from Rev. Ronald Marmaduke, minister of the Bath Congregational Church, which the Seiberlings attended, and an even more embarrassing public rebuke from a dozen local clergy on the eve of the election.[52]

Although Ayres had promised to debate Seiberling after the primary, he refused to set a date, and the Seiberling campaign made his reticence an issue. In early October, when Ayres spoke at a dedication ceremony for a new hiking trail, Seiberling appeared and suggested that they hike together. Ayres responded, "You do your hiking and I'll do my planning." When Seiberling then suggested a photograph, Ayres replied, "Aw, forget it," and walked away. Seiberling told reporters that he had wanted to question Ayres about his conservation votes, "and this is the closest I've been able to come to him in the campaign."[53] Finally, as his situation became more desperate, Ayres relented and agreed to a joint appearance. Their encounter, at a local high school, was relatively restrained until Ayres referred to the dismissive statement of the political science professor. "Shame on you," Seiberling interrupted.[54] Another clash occurred at a dinner meeting of the local chapter of the National Association for the Advancement of Colored People. In a private conversation Seiberling noted that Ayres belonged to many civic organizations but had omitted one important group. Ayres was perplexed. Seiberling's answer: Alcoholics Anonymous. Ayres was furious.[55]

In the meantime, the Seiberling campaign devoted more and more attention to the economy. Seiberling led another hike-in on October 24, but the "final push" emphasized material issues. "We're going to talk about Nixon and jobs," explained Goff. "You don't reach a blue-collar worker when you talk about ecology. But when you talk about his pocket book, he really listens."[56] Other reports suggested that Seiberling's statements about Nixon's economic policies and occupational safety had "turned on" the URW. R. W. Apple concluded that Ayres was "in deep trouble" and in danger of a "major upset."[57]

On November 3, Ayres suffered a "resounding" defeat. Seiberling won 56 percent of the total vote (a margin of 16,000), every Akron ward except the traditionally Republican Eighth, and most of the suburban communities. The victory was even more impressive because the Democrats made only modest gains nationally. In Ohio they won the governorship but lost the U.S. Senate race. Seiberling stood out in a largely inconclusive election.[58]

The election data also underlined the importance of Seiberling's attacks on Ayres and Ayres's blunders. Seiberling recalled that he had "never had more fun in my life than I did the first time I ran for Congress, just outwitting this guy, which turned out to be much easier than I had expected."[59] Rattled by Seiberling's attacks on his record and popular outrage at Nixon's war policy, Ayres had self-destructed. His total vote was 29,000 less than in 1968. Seiberling's total was only 3,000 more than the unsuccessful Democrat's two years earlier, but he persuaded many former Ayres supporters not to vote for the incumbent, or in many cases, not to vote at all. Even with a vigorous union effort, relatively few voters in east and south Akron switched to Seiberling. In only three of the ten Akron wards did Seiberling's vote exceed the Democratic candidate's 1968 total, and the only substantial difference was in the Eighth Ward, where he came within 1,000 votes of Ayres. In the suburban communities he did substantially better, notably in Cuyahoga Falls, which he won, and Bath Township, where he lost by only 400 votes. All together, Seiberling won 60 percent of the urban vote and 51 percent of the suburban vote. Relative to other Democrats, he did better in the more affluent areas and about the same in blue-collar neighborhoods.[60] His identification with the environmental and antiwar movements—not to mention his name and reputation for integrity—appealed to many traditional Republicans while Ayres's attacks had little effect. His uncle Penfield, a lifelong Republican, wrote that "John conducted a very fine campaign . . . he was especially outstanding in his restrained conduct when [Ayres] got very nasty during the last couple of weeks . . . which hurt Ayres and helped John immeasureably."[61]

The cost was not inconsiderable. The Seiberling campaign spent nearly $76,000, more than twice Ayres's total and five times that of the 1968 Democratic candidate. Contributions during the campaign totaled $68,000, with organized labor ($17,000), peace groups ($6,000), and the local Democratic Party ($4,000) making the largest contributions. The largest single contributor, apart from Seiberling himself, was John Behr, Betty's brother.[62] Running an aggressive, professional political campaign was not inexpensive. In at least one sense, however, the 1970 effort was a sound investment. The voters obtained more vigorous representation, and the Democrats found a leader who would quickly have an impact. After 1970 Seiberling never had a serious challenger. In 1972, for example, he spent only $22,000, and after the 1974 race he excoriated the Republicans for running such poor candidates.[63] Prorated over the sixteen years that Seiberling would serve, the $76,000 was a bargain.

Several days after the election, *Beacon Journal* political columnist David Hess wrote a retrospective on the campaign and its likely significance. Like many observers, he was struck by Seiberling's unconventional behavior and appearance. Although tall, lean, and physically fit, his dress was "hopelessly outmoded," including a "formless grey suit, white button-down shirt and narrow nondescript tie" together with a well-worn hat and overcoat that "might have been salvaged from a 1930 rummage sale." His speech, however, was "quick and articulate." "He practices honesty, tact, politeness—to the point of courtly courtesy." An idealist, he planned to be an "issue-oriented" congressman. He described himself as a "moderate liberal with very, very strong convictions on the importance of working for peace through law and a better environment." He had run an "intellectually honest" campaign, in contrast to Ayres's emphasis on "gimmicks, publicity stunts, and trinkets."[64] Now he was ready for even more challenging tasks: ending the war, protecting the environment, reforming Congress, and shifting resources to domestic programs.

When Seiberling first visited Washington two weeks later, he stopped at Ayres's office. The congressman was distraught, "shaking like a leaf. His staff was weeping."[65] Realizing that he was unwelcome, Seiberling beat a hasty retreat. Ayres subsequently landed a perfunctory job in the Nixon administration. On meeting Seiberling in a restaurant several years later, he was his old effusive self. Losing his congressional seat, he said, had led him to quit drinking and keep more regular hours. Seiberling, he insisted, had saved his life.[66]

A Congressional Agenda

The House of Representatives that Seiberling joined in January 1971 was singularly unreceptive to bold policy initiatives, abrupt changes in emphasis, and dramatic internal changes. One source of resistance was structural. Although each Congress adopted its own rules, there were few actual changes. That meant that seniority was the most important criterion for leadership via the elaborate House committee system. Chairing a committee was the objective of every ambitious member. In 1971 committee chairmen were virtually unassailable, and the oldest members, in terms of service and usually age, had a near monopoly of power. During the 1970 campaign Ayres had dismissed Seiberling because of his relatively advanced age: Ayers argued that Seiberling would not live long enough to be influential. Seiberling arrived in Washington a determined opponent of the organizational status quo and soon introduced a bill to set a mandatory retirement age of sixty-five. Although the bill went nowhere, as he anticipated, the sentiment behind it was widely shared by other newly elected members.[67] Seiberling continued to complain about "Chinese warlords, each guarding his own bastion of power" and the "skewed set of values and warped outlook" of the veteran members, but in fact the situation was changing rapidly.[68] In a development of considerable significance for his career, environmental activists toppled five key members of the House Interior Committee, including the antediluvian chairman Wayne N. Aspinall (D-CO), in the 1972 elections. Broader changes were also underway. "Serious proposals for reform, and reforms themselves began to arrive by the truckload on the agenda of the House," writes political scientist Nelson W. Polsby.

They "pared away at the prerogatives and power of committee chairmen."[69] One result was the transfer of many of those "prerogatives and powers" to the heads of subcommittees. Although Seiberling never chaired a House committee, he eventually wielded great power through his subcommittee posts.

A second conservative influence was the makeup of the House. Although Democrats held a commanding majority through the 1970s and 1980s, the numbers were misleading. The large southern Democratic bloc was, with few exceptions, united in opposing new initiatives on civil rights, health care, public housing, and the environment. Since the 1930s the southerners had joined hands with probusiness western Democrats and Republicans to thwart change. After the Republican debacle of 1964 the conservatives' power waned, but then revived with Republican gains in 1966. The late 1960s and early 1970s were frustrating for House liberals. Seiberling complained bitterly that "there is little cohesion within the Democratic ranks. We can't even get firm party positions on a lot of major issues."[70] After the disastrous George McGovern campaign of 1972, the newly reelected Nixon planned to wean enough southern Democrats to give the Republicans control of the House. The failure of his scheme was less important than the light it cast on the tenuous character of the Democrats' dominance.

A third major problem for Seiberling and other liberals was the growth of the imperial presidency. During his first term (1969–73) Nixon dutifully signed a large number of environmental bills and other liberal measures because he believed they were the price he had to pay for a mostly free hand in Vietnam and international affairs. After his dramatic reelection victory, he began to expand his control of domestic policy and the federal bureaucracy. The balance between the branches of government appeared to shift in favor of the executive branch, and congressional leaders, notably Speaker John W. McCormack and his closest associates, were intimidated. "Congress simply isn't doing its job," Seiberling complained, "and the Executive is taking up the slack."[71]

Seiberling made no secret of his intention to challenge the status quo, regardless of the odds. "There's only one way to end the war—end it," he told a Cuyahoga Falls peace group.[72] He was equally adamant about the Cuyahoga Valley, telling John Daily, the Akron park superintendent, "As a Congressman, I want to do everything I possibly can to see that the Valley is preserved."[73] His tactics, however, were thoroughly conventional. He would bore from within, master the procedures of the

House, work harder than most of his colleagues, and form alliances with like-minded associates. He assembled an able staff headed by Donald Mansfield, an Akron native and retired Air Force colonel, who kept that position through Seiberling's congressional career, and Linda Billings, a former staffer for Sen. Gaylord A. Nelson (D-WI) who had helped organize the first Earth Day in April 1970. Seiberling also became active in the liberal Democratic Study Group and the bipartisan Committee on Peace through Law.

These associations soon brought him in close touch with two individuals whose careers would intersect with and greatly influence his over the next decade and a half. Morris K. Udall (D-AZ), the younger brother of the former secretary of the interior, was the leader of the rebellious younger generation of House liberals. Tall—a former professional basketball player—genial, and witty, he was a master of the impromptu quip. But he was also a skilled and ambitious politician who had challenged McCormack for the speakership in 1969 and would seek the presidency in 1976. Like many western representatives, Udall was drawn to public land issues because of constituent pressures, but he also viewed the public domain in larger terms, as a resource for all the people.[74] The other influential colleague was Philip Burton (D-CA). Loud and brash, the stereotypical big-city wheeler-dealer, Burton was a consummate legislator. Unlike Seiberling and Udall, he had little interest in public lands per se: they were simply a stepping stone to his larger goal of dominating the House of Representatives. He jokingly referred to the comparatively reserved and austere Seiberling as "the boy scout" and "the patrician." At a dinner with their wives in early 1973, Burton asked, "By the way, how's your Cuyahoga Park coming along?" Surprised that Burton even knew about the park, Seiberling replied, "Well, we're gonna have to fight to get it passed." Burton offered advice and assistance in lining up supporters. Thereafter they worked together on a wide range of legislation.[75]

Seiberling was soon absorbed in a seemingly endless round of meetings, hearings, conferences, and public appearances. He was assigned to the Judiciary Committee, which he enjoyed and which, during the Nixon impeachment hearings of 1974, provided his first national media exposure. Except for the fact that there were several capable veterans in line ahead of him to chair the antitrust subcommittee, he might have changed course and devoted his congressional years to the issues that had dominated his earlier career. His other initial assignment was the

Science and Aeronautics Committee, which held little attraction for him. When a seat on the Interior Committee became available after the 1972 election, he gladly switched. His goal was to use that position to push for a Cuyahoga Valley national park.

He and Betty rented a small townhouse near the Capitol. Their oldest son attended college in Colorado, and the other two were enrolled in residential prep schools. Betty volunteered as a teacher's aide at a school for handicapped children. "Life is so fragmented," she explained. "A different city, the constant travel, not having the boys home—all of it represents a big change in our way of life."[76] As Seiberling's responsibilities and commitments grew, his workdays became ever longer. Later David Hess would ask rhetorically, "Is success killing John Seiberling?" When Betty was in Washington she insisted that he stop work at 8:00 P.M. When she was away, he often worked into the night, sustained by helpings of mint chocolate-chip ice cream, his favorite sweet. The Seiberlings seldom attended parties or banquets and rarely entertained. He tried to take off Sundays, which they devoted to outings in the region's many parks. Seiberling attested to the "restorative powers of Nature."[77]

Their most immediate and embarrassing problem, however, was financial. In 1969 Congress had raised its members' pay from $30,000 to $42,500 per year, but even the new salary was not enough to pay for two homes plus private school tuitions and frequent travel. Seiberling compounded his problem by promising to return to Akron every other weekend and refusing to charge for speeches. During his first year in Congress his expenses exceeded his income by $18,000. For a family without a private income, this was potentially ruinous. "By this time next year, my assets will be down to my home and my physical possessions," he glumly observed.[78] When several constituents angrily complained that $42,500 was much more than they made, he replied that "it is an expensive existence and a demanding routine." Anyone who worked at the job full-time and "avoids outside connections" would become poorer.[79] Belt tightening and additional salary increases gradually ended the deficits, but in comparison to his earlier salary, or what he could have made in later years as a Washington lawyer or lobbyist, his new career remained financially unattractive.

There were other frustrations. Despite growth of the antiwar movement, Nixon showed little interest in bringing the war to an end, and the congressional leadership was timid and indecisive in reacting to the president's policies. Seiberling became increasingly hostile, leading all Ohio representatives in voting against the president. He called the bombing of North Vietnam "barbaric, hypocritical and insane," but there was little he could do.[80] He also faced new obstacles in his campaign for a Valley park. He tried to publicize other problems by organizing a well-attended conference on housing in Akron and by calling for higher Social Security payments, but his was only one voice among many in Washington. Nevertheless, his voting record won the praises of the League of Conservation Voters and other liberal and labor groups.[81] He summarized his approach and his dissatisfaction when he wrote, "I felt, and I still feel, that the desperate needs of too many people, especially old people and poor people, are being neglected by our government; that people in the lower and middle income groups are bearing too great a share of the tax load; and that too much of the nation's wealth is going down the military rathole."[82]

The one area where Seiberling stood out during his first term was in the campaign against strip-mining. Surface mining had grown rapidly in the postwar years and was devastating large areas of Appalachia, including southeastern Ohio. State regulations were uniformly ineffectual. In practice, the industry was unregulated. Ohio senator Frank J. Lausche had proposed federal regulation in 1967, and the Senate had held hearings in 1968 but had taken no action. In the meantime, local protest groups had sprung up in the Appalachian states. Seiberling was well aware of the situation. He had accompanied his father on a trip to southeastern Ohio in the late 1930s and, as he recalled, "was so shocked by what I saw that I made a quiet pledge to myself to do something."[83] When the House Interior Committee scheduled hearings in 1971, he was eager to act. In March he toured Belmont County, in southeastern Ohio, with Linda Billings and Ted Voneida, an activist from Cleveland. "The devastation we saw was far more extensive than what I remembered seeing. . . . All around us . . . were the sad remains of farm houses, barns, and silos surrounded by eroded gullies, barren slopes, deep gashes in the earth and huge spoil piles of rocks and soil. Whole villages had been destroyed."[84] He took many photographs, with the goal of assembling a slide show for his Washington colleagues—the first example of a tactic he would use repeatedly in subsequent years. He told the Interior subcommittee on mines and mining that strip-mining was "destroying our land before our eyes" and that it was "the most urgent environmental issue facing this country."[85]

What to do about it was another matter. One option was strengthened state regulatory laws, such as the model law Ohio would adopt
in 1972. Another approach, championed in Congress by Rep. Ken W.
Heckler (D-WVA), was simply to ban strip-mining. This approach appealed to environmentalists who had soured on state legislation and to
the United Mine Workers, most of whose members worked in competing underground mines. Seiberling was among the first to cosponsor
Heckler's bill and to work actively with the environmental groups. He
added another provision: government compensation for those who would
lose their jobs because of the closing of surface mines. The Heckler bill,
with Seiberling's amendment, attracted eighty-seven cosponsors and a
national advocacy organization, the Coalition against Strip Mining. No
one actually expected Congress to prohibit strip-mining. But Seiberling
and other opponents hoped that the popularity of the Heckler bill would
force industry allies in the Senate to accept meaningful national regulation, a hope that seemed close to realization after the House passed a
regulatory bill in October 1972. Seiberling never anticipated the prolonged
and torturous negotiations even this modest goal would require.[86]

In the meantime, he had to address several problems that had potential
implications for his own future. The first of these was a result of his
stubborn insistence on charting his own course. Despite his dependence
on union money and union votes, and his general support for causes
dear to the hearts of union leaders, he refused to endorse uncritically
their legislative goals. In fact, he opposed their top priority, the protectionist Burke-Hartke bill. He argued that trade restrictions would lead
to job losses and retaliatory tariff measures and proposed instead that
the government aid companies and workers harmed by competitive im-
ports. The unions did not expect the Burke-Hartke bill to pass without
major revisions, but they sought to recruit the largest possible bloc of
supporters to enhance their bargaining power. Despite "relentless pressure" from the URW, Seiberling was adamant. "A stubborn streak that
impels him to resist such pressures," observed one reporter, may have
been as important as the bill's deficiencies.[87]

A more immediate challenge was the bizarre campaign orchestrated by
a Cuyahoga Falls woman, Mrs. Ben Ruhlin. A member of an evangelical church, she was outraged at the Supreme Court's decision to outlaw
prayer in public schools and by the refusal of liberals such as Seiberling to
support a constitutional amendment reversing the decision. For more than
a year she "pestered" him with billboard attacks and publicity stunts.[88]

In 1972 she recruited a candidate to run against him in the Democratic primary. Seiberling's response was to cite the constitutional separation of church and state and to complain that she was trying "to get the government into the business of propagating religion."[89] He "felt that a very fundamental principal was at stake." In statements that recalled his refusal to discuss his religious beliefs in 1970, he declared his opposition to the amendment a matter of conscience. "I'm not interested in the office unless I can work for the things I believe in. And," he added, "without conscience you have to be a genius at manipulation on the order of Nixon himself."[90]

Still, the immediate problem was political. Seiberling declared his willingness to support voluntary prayer if it was not part of the school routine and assigned a member of his staff to find out if Ruhlin had any public support. After a survey of Akron clergy, the staffer reported that "the feeling among the Akron ministers varies from 'It isn't an issue' to 'Mrs. Ruhlin is helping you.'" One pastor of an evangelical church thought "she *might* be a threat" because he "has to deal with her, and knows how committed and twisted she is."[91] In the end, Ruhlin's campaign was, in the words of political reporter Abe Zaidan, a "non issue."[92] After the primary, in which her candidate received less than 20 percent of the vote, she called Seiberling. "Well, sweetie pie, we had a moral victory." "Well, Mrs. Ruhlin," he responded, "any time I can get 82% of the vote, you're welcome to your moral victory."[93]

By that time Seiberling had assembled a formidable campaign organization of his own. At its core was the group of volunteers that had been so critical in 1970. Harry Hollingsworth again surveyed public opinion, showing that the voters were overwhelmingly concerned about Vietnam and the economy; only 7 percent were unhappy because of Seiberling's opposition to the prayer amendment.[94] The fund-raising group was also active. Seiberling estimated that he might need $40,000, not to mention the $10,000 he still owed from 1970 and $10,000 more he needed to publish newsletters. Most of the money came from Democratic fund-raising events and from well-heeled contributors, mostly corporate executives.[95] A lackluster Republican opponent in the general election ultimately permitted substantial economies. In November, Seiberling won with 75 percent of the vote. "I think my margin will discourage the Republicans . . . from trying to dislodge me in the future," he concluded.[96]

Two other developments of that election season would ultimately prove to be as important to Seiberling's career as his victory. The first was the defeat of Aspinall and other western conservatives who had long dominated the House Interior Committee. The second was the June 1972 burglary of the Washington Democratic headquarters in the Watergate building. (During an Akron appearance in September, Democratic vice-presidential candidate Sargent Shriver had joked about this amateurish effort to disrupt the Democratic campaign.)[97] Despite Nixon's victory, these events would create new opportunities to advance the agenda Seiberling had embraced in 1970 and, above all, to promote his plan for a Cuyahoga Valley national park.

❧ 4 ❧

The Cuyahoga Valley Park, 1971–74

In December 1972 Seiberling won an appointment to the House Committee on Interior and Insular Affairs, a promotion that, more than any other single step, defined his political career and his political legacy. The Interior Committee was his goal for the simple reason that it managed most public lands and all national parks legislation. If there was to be a federal role in the Cuyahoga Valley, it would originate in the committee's work. The Valley park bill that he and Charles A. Vanik had introduced in 1971 had gone nowhere, because no one on the committee had taken a personal interest in it. Now that would change.

Seiberling decided to keep his seat on the Judiciary Committee because of his interest in antitrust issues but soon found, to his surprise, that that appointment also had a bearing on the park campaign. From mid-1973 to mid-1974 the Judiciary Committee was at the center of the storm over President Nixon's misdeeds and in the spring of 1974 conducted the formal impeachment investigation. As the Cuyahoga Valley effort reached its climactic phase, Seiberling was spending fifty hours per week on the Nixon impeachment.[1] That crisis had another related effect. Until 1972, Nixon had routinely signed environmental legislation because it was popular and because his cooperation on domestic issues helped give him a freer hand in international affairs. But as the Watergate scandal became more threatening to his future, he embraced the most conservative and reactionary elements of the Republican Party and became a foe of domestic reform. His successor, Gerald Ford, was a more doctrinaire opponent of domestic spending, with new national parks high on his list of undesirable initiatives. Despite these and other setbacks, the Cuyahoga Valley park became a reality, and Seiberling's position as an influential member of the Interior Committee and the national parks subcommittee was secured. After 1974 public land issues dominated his career.

The timing of Seiberling's new committee assignment was also fortuitous for American public lands generally. The same forces that had inspired the Valley campaign were transforming public perceptions of federally owned lands as far away as Alaska and creating a new political climate. The cumulative results included large additions to the list of national parks and National Park Service (NPS) units and a host of other changes in the character and management of the public lands.

An Evolving Public Land System

For more than a century the public land policy of the federal government had been relatively simple and straightforward: sell (or in some cases, give away) as much as possible to private owners to raise money for the government and encourage economic activity. By the end of the century, the best lands—in terms of immediate economic potential—had been transferred or given away, but approximately one-third of the total remained, including a majority of lands in the arid West and virtually all of Alaska. Although the issue of public versus private ownership would reemerge from time to time, the land controversies of the twentieth century would focus overwhelmingly on the permissible uses of lands in the public domain. How would publicly owned land benefit the public?

By the mid-twentieth century a rough pattern had emerged. On most federally owned lands, commodity production—including mining, logging, grazing cattle and sheep, and other extractive activities—and some services, such as ski resorts, were permitted, even encouraged. For modest payments, foresters, ranchers, miners, and others could extract public resources, much as they could have had they actually purchased the land. In most of the Rocky Mountain and intermountain West, this activity sustained local economies and provided thousands of jobs.

For commodity producers, their employees, and the communities that depended on them, the great issue was the intrusiveness of federal management. The government obviously would play some role, but that in itself meant nothing. What prices would be charged? What restrictions would be placed on leases? Not surprisingly, much of the legislation, and the administrative agencies that applied it, came to reflect the influence of commodity interests. Still, there were significant distinctions. The U.S. Forest Service, which Congress had authorized in 1905 and placed in the Department of Agriculture, had emerged as an elite agency, with high professional standards. It presided over the national forests, mostly remote western lands. However, in 1911, the Weeks Act had authorized the purchase of lands in the East as well; by 1940 there were thirty-seven eastern national forests, many assembled from tax-delinquent, cut-over private lands.[2] The founder of the Forest Service, the colorful and politically savvy Gifford Pinchot, had combined science with idealism in the interest of sustainability; national forests were to be commercial forests whose operations would reflect what nature could create, not what the market would bear. The idea of "sustained yield," sustained in perpetuity, was central to the Pinchot approach and to that of his successors. In the pre–World War II years, the Forest Service was perceived as the embodiment of up-to-date thinking in natural resource conservation.[3]

The Forest Service was, however, the exception. The western grasslands were essentially open range until the 1930s, when the Taylor Grazing Act of 1934 provided for individual leases presided over by a new Interior agency, the Grazing Service. Understaffed and underfunded, the Grazing Service was immediately captured by ranching interests; for the rest of its troubled history it did little more than award leases at attractive rates to the most powerful of its constituents. When Grazing Service officials attempted to introduce modest fee increases in the 1940s, western congressmen slashed their budget to the point of extinction; in some areas sympathetic ranchers chipped in to pay the local administrator's salary. In 1949 President Harry S. Truman combined the beleaguered Grazing Service with the Public Land Office, another moribund agency, to form the Bureau of Land Management (BLM). Without a legislative mandate, additional authority, or much of a budget, the BLM was assigned to oversee more than 400 million acres of western and Alaskan land. Although the first director, Marion Clawson, struggled to remake the BLM in the image of the Forest Service, the ranchers' organizations continued to dominate the agency.[4]

The remaining lands, approximately 52 million acres, or 7 percent of the total in 1970, were devoted to national parks and wildlife refuges. Because of its public role and astute public relations, the NPS, formed in 1916 by an act of Congress (the parks themselves dated from 1872, when Congress set aside Yellowstone and charged the U.S. Army with overseeing it), was soon the best known of the public lands agencies. It was a conservation organization in the purest sense, banning all forms of commodity production, including hunting. It did encourage tourism, and the great western parks soon featured opulent lodges, gift shops, and scenic highways. Congress created an average of ten new NPS units per decade, including numerous historical sites, battlefields, national recreation areas (NRAs), and other parklike lands. By 1960 the NPS managed 22 million acres of public land.[5]

The last and least of the federal agencies was the Fish and Wildlife Service (FWS), another Interior Department unit formed in 1948 from a merger of several wildlife-related bureaus. The FWS had much in common with the BLM: it was chronically underfunded, lacked an explicit congressional mandate, and had little popular support. The refuge system had emerged in the early twentieth century to stop the slaughter of exotic birds, especially waterfowl. Most of the refuges were in coastal areas or along flyways. The FWS's predecessor agencies struggled until the 1930s, when Congress authorized a duck stamp on hunting licenses, with the proceeds earmarked for land purchases and operating budgets. Thereafter the refuges became dependent on hunters and on the businesses that serviced them. Each refuge had its own distinctive regulations, and many explicitly allowed commodity extraction.[6]

In summary, the public lands system of the early postwar years was vast, fragmented, and inchoate, reflecting its evolution in response to diverse problems and needs. It embraced the seemingly contradictory ideas of commodity production and resource preservation and served a variety of business interests. It fostered conservation in the form of sustainable production and resource preservation but had only the most tenuous links to the scientific community. In the 1940s and 1950s all of the public lands agencies faced financial crises. Major changes began in the late 1950s and accelerated in the following decade. Even more dramatic changes occurred in the 1970s, as a new generation of politicians, reflecting the perspectives, intensity, and political clout of the environmental movement, made public land reform a counterpart to the campaign against pollution.

The optimistic, buoyant years of the early to mid-1960s brought to the fore many ideas that had emerged in the preceding decades, symbolized by the impressive ceremony on September 3, 1964, when President Lyndon B. Johnson signed both the Wilderness Act, creating the Wilderness

Preservation System, and the Land and Water Conservation Act, which established the Land and Water Conservation Fund (LWCF) and the Bureau of Outdoor Recreation (BOR). Environmental groups, especially the national organizations that had a large presence in Washington, D.C., by the 1960s, hoped that these and other administrative measures (notably the Multiple-Use Sustained-Yield Act of 1960, which affirmed the Forest Service's approach to natural resource management; the Classification and Multiple-Use Act of 1964, which was a critical step in making the BLM a permanent custodian of public lands; the Refuge Administration Act of 1966, which confirmed the managerial authority of the FWS; the National Historic Preservation Act of 1966, which applied to a wide range of historical and archeological resources; and, not least, the National Environmental Policy Act of 1969, which applied to all the agencies) would make the federal bureaucracy more environmentally oriented and more open to public, as opposed to industry, influence. Their expectations were fulfilled, and in some cases exceeded, but not at once.[7]

The Wilderness Act deserves special mention because of its central role in modern public land management and its impact on Seiberling's career. The product of years of discussion and nearly a decade of lobbying, most notably by the Wilderness Society, the law called for the preservation of certain federal lands in a pristine "untrammeled" state; there could be no highways, buildings, or other developments on wilderness lands and little or no use of machinery in managing them.[8] The Wilderness Act applied to all the federal conservation agencies: the Forest Service, NPS, FWS, and later, partly because of Seiberling, the BLM. The agencies were to study their holdings over the next decade and make wilderness recommendations, but only Congress, by explicit act, could create wilderness areas. By the same token, Congress could make wilderness designations with or without the approval of the agencies. The act also designated 9 million acres of national forest land—land already managed as wilderness by administrative decision—as the first permanent wilderness areas. The Wilderness Act reflected a widely shared desire among conservationists to put parts of the United States off-limits to the seemingly inexorable processes of industrialization and urbanization and an equally pervasive sense that the federal agencies could not be trusted to preserve such areas on their own.[9]

At the time Seiberling joined the House Interior Committee, the results of this avalanche of legislation were still uncertain. The Forest Service was no less closely allied to the timber industry because of the multiple-use act, the BLM was still a ragtag captive of the ranchers, the FWS remained a bureaucratic stepchild, and the NPS continued to build highways, lodges, and visitor centers. The Forest Service and the NPS viewed the Wilderness Act as an obstruction to be avoided whenever possible.[10] The Forest Service, which had been the principal target of the act's proponents, was already involved in a host of lawsuits instigated by environmental groups. The Interior Department's Bureau of Reclamation had been thwarted in its efforts to build dams in western national parks but not elsewhere. In the most celebrated case, it had to abandon a 1950s plan to dam the Green River in Dinosaur National Monument in northwestern Colorado but was authorized to proceed with a far larger project, the Glen Canyon dam on the Colorado River, just north of Grand Canyon National Park.[11] In northeast Ohio, in the meantime, the NPS and BOR had dismissed the Cuyahoga Valley as a suitable site for a park. Would the pace of change accelerate now that the agencies had had time to adapt?

The Forest Service provided one answer. In the late 1960s the chief of the Forest Service and his top managers enthusiastically embraced the timber industry's growing reliance on national forests—a result of the exhaustion of private timber stocks in the postwar building frenzy—and a shift from traditional selective cutting to clear-cutting.[12] They insisted that clear-cutting was simply a technique for encouraging certain shade intolerant species, but it permitted greater mechanization and less skilled labor. Removing all of the trees from an area also increased erosion, reduced soil fertility, and produced the dramatic visual blight that became a hallmark of many national forests. The overall increase in logging was largely invisible to the nonexpert, but clear-cutting was readily apparent to even the most casual observer and became the agency's Achilles heel.

In the same vein, Forest Service managers responded to the mandate of the Wilderness Act with a so-called purity doctrine.[13] The law only required them to conduct wilderness reviews of roadless areas that were officially designated as "primitive." But even within that relatively small group, they could only recommend areas that remained primeval: where there was no history of human activity and where formidable geography made future disturbances unlikely. In the West, wilderness became a synonym for rock and ice; in the eastern national forests, the purity doctrine precluded any wilderness designations whatsoever.

To environmental groups, these responses were a declaration of war, to be fought in Congress and the courts. In 1968, they won congressional

approval for a larger California wilderness area than the agency had recommended. As historian Dennis Roth observes, the California case "was
a strong signal . . . that questions of wilderness allocation would not be
decided exclusively at an executive level in Washington, D.C."[14] A year
later, in a Colorado case, a federal judge ruled that the Forest Service
could not log land adjacent to a primitive area until Congress acted on
a wilderness plan for the area. In the meantime, a citizens' organization
in Montana won congressional support for a wilderness area that was
not officially "primitive." In effect, any roadless area in a national forest had become fair game for a group with political clout. In early 1971
the President's Council on Environmental Quality asked the president
to order a halt to logging and other commercial activity in all roadless
areas. Although Nixon did not act on this recommendation, it was an
indication of how the Wilderness Act had played havoc with the Forest
Service's plans and routine.[15]

The "general uncertainty" over the management of roadless areas led
Forest Service executives to propose a comprehensive Roadless Area Review and Evaluation (RARE) in 1971.[16] RARE would preempt the outside
groups, allow the Forest Service to regain control of forest management,
and also serve as a national environmental impact statement, presumably
satisfying the requirements of the new National Environmental Policy
Act. By the summer of 1972, Forest Service employees had supposedly
examined more than 55 million roadless acres, had hosted hundreds of
public meetings, and had read comments from thirty thousand individuals. In response to this deluge, they set aside more than 12 million of the
55 million acres for further study. The meager total outraged environmentalists. When the Forest Service attempted to log an area that had
not been protected, the Sierra Club sued and won an injunction on the
grounds that RARE was not an adequate environmental impact statement. Acknowledging defeat, the chief of the Forest Service ordered
environmental impact statements for all roadless areas that were to be
opened to logging. RARE had failed to insulate the Forest Service against
its critics.[17]

The purity doctrine had also provided a justification for the Forest
Service's refusal to consider national forest lands in the East for wilderness designation, despite the fact that the NPS had already recommended
some wilderness in Shenandoah National Park and the FWS had recommended wilderness areas in several eastern refuges. Critics suspected
that the purity doctrine had a larger purpose: if the Forest Service

admitted that second-growth forests qualified as wilderness, it would effectively open the door to demands for more wilderness in the vastly larger second-growth forests of the West.[18] Pressured to do something, the Forest Service in 1971 proposed a new designation, "wild areas," for those lands that lacked wilderness qualities but would be devoted to recreation. Most environmentalists were initially suspicious; by 1973 they had concluded that "wild areas" was simply a divide-and-conquer tactic, designed to undercut the wilderness movement. Once again, their opposition forced the Forest Service to admit defeat.[19]

A second and seemingly more encouraging answer to the legislative initiatives of the 1960s came from the NPS. By that time the NPS was organizationally and financially stronger than it had been for several decades. Director Conrad Wirth's "Mission 66" plan, proposed in 1957, had elicited more than $1 billion from Congress, ostensibly to modernize the parks after years of neglect. Most of the money had gone for construction projects. A critic wrote that Mission 66 "has done comparatively little for the plants and animals" and "nothing at all for the ecological maintenance of the system. . . . The agency was successful," he added, "because it decided to compromise its preservation goals by opting for more publicly attractive utilitarian goals."[20] Yet compared to Forest Service policies, the NPS's embrace of tourism and recreation was a comparatively minor blemish. Even its foot dragging on wilderness studies did not produce a comparable uproar because of the system's existing land-use restrictions. Above all, the appointment in 1964 of a new director, George B. Hartzog Jr., an NPS veteran who shared the perspectives of Secretary Udall and most of the environmentalists and was adept at dealing with Congress, seemed to mark the beginning of a new era.

Hartzog's goal was to expand the national park system. "I had a simple credo," he recalled, "take it now, warts and all."[21] In applying this credo he was the beneficiary of the planning the NPS engaged in during the 1950s and early 1960s. Since 1938, when the first seashore (Cape Hatteras) had been created, a top NPS priority had been to add other seashores and lakeshores. President John F. Kennedy had been particularly interested in the Cape Cod seashore, which Congress authorized in 1961, together with a first for the NPS, an appropriation to purchase lands and easements. Point Reyes (California), Padre Island (Texas), and Fire Island (New York) were authorized in the next two years, and others were on the drawing board. The other "frontier" was Alaska, where as many as a dozen parks or park additions were contemplated.

Hartzog's contribution was to add a sense of immediacy and a willingness to work with Congress as it increasingly seized the initiative from the executive branch.

Many obstacles remained. The hostility of the Forest Service, the traditional source of new park lands, became more acute as Hartzog became more active, despite Udall's efforts to negotiate a "peace." By the 1970s the NPS–Forest Service competition had become "the most celebrated interbureau rivalry in government."[22] The timber and mining industries were no less antagonistic and found a sympathetic ear among congressional representatives from the rural West and Alaska. As a result, new park proposals often encountered determined resistance. The epic battles over North Cascades (1968), Redwood (1968), and the proposed Alaska parks all were testimony to the strength of economic interest groups in the heyday of environmental activism.

But the internal obstacles were also formidable. The vast majority of NPS executives thought of national parks as places of majestic, usually mountain scenery with carefully planned facilities for tourists. They had some experiences with historical sites, NRAs (until the 1960s, lands surrounding dams and other reclamation projects), and seashores, but urban parks seemed to threaten the character and mission of the agency. What exactly was a national park, and what was the role of the NPS? The demands of scientists and environmentalists for a biologically sensitive approach to defining boundaries and managing park resources only added to their confusion. The turmoil at the top of the NPS after Hartzog's removal in late 1972—part of Nixon's second-term purge of nonloyal administrators—further complicated the situation.

During Hartzog's tenure, Congress authorized sixty-nine new park units, embracing nearly 3 million acres. Total NPS acreage rose to more than 24 million acres, and the agency's share of all federal lands rose to more than 3 percent. The most controversial and challenging acquisitions were new urban parks in New York (Gateway NRA) and San Francisco (Golden Gate NRA). Others, such as Cumberland Island (Georgia), Sleeping Bear Dunes (Michigan), and Apostle Islands (Wisconsin), were areas of scenic beauty that embodied different land forms. Finally, there were several additions, notably Canyonlands (Utah), North Cascades (Washington State), and Redwood (California), that would have satisfied even the most stringent upholders of park purity.

As a result, the national park system of 1970 was vastly different, far more visible, and politically more controversial than it had been even a decade before. For the NPS itself, the transition was difficult and incomplete, and for conservative politicians, Hartzog's oft-stated goal of a park unit in every congressional district, to ensure continuing financial support, was a nightmare seemingly about to come true. After Nixon's reelection in 1972, the reaction began. The president attempted to extend his influence over domestic policy by replacing agency executives like Hartzog with loyalists (in the case of the NPS, with Ronald Walker, a campaign aide who had no background in park management) and reducing expenditures.[23] In 1973 and 1974 this effort accelerated. Both of these developments, the rapid growth of the park system in the preceding decade and the reaction against domestic initiatives, which greatly accelerated with the Watergate scandal, profoundly affected the prospects for an "urban" park in Ohio.

Cuyahoga Valley, 1971–73

The Cuyahoga Valley campaign had been a springboard for Seiberling's political career but otherwise had produced only uncertainty and disappointment. Locally, at least, the idea of a park between Cleveland and Akron continued to command broad public support. The state also became more supportive after the victory of Democrat John J. Gilligan in the 1970 gubernatorial race and the new governor's appointment of William Nye of Akron to head the Ohio Department of Natural Resources. After losing the 1970 Democratic primary to Seiberling, Nye had supported him in the general election, and the two men had developed a close and sympathetic working relationship, especially since Nye was eager to shift state resources from southern Ohio to the Lake Erie basin. At his urging, Gilligan made a Cuyahoga Valley park the state's number one conservation priority. Seiberling wrote, "We have, for the first time in many years, a really positive interest in Columbus."[24] Although Nye was ready to act on behalf of the state, he believed, like Seiberling, that the area really should be a national park.

That, however, was one of the frustrating problems that beset the project. Should the area be a national park, a state park, or a joint project of the Cleveland and Akron metropolitan park organizations? There was no obvious answer. This uncertainty produced delays and buck-passing. In mid-1971, for example, the local park districts temporarily stopped buying Valley land because the state's interest had driven up prices.[25] But that action only compounded the problem. One critical piece of land, owned by a developer who planned to build four hundred homes, could have been purchased by the Akron park district for $2,500 per acre in 1969 but was not because of the "high" price. A few years later, after one hundred homes had been built, the state paid $9,000 per acre to buy the remaining land.[26] The reemergence of the Interior Department as a participant, and a growing rivalry between the NPS and the BOR, added layers of complexity.

Yet even if the financing had been simpler, there would have been problems because of the multitude of individual and institutional land-owners. Most of the western national parks had been created by simply transferring land from the Forest Service or BLM to the NPS. Eastern parks such as Great Smoky Mountains had been assembled by a combination of transfers and purchases. Whatever problems may have arisen in the process, the final result was a park largely owned in fee by the government. Cape Cod (1961) was the first national park based on collaboration between the federal government, local governments, and private landowners, with zoning as the principal mechanism for maintaining the integrity of the area. Many other new parks of the 1960s and 1970s were "greenline" parks, with large numbers of private inholders.[27] From the beginning, Seiberling and his allies stressed that the Cuyahoga Valley would be based on cooperative relationships and that residents would not be evicted. Shortly after introducing his first national park bill, he reassured a worried constituent that "the common assumption" that the government would buy the land "is totally false." He had made a "great effort . . . to protect the rights of people who presently own land within the proposed park area. It is anticipated that very little land will actually be purchased. Most land will be preserved by zoning, and by scenic covenants."[28] In more expansive moments he foresaw Cuyahoga Valley as a model for urban national parks. To emphasize the potential of this approach, he and Betty donated an easement on their property to the Akron Metropolitan Park District in 1972.

Finally, there were ever-mounting development pressures. Apart from several residential projects on the edges of the proposed park, there were two major threats. In 1971 Cleveland entrepreneur Nick Miletti, owner of the Cleveland Cavaliers professional basketball team, announced his intention to build a 22,000-seat coliseum on land near Interstate 271, just west of the proposed park border. The facility would mean more traffic and congestion and, very likely, additional retail businesses on nearby land. Shortly afterward, the Cleveland Electric Illuminating Company announced its plan to build a large power line across the Valley, because the land there was undeveloped and therefore cheaper. Local residents were outraged at both proposals, and the Peninsula Valley Heritage Association (PVHA), which formally changed its name to the Cuyahoga Valley Association (CVA) in early 1972, led the opposition.[29]

On April 22, 1971, Seiberling and Vanik introduced a Cuyahoga Valley park bill. It called for a Valley park, protections for the headwaters of the Cuyahoga in Portage and Geauga counties, northeast of Akron, and a right-of-way along the old canal route and the Tuscarawas River south of Akron. This third feature reflected a desire to emphasize the Valley's historical importance as well as the need to attract the support of conservative Republican representative Frank T. Bow, who represented the area south of Summit County.[30] In his maiden speech to the House, Seiberling insisted that a federal role was essential to "stabilize land use in the whole Valley" and that the Cuyahoga Valley park would be a notable example of the Nixon administration's announced policy of "parks to the people." The Valley could be either "sacred ground" or "asphalt jungle." Twenty-three of his colleagues, including ten Ohio representatives, signed on as cosponsors.[31] When Akron authorities complained that the headwaters regulations could adversely affect the city's water supply, he agreed to drop that provision.

During the following months, Seiberling did his best to rally public support. He and Vanik held informal hearings in Peninsula, Cleveland, and Akron; devoted much effort to assuring suspicious constituents in Peninsula and other Valley communities that they would not be thrown out of their homes; worked closely with CVA and groups like the Sierra Club to mobilize support; and operated behind the scenes to encourage opposition to Miletti and Cleveland Electric Illuminating. The immediate effects, however, were negligible. The Seiberling bill received no serious consideration because of the absence of a dedicated proponent on the committee and the many competing proposals. During the 1971–72 session, the Interior Committee reported favorably on the Gateway and Golden Gate NRAs (both finally authorized in October 1972) that many proponents considered models for other urban areas. The Nixon administration also grasped this potential and viewed with growing alarm the closely related proposals for the Cuyahoga Valley and the Santa Monica Mountains, near Los Angeles, which would require large-scale land purchases. Secretary of the Interior Rogers Morton insisted that Gateway and Golden Gate were only isolated cases and that "NPS can't afford to run them all."[32]

Despite this wariness, the NPS did become involved. Although he had had contacts with Hartzog before the bill was introduced, Seiberling heard nothing after April 22 and suspected that the NPS had been told not to comment. He then called a friend on the Cleveland parks board, who contacted Courtney Burton, another board member, who was treasurer of the Ohio Republican Party. Burton went to Washington to see Morton and Hartzog. As a result, Hartzog sent two members of his planning staff, Edward Peets and Tedd McCann, to investigate. They arrived in July. As Seiberling reported: "They met with Daily [the Akron park director] et. al., seemed to be impressed, took pictures, visited Blossom, Hale Homestead [the living history museum of the Western Reserve Historical Society], etc. Did a lot of walking."[33] They were pleased, perhaps surprised, at what they found and recommended a more thorough study in 1972. Hartzog approved their report in November, and Morton concurred shortly thereafter.

McCann explained their position. He was "particularly impressed by the favorable 'climate' in the Cuyahoga Valley area . . . [and] the unusual degree of cooperation between the Akron and Cleveland Metropolitan Park Boards." He believed "the Cuyahoga Valley situation offers a unique opportunity for cooperative action."[34] McCann told Linda Billings that the Cuyahoga park "would make a good prototype for the kind of urban parks, local-federal cooperative venture Nixon has talked about." The issue was "a different concept in park development."[35]

In March 1972 McCann returned and spent three months on the extended study. He made a thorough survey of the area, its resources, and recreation potential; talked to various groups and community leaders; and assessed the likely costs. His final report enthusiastically endorsed the park proposal and urged NPS support. It remained in bureaucratic limbo for the next year, the period of the presidential election, the purge of Hartzog and other park expansionists, and the emergence of a new cost-conscious approach to domestic affairs. In June 1973, when Ohio senator William B. Saxbe introduced a Cuyahoga Valley park bill and referred to the NPS's endorsement, John C. Whitaker, the under secretary of the interior, wrote privately: "Does this mean we are supporting an NRA? I thought the Administration's position was that we would take Gateway East and West, but would encourage *state* acquisition for the others."[36] In a meeting with McCann in July, NPS director Walker was blunter: "There is no way we are going to make a national park for some rich Democrat from Cleveland," he said, in an apparent reference to Seiberling. "This will be a park over my dead body."[37]

This was not the only setback. Miletti continued to push his coliseum project despite the protests of the CVA and the Ohio Environmental Protection Agency, which objected to the lack of sewer lines at the rural site. Organized opposition to the park also emerged for the first time. The nominal leader was Ben Richards, a local "character" who had been an outspoken critic of the park plan and Seiberling since the 1960s. The owner of Brandywine Falls, one of the Valley's most notable natural features, Richards hoped to turn his property into a tourist attraction. He and a few other vocal skeptics succeeded in arousing their neighbors' anxieties over property ownership and the prospect of "hotels and honky-tonk camping sites."[38] The irony of their position, as Seiberling and other park supporters often reminded them, was that their protests, if successful, would guarantee an end to the peaceful, isolated lifestyle they had known. Nevertheless, opponents organized a Cuyahoga Valley Planning Association and claimed eight hundred supporters.

The Richards group sought to sabotage the park by persuading the regional planning authority (the Northeast Ohio Area Coordination Authority) to oppose it, which would cut off state funding. The board, consisting mostly of Seiberling supporters, met in early March. The directors of the Akron and Cleveland park systems spoke in favor of the park, as did Bill Nye; Jim Jackson, now president of CVA; and several prominent rubber industry executives. Richards led the opposition. "He made a very lengthy and emotional speech claiming that approval . . . would result in the ruination of the entire Valley and particularly of Brandywine Falls." His complaints went on for such an extended period that the board had to delay its decision until the next meeting, a month later.[39] At the April meeting Seiberling spoke, noting that the park would be created over an extended period and that "at every step of the way, there is access." After hearing more complaints the board voted its approval of the park. The opponents were "frustrated"; the board was "a terrific disappointment." Richards's wife told a reporter that "it['>]s going to take a while for us to get a second wind. I don't know how we're going to react."[40]

But the park supporters were also frustrated. The failure of Congress to take the bill seriously and the Interior Department stalemate meant that federal support remained questionable. Nye was helpful but had a limited budget. A meeting in November of CVA leaders and representatives of the Nature Conservancy and the public agencies at Henry Saalfield's home in Peninsula was inconclusive.[41] The CVA was running popular bus tours of the Valley, with guides such as Jackson and occasionally Seiberling; Jackson was giving illustrated talks on the park plan to community groups; and the Sierra Club was sponsoring hikes to familiarize local people with features of the Valley, but without more certainty about the federal role, these activities had limited impact. What McCann had called a "unique opportunity for cooperative action" had become an example of political paralysis. Seiberling warned of a situation where "some of the substantial supporters of the Cuyahoga Valley cause start to collapse and themselves lend impetus to a 'block busting' psychology."[42]

A Park Emerges

As late as mid-1973 it seemed likely that the results of a decade of agitation would be a patchwork of state and local parks together with housing developments, a major entertainment and shopping complex to the west of the Valley, and an obtrusive power line running across the Valley south of Cleveland. That these were not the eventual results (although the Coliseum survived numerous lawsuits, opened in 1974, operated for twenty years, and was finally demolished, the land ultimately becoming part of the park) was largely a consequence of two other developments of that year. The first was the appointment of Seiberling and a new Republican colleague, Ralph Regula, who succeeded Frank Bow in the Thirteenth District, to the House Interior Committee. Seiberling's appointment marked the beginning of a distinguished career as a champion of environmental causes; Regula's interests were more narrowly focused on his district. In 1973–74, however, they formed a potent lobby within the committee for a Cuyahoga Valley national park. The second development of 1973 was the emergence of the Watergate scandal, which discredited the Nixon administration and emboldened Congress. By 1974 support for a Valley park had become a badge of congressional independence.

Seiberling, Vanik, and Regula introduced a new park bill in April and cosponsored companion bills for studies of an Ohio & Erie Canal historical corridor that would extend south into Regula's district. The park bill called for a 22,000-acre NRA, with 13,000 acres purchased or otherwise preserved by the federal government and cooperative arrangements with other institutions. Ohio's senators, Robert Taft and William Saxbe, agreed to sponsor a similar bill in the Senate. However, the most important potential backer, apart from Seiberling, was Rep. Roy A. Taylor (D-NC), who chaired the national parks subcommittee of the Interior Committee. As a new member of the subcommittee, Seiberling worked to cultivate Taylor, and they quickly developed a "mutually respectful" relationship.[43] In August, Seiberling visited the North Carolinian's home in Asheville, spoke at a Democratic dinner, and joined Taylor on a raft trip on parts of the Chattooga River, which Taylor wanted to designate as a wild and scenic river. The rafting experience was the "highlight" of the trip.[44] By October, Seiberling had persuaded Taylor to hold public hearings on the Cuyahoga Valley bill, a significant breakthrough. Because the bill had the backing of thirteen members of the Interior Committee and impressive local support, a place on the subcommittee's agenda was tantamount to approval.

To make the strongest possible impression, the bill's local supporters began a campaign to enlist as many groups and local government units as possible. Their effort began with a meeting at the Brecksville Reservation on August 30, 1973, that brought together representatives from the two local park boards, the CVA, the Sierra Club, the state, and several public relations firms that had volunteered their services. George Watkins of the Lake Erie Watershed Conservation Foundation presided. Seiberling began with a discussion of the obstacles he faced, warning that passage of the bill might take five more years. "Complacency must not set in. There is need for alternative plans during this five years frustration period." The state's proposed recreation bond issue would be an appropriate "second line of defense." He urged them to refer to the park as "the first urban recreation area in the Midwest (not just in Ohio)." He also announced that he had added a new staff member to work exclusively on park legislation. Loretta Neumann had worked in the NPS's Office of Information and would "keep things moving in Washington" and ensure that people in Ohio were informed.[45]

The most important purpose of the gathering was "to create a clearing house or ad hoc committee . . . to eliminate duplication of efforts, wasted efforts, and oversights and to generate positive action." The George Gund Foundation of Cleveland had already indicated a willingness to support such an organization. A long discussion followed on the appropriate qualifications for an executive director. The consensus was that "it won't be easy to find the right person, at the price we can pay, who is available for what may look like a short-term assignment." Seiberling proposed a steering committee made up of representatives of the park districts, the state, and the CVA to raise money and search for the right person. Watkins agreed to serve as chair.[46]

This approach proved to be highly successful. By the end of the year, the steering committee had obtained $35,000 from the Gund Foundation and $5,000 from the Akron Community Trust. It had also identified a prospective executive director in Harvey Swack, the community relations director of the Cleveland park system, a longtime supporter of the park. Swack agreed to take a leave of absence and fill the new post. At a meeting in Peninsula on February 16, 1974, the steering committee presided over the creation of the Cuyahoga Valley Park Federation, which would coordinate the efforts of the many supporting organizations. Amid the excitement, Seiberling again warned against complacency, because "we may have to ram this bill down the throat of the Department of the Interior."[47] The local Sierra Club newsletter best captured the prevailing mood: "With activity in Washington 'water'-logged, the Ohio home-front is frustrated but churning."[48]

Under Swack, the Federation tried to cast the widest possible net in recruiting participants for the hearings, which were scheduled for March 1–2 in Washington, D.C., and June 6 at the Blossom Center. (At the urging of Sen. Howard M. Metzenbaum [D-OH], Saxbe's successor and a member of the Senate Interior Committee, the Senate subcommittee on national parks had also scheduled a hearing for April 18 in Peninsula.) Swack soon had endorsements from more than fifty local organizations, including the Cleveland and Akron chapters of the League of Women Voters, which prepared an informative guide to the Valley, and Akron's Junior League, which provided a substantial grant and a cadre of active volunteers. In the meantime Neumann had enlisted the national environmental organizations, notably the Sierra Club, Friends of the Earth, Izaak Walton League, and National Parks and Conservation Association.[49]

After the formation of the Park Federation, the most significant remaining obstacle was the hardening opposition of the Nixon administration. After Hartzog's departure, Nathaniel Reed, the assistant secretary, largely ran the NPS. Reed had impeccable environmental credentials but was under pressure to reduce expenses, which meant limiting the number of new park units. The New York and San Francisco parks were highly successful, he acknowledged, but also very expensive. Now others sought to jump on the bandwagon. In a statement that infuriated Seiberling and the other Valley park supporters, he accused them of trying to shift expenses to the federal government. "Like in Ohio, we're owed a national park . . . come in, National Park Service, and do your thing. But where is it going to end?"[50] In a widely cited article in the *Wall Street Journal* Seiberling's bill was portrayed as a "pivotal test" of whether the NPS would go further into the "municipal park business."[51]

Apart from Reed and his allies there was also an ideological faction in the Interior Department, represented by the new director of the BOR, James Watt. Unlike Reed, who came from a wealthy Florida family and had long been devoted to conservation causes, Watt had a modest background and brought a strong fundamentalist religious perspective and a libertarian political philosophy to his work. Saving money was only a secondary concern to him. As BOR director he managed the LWCF, which provided land acquisition funds to local and state governments and federal conservation agencies. But he made it clear that he favored local and state government purchases, even if the costs were higher. He testified at the March 1 hearing that his approach "keeps the Feds out of those local dealings and lets the local people and state people set their priorities."[52] When Seiberling asked Watt's assistant if budgetary concerns dictated opposition to a national park, the man replied, "I do not think it is that at all. I think it is philosophical rather than budgetary."[53] Watt's views marked him as a controversial and unpopular figure in the Interior Department, but they also attracted groups that favored less regulation and greater access to publicly owned resources. His attacks on the Seiberling bill were the opening salvos in a longer campaign to overturn the environmental initiatives of the 1960s and 1970s.

The administration's growing rigidity did not prevent the BOR from announcing that it would provide matching funds to the state for land purchases.[54] In August 1973, the BOR and the Ohio Department of Natural Resources concluded an agreement whereby the federal government and the state committed more than $30 million for Cuyahoga Valley land purchases over the next twenty years. In 1973 alone the BOR provided $6 million in matching funds. Nye was pleased to have the money, but he could not commit the legislature to future appropriations. Seiberling dismissed the plan as slow and costly; real estate speculators would "get there 'firstest with the mostest.'"[55]

The first hearing on the Seiberling bill emphasized the contrasting positions of the park supporters and the administration. Seiberling opened the hearing by introducing thirty-three individuals representing various northeast Ohio groups who had made the trip to Washington. He also listed the many other organizations that had endorsed his bill. Vanik followed with a critique of the BOR plan. Regula spoke briefly. Watt then testified, emphasizing that he represented the NPS as well as the BOR. He insisted that national parks should only preserve areas of "unique national significance" and that the Gateway parks were merely "demonstration-type projects." As for the Cuyahoga Valley, it was "basically a regional, local park, and does not have . . . national significance." "I do not believe," he added, that "we will be proposing many more national recreation areas in urban areas."[56] In a caustic rejoinder Seiberling insisted that "national significance" was a fluid phrase that varied with the "shifting priorities" of the Interior Department, rejected the notion of the Gateway parks as "demonstration projects," and argued that the Cuyahoga Valley had greater significance than the New York harbor. "In the end," he concluded, "it is up to Congress to decide."[57]

Stanley Hulett, Watt's deputy, also testified and reiterated Watt's objections. "At some point . . . you have got to say, when does the Federal Government get out of it? When do local units of government get into it?" He had no objection to the Cuyahoga Valley, but, "What about St. Louis? What about Chicago?" He named other cities. "At some point the Federal Government has got to say, 'Wait a minute.' And the Secretary of the Interior has determined that point is now."[58] Nye, who followed, replied that the Cuyahoga Valley was indeed significant and that a park would not be a precedent for other cities. "So I think it is too cavalier of a dismissal of the natural and historic significance." He added that state matching funds were uncertain.[59]

The other people who testified supported the bill. Some, like Jonathan Ela of the Sierra Club, emphasized the Valley's distinctiveness.[60] Others stressed the Valley's appeal and the large number of local backers.

The Senate hearing in April featured the same arguments and many of the same people. At an earlier hearing Senator Metzenbaum had clashed with Secretary Morton, demanding to know why the policy of "parks to the people" had been abandoned. Morton had replied that it was a "priority problem," a large backlog of projects and relatively little money.[61] At the Peninsula hearing, the BOR's Lew Cherry, representing the administration, insisted that state and local parks were superior. The Ohioans were unimpressed. John Daily, the Akron park director, summarized the consensus when he testified that "we do not have the money to do the job, our sister metropolitan park district to the north does not have the money, and the State of Ohio does not have the money."[62]

The third hearing, in June, was a decisive event in the campaign. Subcommittee chairman Roy Taylor and several other non-Ohio members had reluctantly agreed to attend, mostly as a personal favor to Seiberling. Taylor supposedly told a member of his staff: "Of course, this Cuyahoga Valley is not of National Park caliber, but John is a good member of the Sub-Committee, and we want to help him."[63] Cleve Pinnix recalled that "we all kidded about Oh, my God, Cuyahoga, the river that catches fire."[64] Aware of such remarks, Seiberling's staff made a concerted effort to impress the visitors with two full days of activities. On Friday, June 7, a helicopter transported them to various parts of the proposed park. The tour was followed by a reception at Stan Hywet, featuring a string quartet on the patio, Seiberling's guided tour of the mansion, and dinner at Hale Farm. On Saturday they gathered at Blossom Music Center's outdoor pavilion for the hearing, and then attended a reception and a dinner at Robert Hunker's home in Peninsula, hosted by the CVA. Sunday featured golf at a course in the Valley. Neumann, in charge of the elaborate logistics, worked closely with Jim Jackson in drawing up guest lists, preparing maps for drivers, and instructing the pilot.[65] The hearing itself was a triumph. Eighty-one people spoke, the vast majority in support of the park bill. One of the few opponents, H. C. Katzenmeyer, complained appropriately of being "overwhelmed."[66] At the end Representative Vanik predicted a House vote by mid-August and a Senate vote in September.[67] On the flight back to Washington Sunday afternoon Taylor supposedly remarked: "Now that's a wonderful place, and we must save it."[68]

Though now supportive of the park cause, Taylor had a full calendar of other subcommittee business. He was supposedly "torn between his genuine desire to see the park established . . . and his indecision over how to get it done."[69] The competing bills included Seiberling's proposal to increase the LWCF from $300 million per year to $900 million, a key to the expansion of park systems at all levels.[70] The upshot was that the markup of the Valley park bill did not occur until September 30, when, after minor revisions, the subcommittee voted unanimously to support it.

Several days later Taylor received a letter from Richard C. Curry, associate director of the NPS, objecting to references in the subcommittee proceedings to NPS approval of the park. The NPS, Curry wrote, "strongly recommends against" the Seiberling bill and repeated objections that Watt and others had made at the hearings. He then added that his letter was "prompted by the very deep concern expressed by the field managers in our Midwest Regional Office." They believed that the proposed park "would be impossible to administer."[71] Seiberling responded immediately, denying that he had claimed NPS approval and expressing surprise at the statement that the staff believed the park to be unmanageable. In any case he did not "see how the Committee can seriously consider such a vague statement."[72] In the final months of the session the critical issue would be the willingness of Congress to proceed with a bill that the Interior Department strongly opposed.

During the postelection, lame-duck congressional session, both houses acted without any obvious regard for the administration's position. In late November the House Interior Committee adopted the Seiberling bill by unanimous vote after minimal debate, and Seiberling announced that Sen. Alan H. Bible (D-NV), the chair of the Senate subcommittee on parks, had agreed to act quickly after the House voted. Sen. Henry M. Jackson, chairman of the full committee, made a similar pledge.[73] On December 9, after a brief debate—Regula having recruited many Republicans to support or at least not to oppose the bill—the House passed it by a voice vote. Senator Metzenbaum pushed the Senate bill through the Interior Committee in a day, overcoming the efforts of Sen. Paul J. Fannin (R-AZ) to trade the park for a political appointment that Metzenbaum had blocked. "This was the political game that was played. It was a game of political handball," he recalled.[74] Then, with some high-level arm-twisting by Senator Jackson, the bill to create the Cuyahoga Valley National Recreation Area passed the Senate on December 12. Metzenbaum confessed that the speed of the Senate vote was "simply remarkable."[75] Vanik professed a new belief "that miracles can happen, even in a lame duck session."[76]

There remained the possibility of a veto, despite the appeals of Regula, Taft, and Republican governor-elect James Rhodes, who had defeated Gilligan in November. President Gerald R. Ford, who had taken office on August 9 following Nixon's resignation, claimed to be undecided and took the bill with him to Vail, Colorado, on a skiing vacation. Because of Interior Department objections he delayed a decision until the last possible day, December 27. On that morning Taft spoke with him at length, and Metzenbaum followed a few hours later. At Regula's request, Ray Bliss, an Akron resident who headed the Republican National Committee, added a warning about the political implications of a veto. Ford proclaimed, "It's a tough one."[77] His staff had prepared a list of influential people who supported the bill. After reading it, the president supposedly told his congressional liaison, Bill Timmons, "It looks like everybody who is anybody in Ohio thinks I should sign this bill. It's obvious that if I don't sign it, my name will be mud in Ohio. There must be some merit to it."[78] He decided to sign just before the midnight deadline. Seiberling proclaimed it a "great New Year's present for the people of Ohio." He had thought the chances of success were at best 50–50. "But," he added, "I thought the President would look at the human side of this."[79]

Ford's last-minute, politically motivated decision finally resolved the questions of how big the Valley park would be and who would be in charge. Those decisions were direct outgrowths of Seiberling's role and the success of the Valley campaign. Without a local sponsor, the park bill would have had little chance. Ayres certainly would not have provided the necessary leadership. Had he been elected in Seiberling's place, Nye might have, though he had not been active in the park campaign before assuming his state job. Vanik, Regula, and Metzenbaum were valuable allies but probably would not have had the same level of commitment without Seiberling's presence. Having become convinced of the desirability of a park and the necessity of federal financing, Seiberling worked patiently, tirelessly, even stubbornly to bring it to fruition. This would become his characteristic approach to public lands legislation.

The other essential was the broad support for the Valley park legislation in northeast Ohio. For more than a decade, park proponents had argued that some type of public entity was the only way to preserve the Valley and focus public attention on the river's problems. They overcame the parochial objections of local residents and the more formidable opposition of business interests that were poised to exploit the Valley, and, by mobilizing as the Park Federation and pressuring the state's politicians, the shifting and ultimately negative assessments of the federal agencies, including the NPS. As much as any legislation of the period, the Cuyahoga Valley park bill was a gauge of the environmental awakening of the 1960s and 1970s.

The passage of the park bill marked the culmination of years of work but was only the beginning of a long and often difficult process of actually creating a Valley park. And that process would often tax Seiberling as much as the challenges of earlier years. Still, the park campaign was a major personal achievement, a signal to colleagues and lobbyists that he could get things done. Loretta Neumann had hinted at this achievement when she reported that he was "getting a nice reputation as a 'good guy' (environmentally speaking) on the Interior Committee."[80] From this perspective the Valley park campaign was an important preliminary step toward a larger role in the Congress and in the environmental movement.

❧ 5 ❧

Transition Years, 1973–76

By the end of Seiberling's second term in Congress, he could take some satisfaction in the progress he—and the country—had made. Stopping the Vietnam War had been his most immediate concern of 1970, and it, or at least the direct American role, ended in early 1973. Seiberling continued to oppose the efforts of the Nixon and Ford administrations to provide military and financial assistance to the collapsing South Vietnamese government and would be directly involved in the final resolution of the Watergate scandal. Seiberling was unhappy at Ford's unwillingness to "reorder priorities" but took comfort in the growing independence and assertiveness of Congress, an assertiveness that had allowed him to "ram" the Cuyahoga Valley National Recreation Area (CVNRA) "down the throats of the Interior Department."

Reforming the Congress itself had been his other goal, and here, too, he could point to positive changes. Apart from a number of procedural reforms, Thomas P. "Tip" O'Neill, who succeeded Hale Boggs as majority leader at the latter's death in 1972 and became Speaker in 1977, proved to be refreshingly flexible. By 1975, when Seiberling accompanied him on a tour of the Middle East, they worked together amicably. Seiberling likewise found compatible colleagues on the Interior and Judiciary committees. He continued to criticize the opportunism of many of his fellow representatives but admitted that the old days, when the House had been ruled by a handful of tyrants and reactionaries, were past. In the new setting, hard work and attention to detail provided an alternative route to influence and power. When criticized for supporting a congressional pay raise, he answered angrily that "some of us work damned hard."[1] He and like-minded colleagues only gradually became aware of the rising partisanship that in later years would undermine the reforms of the 1970s and lead to growing legislative paralysis.

At home there was also reason for satisfaction. His candor and independence appealed to many of his affluent neighbors who typically voted Republican, while his voting record and attention to constituent concerns secured his political base among working-class Democrats. He typically received near perfect ratings from the Americans for Democratic Action, the League of Conservation Voters, the AFL-CIO, and consumer groups. His voting record was at or near the top among Ohio politicians in opposing Nixon and Ford. His most difficult relationship was with the local labor movement. One leader summarized it nicely: "We love him, but we sometimes can't stand the way he acts. Frankly, I never could understand the sonuvabitch."[2] Apart from his independence, Seiberling was faulted for having relatively little interest in economic issues. He frequently commented about the ravages of inflation, the need for jobs, the challenges of industrial modernization, and related topics, but, as the unionists sensed, his statements reflected a sense of duty rather than genuine engagement. He was "rarely out in front on those issues."[3] As a union leader noted, "We just can't seem to get him interested in these issues."[4]

His popularity was manifest at the ballot box, where his margin typically exceeded 60 percent of the total vote. His Republican opponents in 1974 and 1976 were local businessmen who sought to gain a higher public profile if not necessarily a seat in Congress. The costs could be substantial. The 1974 opponent, Mark Figetakis, proprietor of a restaurant chain, not only suffered a crushing defeat but soon declared bankruptcy, having spread his attention and resources too widely. Seiberling was known to complain that the Republicans "can't come up with some better candidates to run against him."[5] His most annoying challenge came from Democratic state senator Oliver Ocasek, who represented the northern part of Seiberling's district. A rising power in the legislature, Ocasek spent much of the 1970s trying to redraw the district lines to make himself Seiberling's inevitable successor.

With his initial agenda at least partly completed and his future secure, Seiberling was ready for new challenges. His interest in antitrust remained strong, and he used his seat on the Judiciary Committee to attack the large integrated oil companies and the restrictive rules of professional athletic teams. The recession of 1973–75 dealt Akron's rubber manufacturers a devastating blow and might have provided a new focus for his work, as the union leaders urged. But he sensed that there was little he or any politician could do to reverse the situation, the result of decades of underinvestment, mismanagement, and "decentralization," the local euphemism for the movement of factories and jobs to the low-wage South. He would do what he could to aid the victims, but he was unwilling to devote more of his limited time and energy to what would soon be known as the Rust Belt. Apart from the intractability of these problems, there was the inherent appeal of the Interior Committee. It addressed issues that had excited him ever since his youthful days at Stan Hywet and was at the forefront of a movement that promised to revolutionize the ways that Americans managed their natural resources.

Watergate Resolved

To nearly everyone's surprise, the Watergate scandal emerged as a full-blown political crisis during the spring and summer of 1973. The televised Senate Watergate Committee hearings documented the sordidness of the administration as well as the existence of an Oval Office tape recording system that could provide evidence that would condemn or exonerate the president. By early fall Nixon's dogged refusal to turn over the tapes had persuaded most people that he had something to hide, and his "Saturday night massacre" of October 20 (when he fired the special prosecutor after the attorney general and his top assistant both resigned rather than follow his orders) convinced many people that he had a great deal to hide. Seiberling learned of the "massacre" in Virginia, where he and Betty had gone for a brief vacation. His office was swamped with nearly 500 calls and 5,500 letters, the vast majority calling for Nixon's resignation or impeachment.[6] Seiberling joined many of his colleagues in passing a resolution that called for an impeachment investigation, a move that made the House Judiciary Committee, together with the new special prosecutor, Leon Jaworski (appointed October 31), the center of the storm.

Up to that time the House had not been involved in the investigation. That role reflected the sentiment among many, perhaps most, of the members, and the wariness of Speaker Carl B. Albert. Next in line to succeed the president from October 10, when Vice-President Spiro T. Agnew resigned on unrelated bribery charges, until December 6, when Rep. Gerald Ford was confirmed as Agnew's successor, the Speaker was intent on not appearing eager for the job. Peter W. Rodino (D-NJ), who chaired the Judiciary Committee, was no less cautious. Albert, Rodino, and the investigative staff they assembled between December and March were often criticized for their leisurely pace, but their slow, deliberate approach ultimately paid off. A leading student of impeachment concludes that "the obvious care and caution" of the Judiciary Committee, the special prosecutor, and later the Supreme Court, produced "a widespread sense that impeachment could be a measured and legitimate process. . . . By the summer of 1974 impeachment was no longer regarded as an obsolete, unworkable, or inappropriate provision."[7]

The divisions within the Judiciary Committee were another complicating factor. The twenty-one Democrats and seventeen Republicans were divided into several factions. A liberal group of six or seven Democrats (most observers included Seiberling) harassed Ford and pressed for speedy action on Nixon. At the other end of the spectrum, three cautious southern Democrats became the target of Nixon's defense. The Republicans were likewise at odds: three were considered possible supporters of impeachment, while the rest were Nixon loyalists. All of them, however, were aware of the damage Nixon was doing to the party, and after Ford's confirmation, many if not most of them would have applauded his resignation. Rodino's strategy was to hold the Democrats together, attract a few Republicans, and blur partisan distinctions in order to reach a conclusion that would be persuasive to the full House and the Senate.[8]

Like other liberals on the committee, Seiberling was intensely suspicious of Nixon, even before the scandal became front-page news. He had opposed most of the president's policies and joined more than one hundred House Democrats in boycotting Nixon's second inauguration.[9] In early 1973 he urged a thorough investigation of Watergate to create "the maximum possible embarrassment to the Republicans so they'll never again be tempted to do such a reprehensible thing."[10] In June he told the graduating class at Old Trail School that the country had reached "a critical point in our nation's history." Either it would return to constitutional government or "continue our slide . . . toward the kind of nightmarish, all-pervasive authoritarian state" that George Orwell had described in *1984*. What was needed was "a sense of decency and humanity and . . . personal ethics."[11]

The Ford nomination was a challenge. Ford was honest and seemingly incapable of the kind of scheming associated with Nixon, but he was also narrowly partisan, intellectually undistinguished, and wedded to the political status quo. To Seiberling the nomination was "troublesome." The country needed a vice-president "who can restore the nation's faith." Ford, however, was "disappointing." Nixon "has let us down again." Yet if Congress rejected Ford, "we wouldn't get a better nominee, because Nixon is never going to nominate a first-rate person."[12] During the confirmation hearing Seiberling attacked Ford for his "unseemly" behavior in an earlier campaign to discredit and remove controversial Supreme Court Justice William O. Douglas.[13] Seiberling voted "present" when the Judiciary Committee considered the nomination and was one of thirty-five Democrats to oppose Ford in the final House vote.

Despite his hostility to Nixon, Seiberling was uncertain about impeachment. He told an Akron Democratic dinner in late October that "we're not prejudging this thing."[14] (His mother admonished him to "treat him like a Christian," though later, when she learned more about Nixon's behavior, she was less insistent. "Now I see what you're up against," she remarked.)[15] For several months Seiberling worked to restrain Rep. Robert F. Drinan (D-MA) and other liberals who wanted a quick decision. He later recalled that he had helped Rodino organize the evidence and keep the "hearing in line." "You have to be thorough, methodical—and patient."[16] Two publications that evaluated the sentiments of Judiciary Committee members rated Seiberling differently. In one he was listed as one of eight liberals who were ready to vote for impeachment; in the other he was one of nine who were "maybe yes."[17] In May, when the committee concluded its closed hearings, he assessed the case against Nixon as "borderline," adding, however, that the tapes the president had refused to surrender could "only be unfortunate to the President's position."[18]

He was also uncomfortable with the ever-increasing media attention. The *Beacon Journal*'s David Hess believed that "his long years of lawyerly practice . . . his rather sheltered patrician upbringing, and his proclivity for personal privacy all have strained his ability to stand comfortably in the glare of the national spotlight."[19] Accessible to reporters, he was nevertheless one of the "straight arrows" who did not leak confidential information.[20]

When the committee voted for live television coverage of its final deliberations he tried—unsuccessfully—to limit the extra lights that would be permitted. "We are not going to sit here and sweat and be blinking our eyes while we're carrying out this important responsibility," he complained.[21] The larger problem was the tendency of politicians to perform for the cameras. He would discover, perhaps to his surprise, that in this case television did not detract from the seriousness of the sessions.

Seiberling was involved in two well-publicized clashes with Republican defenders of the president. The first occurred on June 27 as he complained to reporters that Nixon's lawyer, James St. Clair, was drawing conclusions rather than presenting evidence. "When the President has refused to give us the best evidence [the tapes], we should not give a lot of weight to self-serving conclusions." At this point, David W. Dennis (R-IN), one of the most partisan of the Republicans, interrupted. "The Democrats have been nitpicking all morning. Now that St. Clair is presenting the President's side, the Democrats are bringing up points of order and rules of evidence," he charged angrily. Seiberling replied that St. Clair's statement was "full of arguments and conclusions." Dennis replied that the Democrats had voted to allow only five of the Republican's ten proposed witnesses. "We didn't refuse the best evidence," Seiberling interjected. "The hell you didn't!" shouted the "red-faced Dennis." The argument continued as the men stalked away.[22]

The second incident occurred on July 26, as the committee was preparing to vote. Delbert L. Latta (R-OH), another crusty Republican whom Seiberling suspected of joining the committee just to undermine the investigation, attacked Albert E. Jenner, the former minority counsel who had switched sides, for having earlier served on a bar association committee that endorsed legalized prostitution. Seiberling was furious. He demanded an apology "for what I consider to be an unprofessional and certainly an injudicial comment on a complete extraneous matter. . . . It's unbecoming to the dignity of these proceedings and in my time on this committee I never heard this kind of thing." Latta insisted that his comment was germane. Seiberling replied in "a voice quavering with anger" that he hoped "the gentleman would reflect on what he did."[23] Later he described Latta's statement as "McCarthyism, pure and simple." "I wanted to put him in his place," he added.[24]

As the committee began its final deliberations on the impeachment resolutions, Seiberling acknowledged that he would play a secondary role. "I'm type-cast as a northern liberal," and Rodino wanted to avoid the impression of a "liberal plot to get the President." Rodino had asked him to concentrate on several issues, including the cover-up and the Cambodian bombing (the subject of one of the less publicized resolutions). He would "be there on occasion, filling in at times, but not in a highly visible way."[25]

By July 27, when the committee voted on the first impeachment article, obstruction of justice, there was little doubt about the outcome. One of the conservative Republicans, Lawrence J. Hogan (R-MD), announced that he would support impeachment, taking the pressure off the three southern Democrats. All twenty-one Democrats and six Republicans voted for the resolution, a decisive defeat for Nixon. Rodino's cautious approach had worked. On July 29 the committee adopted a second resolution, on abuse of power, by 28–10, and on July 30, it voted 21–17 to charge Nixon with defying congressional subpoenas. It defeated the resolution on the Cambodian bombing campaign and another charging Nixon with income tax evasion. Seiberling predicted that the full House would endorse the committee's decisions by the end of August.[26]

On August 3, Seiberling chaired a panel discussion of impeachment before a large audience at the University of Akron. The evidence against Nixon was "overwhelming," he reported. Still, the crisis was not resolved. If for some reason the House refused to indict or the Senate refused to remove the president, "we will be telling all future Presidents that you can do the same as Richard Nixon and get away with it. . . . If it doesn't work, we're really in a bad way. The President will be powerless his last two years in office, the people will have no faith in the system." The other panel members, two professors and the head of the local League of Women Voters, shared his sense of the historic importance of the Judiciary Committee's actions. The "strongest reaction" came from several members of the audience who were critical of Seiberling's vote against the Cambodian bombing resolution. His answer was simple: congressional leaders had known about the secret bombing campaign. "How could Congress indict the President when they were in cahoots with him?"[27] This did not mollify them. Anticipating this response, he had earlier instructed his staff to send several of the critics copies of a column by Anthony Lewis of the New York Times lauding him for his independence.[28] Several weeks later he and three of the other liberals who had opposed the Cambodian resolution issued a long rationale to their "incensed" constituents.[29]

By that time the issue of impeachment had become moot. Responding to a Supreme Court decision of July 24, the White House released, among others, the tape of Nixon's meetings with his staff on June 23, 1972, which provided the long anticipated "smoking gun" and made his defense insupportable. Every Republican on the Judiciary Committee who had initially backed the president now changed his vote on obstruction of justice. Impeachment became a certainty. Recognizing the inevitability of a Senate trial, Nixon resigned on August 9. Seiberling called his farewell speech "statesmanlike . . . the best I ever heard him make."[30]

Looking back on his experiences, Seiberling found a silver lining. "We were operating on the very foundations of our Constitution in that period," he recalled, "getting back to first principles in order to determine what we should do." Veteran members of Congress had told him that the Judiciary Committee's investigation "had done more for the institution of Congress than any other single thing in their memory." It had produced a "healthy skepticism of presidential power" and curbed the "imperial presidency."[31] That "skepticism," in turn, had led to more aggressive responses to President Ford's foreign policy initiatives and to greater willingness to risk vetoes on domestic measures such as the Cuyahoga Valley park bill. The following years would be a time of unusual opportunity.

Conservation Initiatives

The collapse of the Nixon administration effectively transferred political power to Congress and, to an unprecedented degree, to relatively junior members such as Seiberling. In 1970 Bill Ayres had argued that Seiberling was too old to serve effectively. That argument had been self-serving, but it had also been incorrect. In the mid-1970s Seiberling became a power in the House. Apart from the political vacuum created by the Nixon debacle and Seiberling's personal qualities—his dedication and willingness to put in long hours—a third critical element in his rise was the emergence of environmentalism as a political movement. One of Nixon's more insightful gestures had been to dub the 1970s the "environmental decade." By the time Seiberling came to Washington, a coterie of national environmental groups, including the Sierra Club, Wilderness Society, National Audubon Society, Friends of the Earth, National Wildlife Federation, National Parks and Conservation Association, and Environmental Policy Center, was aggressively promoting policies to reduce pollution and preserve what remained of the natural world. As Seiberling became more deeply involved in the work of the Interior Committee and began to understand the political implications of his interest in public lands, he became more closely associated with these groups. He had been an active Sierra Club member and had worked closely with its northeast Ohio leaders on the Valley campaign, so the association was natural. It would be key to his role as a national political leader.

Seiberling's apprenticeship in national environmental politics began during the crowded days of the impeachment investigation and the struggle for the Cuyahoga Valley park. By the end of 1974 he was reasonably well versed in the causes that would dominate his career. That list included national parks, other public land issues, and the regulation of strip-mining. By 1976 he had sponsored major legislative initiatives in all these areas and had assumed an active role in the policy changes that would redefine public land management.

Alaska

The least consequential of these issues—in terms of his immediate contributions and impact—proved in the long run to be the most meaningful to his career. Until the 1950s Alaska had been only slightly better known to most Americans, including most members of Congress, than Tibet. Statehood, completed in 1959, had resulted from a decade-long marketing campaign by Alaska's territorial leaders, a desire among congressional leaders to show their defiance of the nearby Soviet Union, and a political trade-off: Democratic Alaska for Republican Hawaii. Still, few people knew anything about it or had a compelling desire to inform themselves. That attitude changed in 1968, when a huge new oil field was discovered at Prudhoe Bay, on the Arctic coast. Suddenly Alaska became relevant to the oil industry and, as prices rose and energy "crises" raised the specter of continuing supply shortages, to the American public.

Before Alaska's oil became available, however, a tangle of complex political issues had to be addressed. The first was the Alaskan Natives' long-standing land claims, which included the land over which a proposed eight-hundred-mile oil pipeline (from Prudhoe Bay to Valdez on Prince William Sound, with access to the Pacific) would be built. As late as 1970 congressional leaders viewed these claims as little more than a nuisance. They soon became aware of their error. The Natives' ability to cast their demands as a campaign for social justice, coupled with the environmentalists' eagerness to use the claims as a legal tool to block the pipeline, and therefore the development of the Prudhoe Bay oil field, paralyzed Congress. For nearly two years the deadlock continued, while the oil companies, assured by the state government and the Interior Department that a solution would eventually emerge, quietly prepared to build the pipeline.

The Alaska Native Claims Settlement Act (ANCSA), finally passed at the end of 1971, was radically different from anything that had been seriously contemplated as late as the previous spring. It created a series of new Native corporations and awarded them a total of 44 million acres of land; 12 percent of Alaska, or the equivalent of Missouri; and $1.5 billion. The land grant included the Natives' villages plus other lands that they could select for their economic potential. The law also addressed the future of the remaining Alaskan wilderness. Section 17d(2) directed the secretary of the interior to withdraw at least 80 million acres for a period of five years, allowing Congress to consider the creation of national parks, wildlife refuges, and national forests. Alaska already had three large national parks at Glacier Bay, in the southeast; Mt. McKinley, in the central Alaska Range; and Katmai, in the southwest, plus a series of large wildlife refuges. If Congress followed through on the "d(2)" withdrawals, Alaska would have a disproportionate share of the nation's national park and wildlife refuge lands. Whether viewed as civil rights or environmental legislation, or simply a public lands law, ANCSA was an unprecedented measure, remarkable in scope. Seiberling supported it, though he played no active role in its drafting or passage.[32]

Although ANCSA was driven by the prospect of Alaskan oil, it did not directly address the pipeline issue, and Congress, by not acting, could still decide to leave the oil in the ground. No one seriously believed that would be the outcome, and lobbyists for environmental groups often complained that they could not find a single member of Congress who supported that position. The real question of 1972-73 was not whether to build the pipeline, but what restrictions to include in the legislation authorizing construction. The Nixon administration and the industry's friends in Congress essentially sought to give the oil companies a free hand. The environmental organizations and their allies in Congress sought to impose a variety of constraints to minimize the adverse effects on land and water. Their single most important demand was that the pipeline go overland, through eastern Alaska and the Yukon to Edmonton, Alberta, rather than to Valdez. The Canadian route would reduce the impact on eastern Alaska, a largely roadless wilderness, eliminate the danger of an oil spill in hazardous Prince William Sound or along the Pacific coast, and deliver the oil to the midwestern states. Many midwestern politicians favored the Canadian route because their region faced rapidly rising fuel prices, while California, the destination if the pipeline went to Valdez, had abundant supplies. In addition, environmentalists demanded thorough studies of the geography, flora, and fauna of the affected area (e.g., the impact on permafrost and wildlife migration) and remedial measures for any problems that were uncovered.[33]

The result was extensive litigation and political maneuvering that extended into mid-1973. The delays gave the environmental groups time to combine their resources, as they had done with notable effectiveness in defense of Dinosaur National Monument, and again in the mid-1960s, in defending the Grand Canyon from dam builders, and they gave Seiberling an opportunity to play a role in drafting the final legislation. However, the delays also pushed the critical votes into the summer of 1973, when escalating gasoline prices and fuel shortages created irresistible political pressures for simple, speedy solutions.

Seiberling worked with the environmental groups, strongly favored the Canadian route, and opposed efforts to accelerate the approval process. But his distinctive contribution was an amendment to the pipeline bill that would force the oil companies with Prudhoe Bay leases to divest themselves of any stake in the pipeline. He argued that this requirement would encourage competition, protect consumers from artificially inflated prices, and affirm the historic role of the government in regulating oil shipments. While the amendment reflected genuine concern about monopoly power, it was also a way to bring his particular technical expertise to bear on a contemporary policy issue. The oil companies and their allies strongly opposed it, and many of Seiberling's colleagues considered it a needless complication to an already difficult, politically charged issue. In late July the Interior Committee defeated his amendment by a 2 to 1 margin.

The crucial consideration in the House and Senate debates that followed in July and August was the impatience of Congress with the seemingly endless delays. The oil companies had been waiting nearly four years and had agreed to some improvements, such as elevating the pipeline in permafrost areas. Gasoline and heating oil prices were rising (the Arab-Israeli war and the Arab oil boycott of the United States were still three months away), and popular demands for compensatory action were mounting. Still, many questions remained. The Interior Department's efforts to prepare an environmental impact statement, required by the 1969 National Environmental Policy Act (NEPA), had been a fiasco, a demonstration of how much was not known and could not be extrapolated from other situations with any degree of confidence.[34] Prudence dictated more study, or at least the selection of the Canadian all-land route. Yet Congress—even a Congress that had passed landmark environmental legislation—narrowly endorsed the Valdez route and declared the existing environmental impact statement to have satisfied NEPA, precluding additional litigation. The environmental groups' only option was to challenge the constitutionality of the law, which they declined to do.[35]

Seiberling bemoaned these decisions and joined fifty-nine other House liberals in voting against the final bill. In late July he wrote that the oil companies, "who are themselves largely to blame for the current fuel crisis, are now using it in an effort to stampede the Congress into making an overly hasty choice" between the Alaskan and Canadian routes.[36] When an economist complained about the delays, Seiberling noted sarcastically, "His heart bleeds for the oil cos."[37] After the bill passed the House, he wrote that it "was rammed through under enormous pressure from the oil lobby and in great haste. . . . Both in committee and on the floor, I joined other members . . . in an effort to clean up these defects, but the oil lobby had its steamroller going and rode roughshod over all of our efforts."[38] He later recalled the pipeline bill as a "tragic mistake."[39]

The passage of the pipeline bill had two other implications for Seiberling. First, it and the massive construction project that followed publicized Alaska as no other event since the Klondike gold rush of the 1890s. Alaska was suddenly front-page news. Seiberling's fascination grew to the point that in 1975 he persuaded two other members of the Interior Committee, Alan W. Steelman (D-TX) and Goodloe E. Bryon (D-MD), to join him on an inspection tour. With the assistance of the U.S. Air Force and the National Park Service (NPS), which made the arrangements and assigned Theodore Swem, the principal NPS planner, to accompany them, they spent ten days in Alaska and visited every part of the vast state. Traveling from the Arctic coast to the southeast panhandle, they stopped at areas that had been identified as possible parks, refuges, or other conservation entities. Seiberling was astounded, particularly at the opulence of Alaska's mountain scenery. It was, as he wrote Betty, like "a hundred Yosemites."[40] He took eight hundred photographs, the beginning of a collection that, he believed, provided compelling evidence for preserving wilderness Alaska. He was now better informed about Alaska than most Alaska residents and all of his House colleagues, with the possible exceptions of Steelman, Bryon, and Donald E. "Don" Young, the Alaska representative.

Second, the pipeline authorization was a significant setback for the hitherto triumphant environmental movement. ANCSA had suggested that the Prudhoe Bay discoveries might have a positive outcome; the pipeline bill raised many doubts about that prospect. Faced with immediate economic pressures, Congress had capitulated, endorsing the least responsible of several alternatives. The brutal debates had also engendered an aversion to more Alaska legislation. Congressional leaders were in no mood to take up an Alaska parks and refuges bill, which was likely to be equally controversial. The fate of the d(2) land withdrawals became more problematic.

Parks and Forests

The pattern that had emerged in the Alaska debates—of a Congress unwilling to confront major economic interests but supportive of less controversial public lands initiatives—gave an often frustrated Seiberling opportunities for leadership. Despite the penny-pinching of the Nixon and Ford administrations, the movement for new parks accelerated in the 1970s and enjoyed many successes. Most of the proposed parks were in the East and South and required land purchases. By traditional NPS standards they were shockingly expensive. Between 1971 and 1976 Congress authorized more than $900 million for national park acquisitions.[41] Redwood Park (California) and Big Cypress National Preserve (Florida), with land acquisition budgets of more than $100 million each, were three times the projected cost of CVNRA. Big Thicket National Preserve (Texas), Golden Gate NRA (California), and Sleeping Bear Dunes National Lakeshore (Michigan) were other big-ticket projects, while Cuyahoga Valley (the seventh most expensive), Delaware Water Gap (New Jersey, Pennsylvania), Point Reyes National Seashore (California), and Buffalo National River (Arkansas) were moderately expensive. Seiberling helped finance those acquisitions, aided the NPS in adjusting to its expanded role, and was instrumental in protecting several established parks from large-scale mining projects. He also helped to lay the groundwork for the many additional parks that would be added in the late 1970s.

But parks were not the only public lands that commanded the attention of Congress. By the early 1970s the Forest Service's efforts to sabotage the Wilderness Preservation System had generated widespread criticism of the agency. At the same time, public interest in wilderness preservation was growing rapidly. The result was a series of clashes that led to a substantially larger role for Congress in wilderness politics and anticipated the even more dramatic developments of the late 1970s and early 1980s, when Seiberling headed the House public lands subcommittee.

Seiberling's first and politically most acute responsibility was to see that the CVNRA got off to a successful start. This meant securing adequate funds to acquire land and introduce public services. The immediate obstacle was the hostility of the Ford administration and specifically of Assistant Secretary of the Interior Nathaniel Reed, a traditionalist who looked upon the new urban parks with skepticism, if not disdain. Reed's obvious dislike for the CVNRA and his all-but-announced intention to spend as little money as possible on it earned a rare public rebuke from Chairman James Haley of the House Interior Committee.[42] The administration proposed a meager $1 million for 1975, which the Ohio politicians, led by Rep. Ralph Regula, who served on the Appropriations Committee, raised to $5 million. Ford proposed $5.7 million for 1976, which was again nearly doubled, but that was still not enough to head off dramatic rises in land prices.[43] Seiberling repeatedly expressed his frustration at this penny-wise, pound-foolish approach, which ensured that the total cost would far exceed the $35 million that Congress had authorized.[44] When Ford called for large increases in park spending during his 1976 election campaign, Seiberling observed sarcastically that "there's always rejoicing in Heaven when a sinner repents."[45]

The ultimate answer was to increase the Land and Water Conservation Fund (LWCF), which provided most of the land acquisition money. Because the fund was sustained by offshore drilling lease payments, it was, in theory, immune to the exigencies of the annual budget process. One of Seiberling's first goals as a member of the Interior Committee had been to increase the fund to accommodate the capital needs of the new urban parks. He had proposed an immediate tripling of the fund, to $900 million annually, but then deferred to his more conservative colleagues who voted to stagger the increase over several years until the fund reached $900 million in 1980. He also convinced them to earmark up to $100 million of the annual appropriation for historical restoration, a turning point in the movement to preserve historic buildings. He then had to overcome the opposition of western politicians, who wanted money to develop, rather than to acquire, park lands. By the time their differences had been worked out, nearly two years had passed; the larger LWCF was finally approved in mid-1976.[46]

The expansion of the LWCF was a godsend to the CVNRA. It did not prevent land prices from escalating or the total cost from rising to more than $40 million, but it did enable park authorities to adhere to their acquisition schedule. Indeed, their aggressiveness led to a different type of political challenge in the late 1970s.

The first CVNRA park superintendent, William Birdsell, was an NPS veteran who had served at Gettysburg National Military Park before coming to Ohio in 1971 to oversee NPS properties in the state. He had been an active supporter of the campaign for the Valley park, testifying at the Senate and House hearings. The NPS director named him "key man" for the CVNRA in April 1975 and superintendent in June. Birdsell enthusiastically embraced his new job, working fourteen to sixteen hours a day, seven days a week. His punishing schedule contributed to a heart attack in 1976 when he was only forty-seven years old.[47] Birdsell nevertheless refused to slow down. In an ill-advised move to accelerate the process of land acquisition, he obtained the services of five Army Corps of Engineers agents to augment his tiny staff. The combination of the hyperactive Birdsell and the Corps of Engineers employees, frequently officious and indifferent to individual sensibilities, created ill will among many Valley landowners, who remembered Seiberling's promises that the park would rely on cooperative arrangements with residents.

The other immediate effect of the purchases was to reduce property tax payments to local governments. In 1974 the Ohio Department of Natural Resources employed a consultant to estimate the shortfall. He concluded that only one township and only one school district would be significantly affected, and they would lose 15 percent and 5 percent of their income, respectively.[48] Drawing on the experience of other parks, Seiberling reassured local officials that the losses would be temporary. At a meeting with them in late October 1975, he also pledged to get help from the federal government.[49] He included a payment plan in legislation that had been originally designed to assist western localities with large federal landholdings. By adding a temporary compensation plan for local governments with new parks, he was able to attract eastern supporters who had been indifferent to the earlier measure, and the Interior Committee approved the legislation in March 1976. In August, the House approved his proposal, which provided local governments in the Cuyahoga Valley with a total of $1.7 million over five years, plus a small annual subsidy. The bill, which also provided for the expansion of CVNRA by nine hundred acres, mostly hillsides subject to erosion at the northern end of the Valley, became part of an omnibus parks bill that Ford signed in October 1976.[50]

There were many other occasions to promote national parks during these years, and Seiberling became a champion of the new urban parks. He took particular interest in the proposed Chattahoochee Park, in suburban Atlanta, touring the area with Rep. Andrew J. Young (D-GA), the principal sponsor, and the governor of Georgia, in late 1975.[51] Seiberling recalled that he was "happy" to be "first on the Interior Committee" to visit the area, as he believed "quite passionately in the principle of using federal funds for promoting natural areas in and around our major urban centers."[52]

A different kind of opportunity arose in September 1975, when the *Washington Star* published a long article on a plan by the Tennaco Company to open a large borax strip mine in Death Valley National Monument, adjacent to one of the most popular visitors' viewpoints in the park. Death Valley was one of six national parks that permitted private mines, and it had a long history of borax and talc mining. The NPS had sought to make most of the park a wilderness in order to discourage new mining ventures, but the Interior Department balked, claiming it had no power to intervene. The controversy occurred at the same time that the battle over the federal regulation of strip-mining seemed to be nearing a climax. When other newspapers picked up the *Star* story, the public response was overwhelming. Officials were besieged with letters and telephone calls. Seiberling immediately introduced a bill to ban new mining claims in national parks; five senators, including Alan Cranston and John V. Tunney of California, introduced a similar bill that added a three-year moratorium on current and proposed mining activity.[53]

Seiberling and other members of the House national parks subcommittee subsequently visited the monument and toured the area with an NPS employee who had been a mining engineer and could explain what was happening. Cleve Pinnix of the Interior Committee staff recalled that Seiberling asked "a lot of questions . . . he was trying to learn everything he could about the economics of it."[54] The Senate bill passed with only minor objections. The House measure, officially sponsored by Mo Udall, was more controversial, not because of its likely impact on Death Valley's mines—the legislation banned new claims and mines, not existing ones—but because it threatened a proposed nickel mine on the western edge of Glacier Bay National Monument in Alaska. Newmont Mining, the lease owner, and Don Young prevailed on the Interior Committee to exclude part of Glacier Bay from the ban. When the bill came to the floor, Seiberling successfully led the fight against the Young amendment. The final House bill was identical to the Senate bill, and Newmont later abandoned its proposed Glacier Bay mine. Nancy Lord, secretary of the Kachemak Bay Conservation Society, one of the grassroots environmental groups that had proliferated in Alaska after the oil pipeline controversy, caught Seiberling's attention when she wrote that many Alaskans "feel that you are, in fact, our representative in Congress."[55]

Wilderness

The reemergence of the wilderness movement in the mid-1970s paralleled the interest in parks. The Wilderness Act itself had only created 9 million acres of wilderness, mostly in the Rocky Mountain West and in California, and mostly "rock and ice." The expansion of the Wilderness Preservation System was left largely to the managers of the three federal conservation agencies who were to make recommendations to the president and hence to Congress over the next decade. But as the years passed, very little happened; the federal managers interpreted the charge as a restriction on their managerial powers and an affront to the interest groups that sought to cut timber, build lodges or ski resorts, or in other ways utilize the land and its resources. The Forest Service, with its "multiple use" mandate and close relations with commodity groups, was especially conflicted.

The national forests remained at the center of the wilderness campaign because of their vastness and pristine areas of mature forest and the Forest Service's insular institutional culture. RARE and the purity doctrine had only antagonized environmentalists and inspired more lawsuits. In response to demands for wilderness designations in the eastern forests, the Forest Service responded with another concession that at first seemed to have more promise. At a 1971 Sierra Club Wilderness Conference, Assistant Chief (and soon-to-be Chief) John McGuire proposed a system of "wild areas" in eastern forests. "Wild" wasn't quite "wilderness"—recreational activities would receive more attention than in wilderness areas—but logging and most other commercial activities would be banned. The purity principle would be salvaged, and the Forest Service would decide which areas qualified. McGuire's proposal threw the environmentalists into disarray. National Sierra Club officials were "most suspicious" of the plan, while the leaders of the Friends of the Earth and the Wilderness Society rejected it out of hand.[56] But some midwestern and New England Sierra Club activists were receptive, and the national leaders of the Izaak Walton League enthusiastically endorsed it as a way to make peace with the Forest Service. For more than a year there were debates within and between groups. A series of conferences, culminating in a meeting at Knoxville in December 1972, and a daylong meeting of the Wilderness Society and Sierra Club staffs a few days later, produced a consensus. The Forest Service could have its wild areas as long as it supported eastern additions to the wilderness system.[57]

In early 1973 Sen. Henry M. Jackson (D-WA) and Rep. John P. Saylor (R-PA) introduced an Eastern Wilderness Areas bill that created twenty-eight wilderness areas in eastern national forests. McGuire realized that his plan had backfired, potentially creating more, not less, wilderness. The wild areas idea disappeared in 1973 as environmentalists and congressional leaders decided how many new wilderness areas to create.

The final legislation was disappointing to the environmental groups. In June 1974 the Senate passed a modified Jackson bill, creating nineteen wilderness areas and forty wilderness study areas. It also improved on the Wilderness Act by banning grazing and mining claims in eastern forests. Proponents proclaimed a "solid victory."[58] The House proved to be less helpful. The public lands subcommittee, under John Melcher (D-MT), a friend of the Forest Service, was slow to act and then decided that only potential wilderness areas that had the explicit support of the local congressional representative would be considered. This stipulation, forcing the individual representatives to take a public stand, led to the deletion of two areas in Missouri and one in Michigan, a reduction in the number of wilderness study areas from forty to seventeen, and the elimination of the other reforms. The senators concurred, and President Ford signed the bill in early January 1975.[59]

Despite the seemingly meager results, the Eastern Wilderness Areas Act had broad implications for Seiberling's career. The events of 1971–74, the lawsuits, RARE, the abortive wild areas campaign, and the Eastern Wilderness Areas Act (together with the later Endangered American Wilderness Act), emphatically underlined the ability of groups and individuals apart from the Forest Service and the other land management agencies to propose and campaign for new wilderness designations. Congress would respond as readily to citizens groups as to the agencies. The eastern wilderness controversy also demonstrated once more the importance of strategically placed individuals in the Congress. John Melcher was hardly another Wayne Aspinall, but he was closely identified with western rural interests. He ran successfully for the Senate in 1976 and was succeeded as chairman of the public lands subcommittee by Teno Roncalio (D-WY), a more sympathetic figure, and then, in 1979, by John Seiberling.

Land-Use Planning

Three other legislative battles dealing with land and land management issues illustrated the residual strength of groups that had a financial interest in preserving the status quo, even in the face of rising environmentalist pressures. In the first case, a land-use planning bill that Seiberling strongly supported "got clobbered by what we would now call the 'Wise Use' movement," Sierra Club lobbyist and Seiberling ally Charles "Chuck" Clusen recalled two decades later.[60] In the second, environmentalists, aided by favorable court decisions, mounted a campaign against clear-cutting in national forests, which, like strip-mining, had become a potent symbol of environmental degradation and of the failure of government to uphold the public interest. The campaign failed in its immediate objective but did succeed in opening new avenues for protests and appeals. In the third case, Seiberling and his allies were able to rescue a long-delayed organic act for the Bureau of Land Management (BLM) that, at a time of heightened interest in national parks and wilderness designations, remained a relic of an earlier era when commodity producers brooked no opposition in the western states and Alaska. The final result, the Federal Land Policy and Management Act (FLPMA) of 1976, was a tentative but meaningful step toward a more professional and balanced approach to land management in the West.

Land-use planning legislation was supposedly President Nixon's top environmental priority, and his administration continued to support it until the impeachment crisis of 1974. Indeed, Secretary of the Interior Rogers Morton, who was to administer the program, was forced to reverse himself on the eve of the congressional vote. The actual bill was comparatively toothless, providing grants to states that voluntarily set up a planning mechanism similar to the transportation and housing planning systems that were already in operation. The states would be in charge, and many questions remained about the likely effects of the legislation. Environmentalists worried that it might allow state governments controlled by prodevelopment interests to override local controls. Seiberling, for example, received a long critique from James Alkire, director of the Akron Planning Department, who was highly critical of the House bill.[61] Nevertheless, the Senate passed a land-use planning bill in 1972 and 1973, and most House liberals, led by Udall, supported similar legislation.

Seiberling was active in the committee deliberations, sponsoring several amendments proposed by environmental groups. His most important contribution was an amendment requiring the state authorities to consider "the maintenance of adequate open space land in urban and suburban areas." He believed that he and Rep. Charles A. Vanik "could have a very good floor colloquy using the Cuyahoga Valley Park as an example of the kind of open space preservation that these sections of the bill are intended to cover."[62]

As the bill neared floor action in the House, the focus of the debate shifted. Rather than criticizing specific provisions, opponents, backed by real estate and land development interests, attacked land-use planning in general as an assault on personal freedom and property rights. Orchestrated by Rep. Sam Steiger (R-AZ), an "unreconstructed ultraconservative" and "spokesman for special interests," in Seiberling's words, and joined at the last minute by the embattled president, the Rules Committee tabled the bill, and a procedural motion to bring it to the floor failed by a small margin. Most observers blamed Nixon for the defeat. In Seiberling's view, his shift was "a sop to the ultra-rightwing in the Senate whose votes he is going to need in case he's impeached."[63]

In 1975, with Nixon gone, the results were no better. Loretta Neumann complained that "Steiger has been rounding up his troops and generating mail against [Udall's bill], but the environmentalists haven't been on the ball at all."[64] With several stalwart supporters wavering in the face of constituent pressures, Udall brought up the bill in committee in mid-July. The committee vote was 19–23, effectively killing it. Seiberling explained that it "was the victim of a campaign of extraordinary and inexplicable misrepresentation." Right-wing groups had used it as "a shibboleth for their own biases."[65]

The campaign to restrict clear-cutting in national forests was an outgrowth of federal court decisions in West Virginia (1973) and Alaska (1975) that declared clear-cutting a violation of the Forest Service's organic act. Timber industry allies then proposed legislation that would restore the Forest Service's authority to specify harvest methods; environmentalists campaigned for a nationwide ban.

In the House the legislation was managed by the Agriculture Committee, which was sympathetic to the timber industry and largely indifferent to environmentalist pressures. Accordingly, the committee bill simply gave carte blanche to the Forest Service to use whatever methods seemed appropriate—in effect, an endorsement of clear-cutting. Seiberling opposed the final bill, which passed 305 to 42.[66] The environmental groups were more successful in the Senate, which passed a compromise bill. The final National Forest Management Act of 1976 did not prohibit clear-cutting, but it did force the Forest Service to prepare more elaborate and transparent forest plans, creating new opportunities for opponents of clear-cutting and other Forest Service policies.[67]

The proposed BLM organic act dated from the early 1960s, when Representative Aspinall successfully proposed a study commission to review and synthesize a century of public land regulations. The commission, with Aspinall himself in charge, reported in 1970. Among its many recommendations was a proposal to upgrade the BLM, the haphazard, industry-dominated agency that presided over western public lands not included in the national parks, national forests, or wildlife refuges. An organic act would give BLM managers powers comparable to those enjoyed by the Forest Service and NPS. The devil, however, lay in the details. Aspinall, arguably the most ardent defender of commodity interests in Congress, had no desire to diminish their influence, and his views were shared by influential allies in the other western delegations. The issue, then, was whether a desirable administrative reform should be combined with major policy reforms. Aspinall's successors (following his 1972 reelection defeat) opposed any meaningful change; Seiberling and the environmentalists fought to reduce the agency's industry bias at the same time they elevated it.

Surprisingly, the one feature of this conflict that occasioned little controversy was a requirement that the BLM join the other conservation agencies in evaluating its lands for possible inclusion in the Wilderness Preservation System. This was primarily the work of Harry Crandell, a former Fish and Wildlife (FWS) official who had gone to the Wilderness Society in 1970 as its chief wilderness lobbyist. In 1975, when internal discord at the Society led to mass firings, Crandell found himself out of a job. To his surprise Melcher asked him to join the public lands subcommittee staff. Crandell promoted a wilderness review plan that, he argued, was essential to the bill's passage and arranged for friends who worked for Sen. Lee W. Metcalf (D-MT), an influential member of the comparable Senate subcommittee, to make a similar case.[68]

In other respects, Melcher's version of an organic act was extreme, even outrageous. His 1974 bill gave new powers to mining companies, streamlined procedures for the sale or donation of public lands, amended the Endangered Species Act, and liberalized grazing leases. Environmental groups mobilized to amend or defeat the bill and argued successfully that it was unacceptable.[69] Melcher brought up a slightly modified bill two years later and set off another storm of protest. He won the endorsement of the Interior Committee despite the vocal opposition of prominent Democrats, including Seiberling, Udall, James H. Weaver (D-OR), Paul E. Tsongas (D-MA), Teno Roncalio, and Phil Burton (D-CA), the group that would dominate the committee after the 1976 election. They complained that Melcher's bill provided "special treatment" for mining and livestock interests, the "most flagrant example" of which was an "absurd" provision that forced the secretary of the interior to review all public land withdrawals every five years and to justify their status. (Withdrawn land was off-limits to new mining claims and other commercial ventures.) They were no less outraged by a new grazing fee formula that promised to lower the already heavily subsidized fees that ranchers paid. Another complaint was the bill's failure to address the problem of law enforcement on BLM lands, which meant that almost anything movable was fair game for thieves.[70] These objections, and the lobbying of the environmental groups, caused many eastern representatives to withhold their support. The bill passed in July 1976 by a narrow 169 to 155 margin, with 106 abstaining. That was close enough to force Melcher to include Seiberling, Udall, Weaver, and Burton on the conference committee.

Seiberling, who had introduced several successful amendments during the floor debate, played a leading role in the conference deliberations. His continued objections to the most controversial sections of the bill gradually wore down Melcher. Finally, he and his allies, including several senators, eliminated the most obnoxious features of the House bill, including most of the restrictions on land withdrawals and the new grazing fee schedule. They also jettisoned several qualifications that had been added to the wilderness studies, including a "once and for all" proviso that closely resembled the so-called hard-release formulas that would be proposed for national forest lands in later years. On a positive note, they were able to insert a land-use planning provision that had originally been part of the proposed land-use planning act. The final bill also increased the police powers of the BLM.[71]

The Challenge of Strip-Mining

The continuing effort to regulate strip-mining illustrated both the power of entrenched economic interests and the impasse that had developed between Congress and the new president. An extended conflict in 1973–74 that tied up Congress for months resulted in a severely weakened bill that President Ford ultimately vetoed; an almost identical standoff led to another veto in 1975. These battles were a prelude to the successful legislation of 1977, but they had another effect that may have been as important. The fight over strip-mining—long, arduous, dependent on technical distinctions that most people did not understand—solidified Seiberling's reputation as a tough, patient champion of environmental causes.

Until 1973 the campaign against strip-mining was based on the simple, appealing idea that it was so destructive that it ought to be prohibited. As historian Chad Montrie shows, the abolition effort galvanized activists throughout Appalachia, including southeast Ohio.[72] It took concrete form in a bill introduced by Rep. Ken Heckler (D-WVA), cosponsored by Seiberling. In October 1971 activists formed an umbrella organization, the Coalition against Strip Mining, to represent them in the congressional fight, naming Louise Dunlap of the Environmental Policy Center, as chair. Dedicated, passionate, and wholly absorbed, Dunlap became an influential advisor to Heckler and Seiberling as well as a link between the grassroots groups and their congressional allies.

As it became apparent that Congress might be receptive to regulatory proposals, the abolition movement faded. Many backers, like Seiberling, saw it as the ideal solution but, given the political power of the coal industry, an exceedingly unlikely one. Seiberling told one interviewer that he wanted tough regulations to "prove that even strict controls won't work."[73] Dunlap and her followers continued to call for an end to strip-mining but devoted more and more of their energies to regulatory proposals. Their new interest seemed to pay off in October 1972, when the House overwhelmingly passed a comparatively weak bill. The Senate did not act and the legislation stalled, but prospects for a new, tougher bill in the next session were favorable. Seiberling promised to "continue to work for a bill to impose rigid controls on strip mining . . . if not abolish strip mining altogether."[74]

For the next year reformers fought the coal and electric utility industries. The legislation was managed jointly by the House environment and the mining subcommittees, headed respectively by Mo Udall and Patsy T. Mink (D-HI), who, like Seiberling, favored strict controls. But the subcommittees also included many representatives of western and southern mining states. Udall and Mink held well-attended public hearings in April and May 1973 and conducted field inspections of Appalachian mining areas (Kentucky, West Virginia, Pennsylvania, and Ohio) in May, with Seiberling participating. Environmentalists won an important victory in August when the subcommittees voted to use Udall's relatively stringent bill as their mark-up vehicle. Seiberling, who had been "intimately involved" in drafting the bill, was "delighted" at the outcome of the vote.[75] Industry allies, led by Sam Steiger, responded with delaying tactics, partly to allow rising energy prices to generate public pressure against regulation. As a result, twenty-four mark-up sessions were necessary before the subcommittees completed their work in November. Action by the full committee and the House was postponed until the spring. The Senate passed a weaker bill in October.

Seiberling introduced two controversial amendments. The first was to ban strip-mining in national parks, national forests, and other federal conservation units. This was partly a response to mining in Ohio's Wayne National Forest, the only national forest with active mine operations at the time. The other amendment levied a $2.50-per-ton reclamation fee on all coal production, with generous deductions for certain mining expenses. Seiberling's primary goal was to provide for the reclamation of abandoned lands, a serious problem in the Appalachian states. A secondary objective was to encourage underground mining at the expense of strip-mining. The deductible costs included safety equipment and the black-lung benefits that Congress had decreed in the late 1960s. These benefits had raised the cost of underground mining and made western strip-mining more attractive. The Interior Committee staff estimated that underground mines could offset $2.25 of the $2.50 tax, strip-mine operations only about $1.50. Three-fourths of the reclamation fund would come from western operations, while most of the expenditures would be in the East.[76] Coal and utility lobbyists strongly opposed the Seiberling amendment. "Frankly, we were shocked," explained one. "We thought that Seiberling was consumer-oriented, but this seems like a way of punishing consumers."[77]

An added factor was the Nixon administration, which became an active opponent as it became increasingly dependent on congressional conservatives. Federal Energy Administrator William E. Simon and Interior Secretary Rogers Morton took the lead, writing Interior Chairman Haley and others that the proposed regulations would curtail energy supplies.[78] Seiberling was "sickened" by their efforts. "Once again . . . [Nixon officials] have met behind closed doors . . . to draft a policy favorable" to industry.[79] In the following months, as the administration became a de facto partner of the coal companies, the heads of the Environmental Protection Agency and the Council on Environmental Quality publicly dissented from the administration's position. Udall expressed the consensus among congressional leaders when he complained that "every single decision made down at the White House is related to the President's impeachment difficulties, and everything is being slanted to be of assistance in that effort."[80]

The combination of intense industry lobbying and pressure from the administration made it unlikely that the more controversial features of the legislation would survive. Seiberling agreed to revise his amendment, but the Interior Committee voted to substitute another reclamation plan that reduced the tax and eliminated the distinction between underground and surface mining. What had started as a plan to aid the eastern mines became another burden for them. Dunlap and the environmental groups pledged to oppose the final bill, unless the Seiberling amendment or Heckler's substitute won on the House floor.[81]

More months of wrangling followed. The House finally passed a bill in July 1974, and a conference committee, on which Seiberling served, attempted to reconcile the House and Senate versions. In the process the most controversial provisions were dropped—the final bill included a flat 35-cents-per-ton reclamation tax, too little to undertake more than a minimal effort. Another potentially more radical measure, introduced by Sen. Mike Mansfield (D-MT) that banned strip-mining leases when government only owned the mineral rights to the land, was also discarded. The most significant remaining restrictions were a requirement to return the land to its approximate original contour and Seiberling's ban on strip-mining in national forests and parks (but not other conservation units). Seiberling wrote that he was "disappointed"[82]: "I worked hard both in the Interior Committee and in the House/Senate Conference Committee," he recalled, "to provide a differential that would take into account the differences between deep and strip mining. . . . Both sides were committed to some type of Abandoned Mine Reclamation Fund, and the per-ton fee was the compromise. I attempted to include a system of credits in the fee, but was defeated."[83]

Even this watered-down version was not acceptable to the coal producers. Their continuing intransigence was symbolized by Steiger's threat to punch Seiberling "in the face" after he challenged some of Steiger's claims.[84] When the bill finally passed and went to President Ford during the postelection lame-duck session, he dutifully refused to sign it, arguing that the reclamation fee was too high.

The bill's supporters were determined to avoid a repeat of this experience in 1975. The Democrats made substantial gains in the 1974 congressional elections, electing fifty-two new House members and several additional northern senators. The House and Senate Interior Committees were largely unchanged, however, and the only major difference in the 1975 bill was Seiberling's successful proposal, in committee, for a reclamation fee of 35 cents per ton on strip-mined coal and 10 cents per ton on underground coal, supposedly a concession to Ford. (In the final version, the underground tax was raised to 15 cents per ton.) The Senate passed the new bill on March 12; the House followed on March 18. The conference committee adopted several amendments that addressed the administration's complaints, "substantially" weakening the bill but going "a long way" to accommodate the president. The conference report was adopted by both houses in early May. Ford, now firmly in the antienvironmentalist camp, followed with a veto on May 20.[85] The bills had passed both houses by more than a two-thirds majority, so a successful override seemed likely.

During the following weeks, industry and administration lobbyists focused on the House, as a Senate override was a foregone conclusion. Passage of the bill, they predicted, would mean job losses, higher prices, and increased dependence on imported oil. At an Interior Committee hearing on June 3, Secretary Morton and Energy Administrator Frank Zarb presented the administration's case. Udall and Seiberling challenged them, insisting that their arguments were dishonest and misleading, a "smoke screen" for subservience to the coal industry.[86] Nevertheless, the attacks had an effect, and by the eve of the vote the outcome was in doubt. On June 5 the House failed by three votes to override the president's veto.[87]

Later that year, Representative Melcher, who supported the environmentalists on strip-mining, tried to attach a "scabbed down" version of the strip-mining bill to a coal leasing bill the administration supported. Udall and most of the environmental groups backed this measure.

"We've got to keep the issue alive," Udall told a reporter, "and the only horse around is Melcher's." But Representative Mink and many others preferred to wait until 1976 and pass a stronger bill. The Interior Committee agreed, defeating Melcher's proposal by one vote.[88]

The situation did not improve in 1976. With key congressional leaders, including Udall and Jackson, campaigning for the presidency and other Democrats reluctant to revive controversial measures in an election year, the strip-mining bill went nowhere. The Rules Committee sabotaged a bill adopted by the Interior Committee, and another bill stalled as the election process became all-absorbing. The Ford administration opposed all these measures, "firmly convinced," in the words of the acting secretary of the interior, that "a major new all-embracing Federal Surface mining program could have a devastating effect on coal production."[89]

In August, Seiberling reflected on these events and indirectly on the five-year campaign that preceded them. He bemoaned the failure of Congress and the president to devise a coherent and responsible energy policy with attention to renewables such as solar and wind, but even that paled beside the collapse of strip-mining reform. "Of all the disappointments I've had, this is the biggest one. . . . It makes you weep to see what's happening, whole towns destroyed, people impoverished, tax bases eroded, landscapes ravaged, streams silted and spoiled. It's a disgrace."[90]

This experience had a lasting impact on Seiberling. The strip-mining bills addressed a problem that only government could correct. And yet government was paralyzed because of the entrenched power and financial resources of groups that opposed regulation, coupled with the indifference of many in the Congress who were not directly involved. How then could reformers overcome the conservative inertia inherent in the system? There was no obvious answer, but the events of the mid-1970s pointed to several possibilities. In the Cuyahoga Valley park campaign, a variety of competing approaches had produced mostly frustration and disappointment until Seiberling had decided, in effect, that a national park was the solution and proceeded accordingly. Aggressive leadership had been essential. A second requirement was public pressure. The defenders of the status quo would almost always have superior financial resources. Reformers could succeed only by mobilizing a larger and more devoted constituency. There were many activist organizations in Appalachia, but they never succeeded in neutralizing the power of the coal companies or mobilizing large numbers of supporters outside the area. On controversial issues such as strip-mining, or even more so, the fate of Alaska's vast d(2) lands, public pressure would be indispensable to success.

6

Wider Horizons, 1977–78

John Seiberling's friends tell a story about him that illustrates his approach to practical politics as well as his role in Congress. The House was considering a bill to create new federal judgeships, and Seiberling's assignment was to negotiate the details with Sen. James O. Eastland (D-MS), the crusty, authoritarian chairman of the Senate Judiciary Committee. Seiberling arrived at Eastland's office; the men engaged in a cordial discussion and worked out the differences between the House and Senate bills. Eastland then invited Seiberling to remain for a glass of bourbon, a rare compliment for a northern liberal. Seiberling, however, rose, thanked Eastland, explained that he had other work to do, and rushed out. Eastland, incredulous, turned to an aide: "You know, that sumbitch don't like whiskey."[1]

After three terms Seiberling remained a reluctant politician, hostile to the political culture of Washington, suspicious of insiders, and impatient with the endless delays, the hypocrisy, and obfuscations. "The House is a club, a place where camaraderie is highly valued," explained Linda Billings, "and John is the odd man out. He isn't palsy with people." Michael Straight, another staffer, explained that he "is not the sort who goes out and has a beer with the boys. He isn't interested in playing those games." Seiberling agreed. "I basically am a private person. . . . I value my solitude, which I don't get very much of these days. I value my family life, which is rather meager. I try to do my own thinking. I'm not as gregarious as the typical politician."[2]

But the political paralysis of 1975–76 was also an influence. Before the impeachment crisis, the wheeling and dealing at least had produced results. Now with the Democrats entrenched in Congress, a beleaguered and stubborn president in the White House, and the 1976 elections on the horizon, very little was being accomplished. As Seiberling had feared, Ford had become increasingly rigid and conservative. In early 1976 Seiberling told a reporter that "the past year or so has been the most frustrating of my time here." He talked about quitting. "I don't know whether I could endure another four years of divided government here."[3]

Seiberling's personal financial situation also contributed to his sense of frustration. In a feature story, James Reston of the *New York Times* described him as a "handsome, rich, middle aged man," a common characterization because of his family name.[4] He may have been handsome and middle aged, but his income was $43,000 in 1974 and $45,000 in 1975, with his congressional salary accounting for nearly all of that. Two mortgages, biweekly commutes to and from Akron, and mounting college expenses took their toll. Seiberling's deficit was approximately $10,000 per year through 1976.[5] Betty had become a Capitol Hill real estate agent, but she was not able to make up the difference.

One source of solace was the Bath Township home with its panoramic views, lush forests, and comparative isolation. "In spring, summer, and fall," Seiberling explained, "I get out on my riding mower. Between the noise of the mower and being away from the telephone, where there's nobody around, no one can get at me. That's one of the nicest relaxations I have."[6] There were also infrequent family vacations at Colorado or other western ski resorts. One of the compensations of service on the Interior Committee was the opportunity to visit national parks and other public lands. The Alaskan trip in 1975 proved to be one of the most instructive of Seiberling's life.

Yet there was another side to this story. By the mid-1970s Seiberling was a rising star in Congress, known for his patience, hard work, and mastery of issues. His general indifference to newspaper headlines and television coverage—he refused to hire a publicist or press secretary—and lack of ambition for higher office also distinguished him from many colleagues. In the congressional world he was a rare and valuable commodity. In the community of liberal reform organizations he was known as a man of convictions, eager to act on them.

As Seiberling explained, he "tried to think for himself," though the results sometimes upset old friends and constituents. On international economic issues his commitment to free trade often put him at odds with the URW and other Ohio unions. He also had uncomfortable exchanges with representatives of Akron's gay community. Ironically it was his nemesis among Ohio Democrats, the conservative, authoritarian Rep. Wayne L. Hays, who helped him remove the one questionable mark on his liberal record. In 1975, as chairman of the House Government Affairs Committee, Hays pushed through legislation to increase office budgets, allowing Seiberling, among others, to terminate a special fund, sustained by wealthy friends, that he used to publish newsletters.[7] Actually Seiberling was doubly fortunate: he received the extra appropriation but no longer had to tolerate Hays, who was soon forced to resign in a sex scandal.[8]

National Politics

As the presidential election approached, Seiberling was most certain about whom he did not want. In the Democratic primaries he worried about the strength of George C. Wallace among blue-collar voters, including many in the Fourteenth District. Wallace, he explained, would be a "disaster" (though he hastened to add, if Wallace were facing Ronald Reagan, who was then campaigning against President Ford in Republican primaries, he would vote for Wallace).[9] He briefly proposed to lead a slate of uncommitted delegates to the convention as a way to undermine Wallace. But when Wallace was wounded by a would-be assassin and forced to drop out of the race, Seiberling immediately abandoned his plan. The remaining choices were Jimmy Carter and Morris Udall. Seiberling was "suspicious" of the little-known Carter and personally close to Udall, but he was not convinced of Udall's electability. His reticence was a bitter pill for Udall, painfully aware that the Ohio primary was his "last best" chance to secure the nomination. When the Arizonian appeared at an enthusiastic, union-sponsored rally at Akron's Our Lady of the Elms School, he tried to put Seiberling on the spot: "I want John's stand-up endorsement because he is well-respected down there." Seiberling, however, demurred. He explained that he had cast his absentee ballot for Udall "because he is a man of intellect and has an outstanding record . . . but I can't tell other people how they ought to vote." He hoped that "my example will prompt them to do it voluntarily."[10] This semiendorsement probably swayed few Summit County Democrats. Presumably it reflected a desire to remain uncommitted as well as a realistic assessment of Udall's chances. That judgment seemed justified when Carter won Ohio and Summit County by healthy margins.

By mid-July, when he returned home from the Democratic National Convention, Seiberling was confident that Carter could win and be an effective president. "Congress obviously needs the kind of strong leadership that he can give," he told reporters. Compared to Ford or Reagan, the former Georgia governor was "not only acceptable, he's inevitable."[11] As he predicted, Carter won, taking Ohio by a comfortable margin and helping the state's Democrats score major upsets. Howard M. Metzenbaum, who had earlier filled an unexpired term in the U.S. Senate, defeated incumbent senator Robert Taft (during the campaign both men claimed credit for the creation of the CVNRA); Metzenbaum subsequently won a seat on the Senate Interior (Energy) Committee.[12] The Democrats also gained two more seats in the House. Seiberling won with 75 percent of the vote and the largest total in his electoral career.

With the political bottleneck seemingly broken, the competition for positions and influence in the Democratic congressional caucus became more intense. In the House, Interior Committee Chair James A. Haley had retired, and Patsy Mink had been defeated in a Senate race, so there would be at least two major positions to be filled. There were also several open leadership positions on the House Judiciary Committee. In mid-November the environmental organizations launched a campaign to persuade Carter to name Seiberling secretary of the interior.[13] New York Times columnist William V. Shannon speculated about various candidates and concluded that former Idaho governor Cecil D. Andrus and Seiberling were the best choices. Andrus, a westerner with a good record as governor, was the orthodox, safe choice. Seiberling would be strongly opposed by mining and other commodity interests.[14] Seiberling was "privately elated by the speculation" but did not take it seriously, did not expect to be asked, and had no intention of giving up his House seat for a cabinet position.[15] On December 5, he had an extended telephone conversation with Frank Moore of Carter's staff. Moore explained that Andrus was Carter's choice: he had stood up to the Nixon administration, had good relations with cattle ranchers and hunters, and had the support of most environmental groups.[16] Seiberling later explained, "I wasn't seeking it so I wasn't disappointed." Andrus "hasn't had a perfect record on the environment, but he has had a good one."[17]

Seiberling's ultimate assignment, a new subcommittee on Alaska lands, was an outgrowth of a remarkable series of events that no one could have foreseen. First was the retirement of Speaker Carl B. Albert and the subsequent elevation of the majority leader, Thomas P. "Tip" O'Neill, to the speakership. That provoked a heated contest for the majority leader's position. The principal contenders were James C. Wright, a conservative Texan, and Seiberling's friend Phil Burton, the California liberal. After a tense campaign, Wright won by a single vote.[18] Wright had been chairman of the patronage-rich Public Works Committee, and Rep. Harold "Bizz" Johnson (D-CA), an able but conservative northern Californian, whose district was heavily dependent on the timber industry, was next in line for both Public Works and Interior positions. Environmental leaders plotted to persuade him, or if necessary, force him to opt for Public Works, because Mo Udall was next in line for the Interior post. Johnson ultimately chose Public Works; Udall took over the Interior Committee; Seiberling assumed the Alaska post; and Burton, determined to make his mark as a legislator, unexpectedly took over the national parks subcommittee.[19] For at least a century the Interior Committee had been the preserve of commodity-oriented westerners. Now, overnight, with Udall, Burton, and Seiberling slated for leadership positions, it became a center of environmental activism.

The next six years, until Burton's sudden death in June 1983, were arguably the most productive and challenging in the committee's history. Having largely abandoned his hopes for higher office, Udall determined to make the most of his position in the Congress. His genial personality, ready wit, and political sophistication helped calm the tensions that emerged as his energetic colleagues jockeyed for attention. His most important tactical decision, which reflected his personal preference as well as the combustible nature of the committee membership, was to give the subcommittees substantial autonomy. As Cleve Pinnix, a staff member, recalled, "With Mo as the committee chair, they were going to have a guy who was basically going to let [Burton] and Seiberling and the other people do what they wanted to do and get some of these things accomplished." Under his watchful but permissive eye "they basically were . . . 'slicing and dicin'.'"[20] Alaska was certain to be a challenging assignment. When Teno Roncalio (D-WY) complained that his public lands subcommittee agenda was already full, Udall, in accord with the "slicing and dicing" formula, carved out a new position for Seiberling.

While Udall and Seiberling had worked together and shared many values, Burton brought a different perspective to the committee. He represented an urban district and had no evident interest in nature or physical activity; supposedly he only went outside to smoke. Mutual friends recall hilarious exchanges when Seiberling tried to persuade him to join a tour of potential California wilderness areas.[21] Burton was also famously confrontational, belligerent, and profane, a man of "prodigious appetites and passions."[22] He intimidated the Republicans or bought them off with minor concessions, reserving most of his energies for fellow Democrats. Pinnix, who worked with him on national parks issues, recalls that "he just pissed all over Jimmy Carter any time he got a chance" and "had a lot of contempt for Mo Udall."[23] In his new role, Burton operated more or less independently with remarkable effectiveness.

To the surprise of nearly all their acquaintances, Seiberling and Burton got along well. Pinnix recalls their odd-couple relationship. "I mean, here is this patrician, 'Mr. Rational' in John Seiberling, and here is this lunatic, from San Francisco. . . . [Burton] seemed to have an implicit trust that John was going to do it right, and at the same time he would kid John about being a Boy Scout, and about thinking the world was on the level. . . . He would sort of rag John about 'You've got to remember none of this is on the level, and you've got to do things behind the scenes to organize it.'"[24] Dale Crane, another staffer, believed that "Phil admired John . . . because perhaps he wasn't the drinking buddy, typical politician kind of person. . . . And I think John admired Phil because he was so damned good at politics."[25] They remained friends, Seiberling recalled, because he "didn't mind telling Burton when he was off base. I was the only one who would. . . . He never got mad at me the whole time."[26]

Burton was an invaluable source of tactical advice. Pinnix recalls evenings at Burton's home: "John would come over, and he and Phil would spend some time . . . talking about Alaska lands strategy. . . . There were a couple of times when he and John would have long, detailed conversations about who was going to vote in what way and what was influencing it. . . . And it seems like John and Phil really just . . . were complete allies, and Phil was giving John whatever he could in terms of support."[27]

With a new, more cooperative administration, such friendships had great promise. The first real test was the controversial strip-mining bill. Carter had pledged to sign it, and Udall took the lead in revising the legislation. He organized a tour of mine sites in Virginia, West Virginia, and Pennsylvania (with Seiberling participating) in March, pressured the Interior Committee to adopt a bill similar to the 1975 bill in April, and won a lopsided House vote (241 to 64) later that month. Udall's success reflected both his negotiating skills and the many loopholes that remained in the legislation. Secretary Andrus complained that it did not protect agricultural lands in the Midwest and that it permitted a new, destructive technique known as mountaintop removal. To finance the reclamation fund, the new House bill levied a tax of 35 cents per ton on underground coal and 50 cents per ton on strip-mined coal.[28] (The 1975 bill had called for 15 cents and 35 cents, respectively.) The Senate passed a bill in May, after coal state Democrats, over Andrus's objections, pushed through a number of weakening amendments. The final Senate bill had two hundred provisions that differed from the House bill.[29]

Seiberling agreed to serve on the conference committee, which met through June and early July. He played an important role in preserving the high reclamation standards that were a feature of the House bill and in eliminating some of the more offensive provisions of the Senate bill, but he was not able to stop a reduction in the tax to 15 cents per ton on underground coal and 35 cents per ton on strip-mined coal, creation of an eighteen-month grace period for small mines—nearly two-thirds of the total—and retention of mountaintop removal. The House and Senate passed the legislation in late July, and Carter reluctantly agreed to sign the "watered down" measure.[30] The grueling conference committee sessions were a particular burden for Seiberling, because they came at the same time his subcommittee on Alaska lands was completing a marathon series of hearings that took him to all parts of the country. An Akron area reporter noted in early July that "he looked haggard."[31]

Despite the importance of the strip-mining legislation, the paramount issue of that spring and summer was the fate of the 80-plus million acres of federally owned land in Alaska that had been set aside under section 17d(2) of ANCSA for possible additions to national parks, wildlife refuges, wild and scenic rivers, and national forests. Congress had given itself a five-year deadline, which was to expire at the end of 1978. The need for immediate action was also obvious. The Valdez pipeline had just gone into operation, which effectively opened thousands of square miles of Alaskan wilderness, nearly doubled the state's population to more than 400,000, and transformed a nearly bankrupt state government into one of the nation's most profitable public entities, inspiring endless development schemes by the state's tireless, avaricious promoters. By 1977, Alaska had selected about 70 million acres of its promised 104-million-acre statehood allotment, and the Native corporations were in the process of choosing the 44 million acres awarded them by ANCSA. Nearly all of this land, plus more than 90 percent of the remaining public lands managed by the

Forest Service and the Bureau of Land Management (BLM), was open to mining, gas and oil drilling, logging, and other extractive activities. Most of it was de facto wilderness and, until the pipeline, likely to remain that way. Now it was clear that prompt action would be necessary if any substantial part of Alaska was to be preserved in its natural state. President Carter, responding to the pleas of environmental groups, made an Alaskan land settlement his number one environmental goal.

To shepherd the legislation, which the national environmental groups prepared with the help of their Alaska allies and sympathizers in the National Park Service (NPS) and the Fish and Wildlife Service (FWS), Udall decided to create a special subcommittee on General Oversight and Alaska Lands. Seiberling would be its chair, but the two men would be partners. (Seiberling, however, would have sole responsibility for the "oversight" function, that is, overseeing the Interior Department agencies, a major assignment in itself.) Udall would be the principal sponsor of the Alaska legislation and lend his moral and political support to the campaign. Seiberling would do the rest: direct the staff, conduct the hearings, and maneuver the revised bill through the subcommittee. Their collaboration depended on trust and confidence, in particular Udall's confidence that Seiberling would play his large and difficult role effectively.

There were several reasons for this strategy. Guiding the legislation through the committee and the House would be difficult and time consuming, probably more than the public lands subcommittee could undertake with any expectation of success. Seiberling was one of the few House members who knew something about Alaska, and the only one in a leadership position. His 1975 trip had awakened him to Alaska's scenic beauty and emptiness and the dangers inherent in economic development. As he recalled, "Alaska is the only state . . . where you can see 95 to 99 percent of the land looking as though still in the hands of the Creator. This is the thing that really gripped me about Alaska, something you can't experience in many places in this world. . . . This was a chance to preserve a significant part of America's wild heritage."[32] Another advantage was the remoteness of Alaska from the Fourteenth District. "The public in my district didn't give much of a damn about it," he recalled. "I was trying to educate the country."[33] In practical terms he would be free from the pressures that other representatives, especially those from western states such as Roncalio, would have confronted. The other members of the new Alaska subcommittee included Austin J. Murphy (D-PA), from western Pennsylvania, a close friend of organized labor; James D. Santini (D-NV), an ally of the mining industry; Lloyd Meeds (D-WA), who represented union groups with interests in Alaska; and Don Young, the leader of the Republican contingent and a colorful champion of the state's business interests.

To head the staff Seiberling chose Harry Crandell, who had most recently worked for the House public lands subcommittee. When the subcommittee chairman, John Melcher, was elected to the Senate in 1976, Crandell once again found himself out of a job. He was contemplating his future when Roncalio told him about Seiberling's new subcommittee and urged him to "get your sweet ass downstairs and talk to John Seiberling."[34] Crandell brought to his new position long experience, a thorough knowledge of Congress and the public lands bureaucracy, and a lifelong interest in wilderness. He was aided by two young idealistic attorneys, Stanley Sloss and Roy Jones, and Loretta Neumann, who transferred from Seiberling's personal staff. Bill Horn, an Alaskan with ties to the Anchorage business community, became the minority staff representative.

In January they began work on legislation that reflected years of preparation and a new, broader, and more scientific approach to land-use planning. Because Alaska was lightly populated, had virtually no agriculture, and had formidable mountain ranges, vast wetlands, and wildlife (caribou, grizzlies, and Dahl sheep, for example) that required largely undisturbed areas, it was possible and desirable to consider whole ecosystems rather than specific mountains (such as Mt. McKinley), notable natural phenomena (such as the volcanic eruption site at Katmai in western Alaska), or other customary park or refuge attractions. They also had an indispensable partner in the Alaska Coalition, an alliance of the national environmental organizations and the local and regional groups that had emerged in Alaska since the pipeline conflict. Seiberling's goal was to come up with a bill that was ambitious enough to satisfy the Alaska Coalition and realistic enough to pass the Congress.

D(2) Debates

Although Congress had devoted little attention to Alaska after the passage of the pipeline bill in 1973, the public land agencies, the environmental organizations, and various groups of Alaskans had not forgotten about the d(2) withdrawals or the deadline. Their deliberations and conflicts shaped the legislation that Seiberling was to shepherd through

Congress and ensured that the eventual Alaska National Interest Lands Conservation Act (ANILCA) would be the most important public lands initiative in many decades.

Because ANCSA had not specified which agency or agencies were to manage the 80 million acres, the act had set off an intense bureaucratic turf war. In December 1971 Assistant Interior Secretary Nathaniel Reed had charged the NPS and the FWS to "pick out the vital land masses." To guide this effort he assigned Assistant NPS Director Theodore Swem to take charge of the "greatest challenge and opportunity" of their lives.[35]

They needed little persuasion. The NPS had been involved in Alaska since the creation of Katmai National Monument in 1917 and the transfer of Mt. McKinley National Park to NPS management in 1920. Glacier Bay National Monument was added in 1925. Additions to Mt. McKinley in 1922 and 1932, to Katmai in 1932 and 1969, and to Glacier Bay in 1939 doubled the total acreage and made the Alaskan parks notable examples of ecosystem preservation. The three Alaskan parks accounted for more than half the total national park service acreage, though less than 1 percent of public visitations in the years preceding ANILCA. Federal wildlife agencies had also been active in Alaska since the 1890s, and their responsibilities had greatly increased in 1960 with the creation of three huge new refuges, including the Arctic National Wildlife Range in the northeast corner of the state, designed to preserve part of the Arctic coast and facilitate the annual migration of the large Porcupine caribou herd.[36]

The Forest Service had likewise had a large and significant presence in Alaska. Southeast Alaska's Tongass National Forest, at 17 million acres, was the largest national forest (larger than West Virginia), and the Chugach National Forest, just to the north, at 6 million acres, was second largest. The Tongass surrounded all of the major population centers of the pre–World War II years and was the focus of government-backed efforts to provide jobs and business opportunities for Alaska residents. In the 1950s the Forest Service negotiated deals with several paper companies to harvest most of the lush lowland forests and convert those areas into enormous tree farms. As more and more square miles were cut, critics of the plan became more outspoken and local protest groups had formed. By the 1970s the battle lines were drawn. For the next two decades, the Forest Service, closely allied with Alaskan industrial and commercial groups, would be locked in an extended, bitter, and occasionally violent campaign with environmental activists who sought to preserve parts of the Tongass forest as wilderness.[37]

The rivalry between the Interior agencies (the NPS and the FWS) and the Forest Service became heated as Secretary of the Interior Rogers Morton allocated the 80 million acres. He made his initial d(2) selections in March 1972, largely following the recommendations of the Swem committee, which emphasized parks and refuges. In September 1972, he made his "final" d(2) recommendations. They included only minor concessions to the Forest Service and the state, which was attempting to use its selections under the statehood act, to sabotage the d(2) allocations. Still, Morton did not have to make definitive recommendations until the end of 1973, so the controversy, pitting the NPS and the FWS against the state, the Forest Service, and even the BLM, which would continue to administer what was left over after the various allocations and selections, continued. By mid-1973, Morton's influence within the Nixon administration began to wane as the campaign to rally political conservatives took precedence over other considerations. In the following months he essentially capitulated to the Forest Service, noting that Congress would make its own decisions on d(2) lands. His December 1973 recommendations called for only 32 million acres of new parks and 19 million acres of national forest additions in new and existing forests. Agency executives, state officials, and environmentalists were equally displeased.[38]

The other effect of section 17d(2) was to mobilize the environmentalists, ultimately inspiring the largest and most complex campaign in conservation history. The pipeline battle had left them dispirited and uncertain about their next steps. Former Sierra Club president Edgar Wayburn organized an Alaska task force within the club and persuaded Sen. Henry M. Jackson to introduce several d(2) bills for it. Jackson, however, made no effort to push the Alaska bills, causing Wayburn to bemoan the "lack of demand from constituents."[39] Another problem was the internal upheaval in the Wilderness Society, which left the organization paralyzed and financially strapped. Finally, there was no shortage of other competing issues and campaigns to occupy the activists' attention. Since the deadline for d(2) legislation was still several years in the future and Congress seemed uninterested, it was easy to defer any definitive action. Environmentalists could take heart from the success of Seiberling's effort to ban mining in national parks, including Mt. McKinley and Glacier Bay.

The growth of a vigorous environmental movement in Alaska was another positive sign. Most Alaskans, who subscribed to the traditional view of the federal government as a hindrance to the state's economic progress, had little enthusiasm for new parks and wildlife refuges. In an effort to

head off more ambitious legislation, the state's congressional representatives introduced d(2) bills that provided for minimal additions, confined
largely to "rock and ice," mountaintops that had no obvious economic
value. But then the pipeline boom led to a large population influx, rising
consumer prices, an escalating crime rate, and other evidence of social
disorder, while most of the new wealth went to real estate speculators,
bankers, oil industry executives, and construction workers, most of whom
came from outside. For the first time large numbers of Alaska residents
began to question the basic premise of the state's political elite: that the
state's natural resources could and would create a stable, growing, and
prosperous economy.

Public disillusionment enhanced the influence of the state's growing
environmental community. Alaskans had supported a variety of conservation efforts since the late nineteenth century but did not organize
statewide until the late 1950s, when the Wilderness Society enlisted many
of them in the campaign for an Arctic wildlife range. The leaders of that
effort then created a permanent organization, the Alaska Conservation
Society (ACS). In the following decade the ACS successfully opposed a
variety of development projects, monitored state government, and encouraged the formation of local environmental groups. Its greatest single
achievement came in 1974, when Jay Hammond, an ACS member, critic
of the oil boom, and champion of the fishing industry and the traditional
economy, upset the favorite in the Republican primary and defeated the
incumbent governor in the general election. Hammond pledged greater
sensitivity to environmental concerns and appointed a number of ACS
members to posts in his administration.[40]

The ACS was moderate, respectable—many of its leaders were scientists—and highly effective in countering the more extreme plans of the
state's leaders. But it was uncomfortable with the activist spirit of the
1960s and too close to the local establishment to suit many of Alaska's
new arrivals, particularly those from California and other states where
environmental activism had become popular and acceptable. In the
early 1970s they organized chapters of the Sierra Club and Friends of
the Earth, as well as a host of local groups that extended the work of
the ACS and attacked the Valdez pipeline. With disillusionment over the
pipeline boom growing, the state's environmental organizations gained
credibility and members. They also found a way to coordinate their
efforts. Since the enormous distances between the state's urban centers

made statewide meetings prohibitively expensive, they created regional environmental centers where members of the various organizations could gather to address problems of that area. The Juneau center focused on the Tongass, the Fairbanks center specialized in Arctic issues, and the Anchorage center emphasized urban and statewide political problems. By 1977, Alaska's environmental community probably had the highest per capita membership rate of any state.

Regardless of affiliation, the Alaskans realized that their role in the d(2) controversy would be critical, because Congress would be reluctant to act without evidence of local support. Their first task was to develop their own d(2) recommendations. To that end they held an environmental "summit" meeting in Fairbanks, February 19–20, 1975. After long discussions, leaders of the ACS, the environmental centers, the Sierra Club, the Wilderness Society, National Audubon Society, and others agreed to back a bill for parks and wildlife refuges totaling more than 100 million acres and large "instant" wilderness (designated by Congress without agency review) areas. Brock Evans, the Sierra Club representative at the meeting, reported that it resulted in a "good basic consensus. . . . The ACS people came much further in adopting a national outlook than anybody thought they would, including themselves."[41]

With the national organizations beginning to mobilize, the Alaskans held a second "summit" on May 15–16, 1976, at the Mt. McKinley Park hotel. This meeting reaffirmed the consensus of 1975, incorporated the demands of Alaskan Natives for subsistence rights in the new conservation units, and added an element that the national organizations had been reluctant to embrace: millions of acres of "instant" wilderness in the Tongass and Chugach national forests. This had been the principal demand of the southeastern groups, and the other Alaskans insisted on honoring it, even though it was unrelated to the d(2) allocations. The representatives of the national organizations also agreed to give Alaskans prominent roles in the forthcoming campaign.

The final plans for the campaign were completed in a series of meetings between representatives of the Sierra Club, National Audubon Society, Friends of the Earth, and Wilderness Society between July and October 1976. The bill they endorsed provided for ten new parks totaling 64 million acres, additions to the three existing parks totaling 8 million acres, nine new and two enlarged wildlife refuges totaling 46 million acres, twenty-three wild and scenic rivers, and additions to the Tongass and Chugach forests totaling 1.6 million acres. It also designated 145 million acres of wilderness (most of the new parks and refuges, together with large areas of the existing parks and refuges and 5 million acres of national forest lands).

To rally public and congressional support for the legislation, leaders of the Alaska campaign revived the Alaska Coalition (originally created for the pipeline fight) and mobilized the national organizations, the Alaska groups, and others, such as garden clubs, civic organizations, and a handful of unions. The national organizations assigned staff members to the Coalition staff and paid the bills. Chuck Clusen and Douglas Scott, Sierra Club staffers who had worked closely with Seiberling since 1973, served as chair and chief lobbyist, respectively. Their goal was to draw on members of the various groups and other volunteers to create an effective grassroots organization in every congressional district. Their prospects received a major boost with the election of Carter, the elevation of Udall, and the creation of the Alaska lands subcommittee.

Galvanizing a Nation

Stan Sloss recalled the dramatic events of the spring and summer of 1977 with an analogy to the 1944 Normandy invasion. It was as if General Udall, in the role of Eisenhower, had gotten up before the troops on the eve of the invasion. "It's going to be a tough fight but our side is right and we have a superior plan of attack. With courage, hard work, and resolve we will win. Now here's General Seiberling, who will explain how we're going to do it, what resources and supplies we will need, and what role each of you is going to play."[42] Seiberling understood that such a role was a huge undertaking. As he later explained to a critic in Ketchikan, Alaska, "There's no political gain for me in this legislation, only headaches."[43] But he also realized that the Alaska legislation was an opportunity to show that he could take on a large project and bring it to fruition. Udall and his colleagues had entrusted him with the president's top environmental goal and a project the environmental groups had worked on for years. His reputation would rise or fall with the result.

But he also had a broader, more personal goal. He hoped to make available to younger Americans, living in a highly urbanized society, the kinds of opportunities he had known at Stan Hywet. The CVNRA and parks like it were a step toward that end. Yet they lacked the dramatic mountain landscapes, the grand vistas that, in his mind, were essential to an appreciation of the natural world in all its diversity. At one time Appalachia had provided that type of opportunity. But much of it had been destroyed through a "hit or miss, every man for himself and never mind the consequences" approach to land utilization.[44] Strip-mining regulations would partially compensate, but it made more sense, and was far cheaper, to preserve vital areas from exploitation. To Seiberling, then, the proposed Alaskan parks and refuges were essential features of an effort to "give people, particularly young people, a sense of the order of the natural world so they don't feel totally adrift in the chaotic world of man's own creation."[45]

From a practical perspective, the subcommittee's challenge was to refine the Udall bill so that Congress would pass it over the likely opposition of the state's elected officials and other champions of Alaska industry. Given the congressional tradition of deference to local opinion, this was an ambitious undertaking, mitigated somewhat by the support of the Carter administration and the fact that most Alaska officeholders (Representative Young, Sen. Ted Stevens, and Governor Hammond) were Republicans, and the notable exception, Sen. Mike Gravel, was a loner and an eccentric, unpopular with his colleagues. Still, the subcommittee would have to show that the national interest outweighed the parochial interests of Alaska residents and that there was, in fact, substantial support within the state.

The best way to document a national interest was to hold hearings throughout the country. The subcommittee staff planned daylong sessions in major cities, to be followed by hearings in various Alaskan communities that would allow environmental groups there to show that the state was divided. Accordingly, they planned hearings for Chicago (May 7), Atlanta (May 14), Denver (June 4), Seattle (June 18), southeast Alaska (July 5–9), Anchorage (August 17), and Fairbanks (August 20), and town meetings in eleven "bush" communities (August 8–19). In addition there were to be Washington hearings in late April and early May, and extra sessions for officials from federal agencies with an interest in Alaska during the summer and again in mid-September. A session scheduled for San Francisco had to be cancelled because of Seiberling's participation in the conference committee on the strip-mining bill. The Washington hearings began with a slide show of photos Seiberling had taken on his 1975 tour of Alaska. Displays of his photographs were also used to educate colleagues during the House deliberations.

Seiberling was the only subcommittee member who attended every session. Udall appeared irregularly, though he did spend a week in Alaska, and Rep. Paul Tsongas (D-MA), who would play a critical role in the eventual outcome, only attended the Washington hearings. All the other Democrats on the subcommittee, except the nonvoting representatives of Puerto Rico and the Virgin Islands, made at least one trip; apart from Don Young, the Republicans rarely attended and played little role in the hearings. Because of the large number of people who wanted to appear, it was essential to have at least one other Democrat besides Seiberling at each hearing so there could be concurrent sessions; in some cases there were as many as four simultaneous sessions in separate rooms. Seiberling usually assigned the environmentalists to the other representatives while he listened to the critics.

A typical session featured Seiberling and Young, representing the bill's opponents. While Seiberling urged the audience to think broadly and to consider the needs of future generations, Young, who lived in a rural village and was married to a Native woman, played the role of the practical man, focused on immediate concerns, suspicious of lofty goals and especially the effete concerns of eastern elitists. Like most Alaska politicians, he combined populist rhetoric with vigorous support for outside business interests. He and Seiberling clashed at almost every session. Young typically tried to taunt the bill's supporters into making outlandish claims that would expose their naiveté and impracticality. Seiberling defended them and sought to show, by implication, the fate that awaited Alaska if a strong bill were not enacted. For his purposes, Young was the perfect villain. The Alaskan's rudeness, fractured syntax, and contempt for anything that could not be measured in dollars and cents were constant reminders of what might lie ahead in the absence of forceful action by Congress.

The Alaska Coalition's recruiting efforts succeeded in attracting standing-room-only crowds at the early hearings. More than 300 people signed up to speak in Chicago, many traveling long distances from Ohio, Minnesota, Missouri, and other states. In Atlanta, 177 testified; in Denver, 299. In Seattle, 1,200 appeared, including several hundred Californians who had expected to testify in San Francisco, overwhelming Seiberling and Young, the only subcommittee members who attended. Up to that point there was virtually no opposition to HR 39. When Young attacked prominent mountaineer and Seattle business executive James Whittaker, Whittaker responded by belittling Young for his narrow perspective. The audience erupted in cheers, and the confrontation was widely featured in newspaper accounts of the session.[46]

In Alaska, the opponents were more numerous. At Sitka, the Alaska Lumber and Pulp Company and the local chamber of commerce went to great lengths to ensure that opponents dominated the hearing. Of the 150 individuals who testified, 130 opposed the Tongass wilderness provisions. However, they focused exclusively on the Tongass, seemed to know nothing about the rest of the legislation, and resorted to tactics, such as chainsaw demonstrations outside the building, that suggested coercion and possible violence. The hearing at Ketchikan, on July 9, was similar. The town was notorious for its hostility to environmentalists, and a group of local fishermen sent Seiberling a message indicating that they were afraid to speak.[47] The actual testimony was less one-sided than Seiberling and his allies expected and gave him ample opportunity to lecture the crowd about irresponsible corporate influences.

The larger Alaska towns were more evenly divided, underlining the strength and vigor of the Alaska environmental organizations. The Juneau hearing was a standoff, with 100 people in favor and an equal number in opposition. When Seiberling returned for another round of hearings in August, the results were even more favorable. At Anchorage, 277 people spoke, with 136 in favor, 131 opposed, and 10 neutral. At the Fairbanks hearing, 294 testified, and again, the pro-environmental groups came out ahead. The state's political leaders were disheartened.[48]

The hearings thus achieved their original goals of demonstrating public support for the legislation and casting doubt on the objections of Alaska's elected leaders. They also provided suggestions for fine-tuning the legislation, something Seiberling asked for repeatedly. One recurring theme was the disillusionment of Alaska's Natives with ANCSA, largely because of delays in transferring land to the Native corporations. That and the related issue of subsistence hunting and fishing in prospective parks and refuges were critical considerations for the Native communities. The other major controversies involved the amount of "instant" wilderness. Assuming that any amount they proposed would be substantially reduced, the authors of the Udall bill started with an unrealistic 145 million acres, which became a lightning rod for opponents. Related concerns, such as the use of snowmobiles for hunting and trapping and motorized access to private inholdings in wilderness areas, were almost as controversial. Seiberling agreed to reduce the total and insisted that the other problems could be managed. In the end, though, two wilderness-related issues defied compromise. The first was the proposed Tongass wilderness designations, which included prime timber areas such as Admiralty Island that were vital to preserving the region's bear population. The second was the Arctic coast of the new Arctic National Wildlife Refuge, a greatly expanded successor to the Arctic National Wildlife Range, another critical wildlife area coveted by oil companies.

Apart from emphasizing the breadth of public interest, the most notable feature of the hearings was Seiberling's persistence and tenacity. He became "ironpants," capable of listening to the same points over and over for hours without a break and without evident impatience or boredom. Indeed, he seemed to delight in the fact that most of the people who testified had never spoken at a large public gathering and made simple, heartfelt statements, pro or con. He enjoyed debating opponents and typically closed the session with an expression of personal philosophy, in several cases with poetry, recited from memory. The Alaska hearings were evidence that ordinary people, not just Washington lawyers and lobbyists, were concerned about government and public policy.

In his statements Seiberling repeatedly emphasized several themes. One was the value of preserving wilderness. "This legislation would protect another resource," he told the audience in Atlanta, "probably the scarcest one in all of this modern world, that is, wilderness. Wilderness is a resource. It is not only a physical resource . . . it is a spiritual resource."[49] He reminded a sympathetic audience in Denver that "when you destroy a wilderness, in Alaska particularly, then it's gone forever. . . . If you leave it alone, it will always . . . be there if you later need to develop it."[50] He reminded the hostile crowd in Sitka that "open space is a very important need. . . . Since the Federal government happens to own tremendous acreages here in Alaska, it makes sense to use some of that acreage [for open space],"—a reply to the opponents' charges that parks and refuges "locked up" land.[51] On another occasion he compared the Alaska legislation to the building of the cathedral at Chartres. "I really feel that we are doing the same thing in trying to save some of the great treasures of nature for future generations."[52]

Another recurring theme was the beauty of Alaska. "Alaska is the most beautiful place in the world as far as I am concerned," he told the Denver hearing.[53] In Juneau, he confessed that he considered Alaska "to be the most beautiful place I have ever been in my life. And whenever I have had an opportunity, this has been the place I wanted to go."[54] After flying over the Stikine River Valley, halfway between Juneau and

Ketchikan, he recalled, "I just felt lyrical. I started whistling Bach and Mozart and I felt . . . I've seen everything. . . . I'll admit I'm high on Alaska and I'm hooked."[55] "For years I've been asking myself," he told the Anchorage crowd, "what is it about the Alaska landscape that is so unique. It isn't just the wilderness. It's the undisturbed wilderness. . . . Alaska has the opportunity to take some areas that are significant in size, keep them the way the Creator fashioned them. . . . The abstract designs are absolutely beyond the wildest imaginings of Picasso or any other great artist."[56] He repeated this point in Fairbanks, commenting on his impressions of Alaska from a small plane. "One of the things . . . is the fantastic array of abstract art everywhere you look. The forms of the land and vegetation are striking like nothing else I have ever seen. . . . Nowhere else that I have been can one see so clearly the hand of the Creator." It "reminds man of his place in the scheme of things . . . and that he is not the Creator. He is the beneficiary of a system of life that he can destroy but did not create."[57]

He also compared Alaska with Appalachia, warning of what could lie ahead. The danger, he told the Atlanta hearing, was the "uncontrolled, unplanned exploitation of the land. What happens is, profit for a few, and destruction, devastation and poverty for the many."[58] Mining areas in Appalachia, he warned Juneau's mayor, "will make your heart break. . . . Economic development in itself can be devastating, and each one takes another slice of the salami [a favorite metaphor] and what you end up with is an incredible garbage pile."[59] "There is this fear that we are going to have another Appalachia ripoff up here," he told the largely hostile crowd in Ketchikan.[60]

The immediate threat to Alaska came from corporate interests, mostly from outside the state. "My son asked me once why I worked so hard for the environment and on antitrust law; and I said during 17 years in a corporation and for 5 years before that as a corporate lawyer I saw a lot of things and I'm trying to create a better way here."[61] He told the Denver crowd, "We are doing battle with tremendous corporate interests, tremendous collective corporate interests. . . . [Yet] as long as we have our democracy, the ordinary people like ourselves . . . are in the end going to prevail if they persevere." He was most explicit in his Seattle summary: "Every single interest group from the oil companies right on, who want to rip-off the public, rape the public, are trying to hide behind two false fronts. One is jobs, the other is energy. I get it every day of the year."[62]

He explained that "industry can mobilize large amounts of money and they can use the mass media and they can use—I won't say the big lie technique but the phony issue technique." The result is "misapprehension and fear stirred up by a very small number of people whose personal greed . . . has motivated that."[63] Later, reacting to a sign in a Sitka shop accusing him of representing the rich, Seiberling noted that his constituents "will be highly amused. . . . The people who would be most amused, except that they are not very amused, would be the rich. I try to represent all the people of my district, but there are some, and mostly they are very wealthy, who do not take kindly to my position."[64]

Underlying the corporate threat was the political naiveté of most Alaska residents. He told the Seattle audience that "some of the labor people have been sold a bill of goods by some of the management people who . . . have spread a lot of unsubstantiated statements to cast fear of loss of jobs."[65] On another occasion he recalled seeing a mother and child outside a union hall in Ketchikan. "'Mommy, what are all those signs about?' And then she said, 'Oh, I know, it's that man who wants to stop all cars and all the airplanes and all the boats.' And I thought, well, that pretty well sums up the reach of the kind of campaign that is going on."[66]

Alaska governor Hammond had proposed a joint federal-state land management commission in an ill-disguised effort to give the state veto power over federal government policies. Seiberling "had to tell him candidly that as it then stood it didn't have a prayer in Congress."[67] He added that "it shouldn't be necessary for the people of Alaska . . . [to] wait until they have created a mess before they realize they can learn something from the other 49 states."[68] Ultimately, he told the Anchorage audience, "it isn't your lands. It's the lands of the American people. That's the thing you don't seem to recognize."[69]

He insisted, however, that he was not inflexible. "It is a matter of balancing. I hope the environmentalists and industries will all recognize that we have to give."[70] On another occasion he observed, "We have got to make adjustments in order to work out accommodations for everybody. There's enough room in Alaska. There's enough room in this country for every lifestyle."[71]

Finally, his Alaska travels had given him a new appreciation of Native interests and concerns. "I have a very tremendous warm feeling about the Alaska Native people." They have "a simplicity and warmth that perhaps comes from the fact that they are not too far removed from nature."[72] That sensitivity had practical implications. "In no way would I support wilderness designations that would prohibit the Native corporations from taking whatever action on their own lands they feel appropriate."[73] On another occasion he suggested that there was no way to protect Native subsistence rights except "putting it strictly on a racial basis."[74] And on delays in land transfers: "It's an intolerable situation."[75]

Seiberling's personal feelings about the hearings were best summarized in an exchange with Terry Tempest Williams, at that time a New Mexico science teacher and aspiring author. After listening to Williams read from a journal she had kept during an Alaska trip, he congratulated her on her "degree of sensitive thinking and beauty of expression." He then contrasted her approach with the "crassness" of Washington, which could be "very disheartening at times." He much preferred to "come out and listen to the ordinary people who are approaching something not from the standpoint of selfish profit but of what is in the public interest."[76]

Victory and Defeat

Seiberling returned to Washington in mid-August, buoyant and reinvigorated by the success of the hearings. He was more convinced than ever that he was on the right course and that his opponents, the Alaskans in particular, were simply apologists for entrenched economic interests. They were the ones who sought to lock up the state, transforming it into another Appalachia. Yet for all the bluster of the Alaska hearings, some useful criticism had emerged. Seiberling was convinced of the need to facilitate land transfers to Native groups and to guarantee their rights to hunt and fish for food in the parks and refuges. Traditional activities, including the use of motorboats and snowmobiles, also had to be protected, even in wilderness areas. He also recognized that the 145 million acres of wilderness was unrealistic.

In September and October, Seiberling and his staff drafted a revised version of the Udall bill. The new bill called for 104 million acres of parks, refuges, wild and scenic rivers, and national forest additions, with 84 million acres of instant wilderness. They redrew the boundaries of some units to exclude areas of potential value to miners and relaxed federal restrictions on subsistence activities in parks and refuges. They also added several cooperative management areas to give the state and the Natives a voice in policy making. Seiberling pointed to the new bill as evidence of his flexibility. He planned to begin the mark-up sessions in November.

Given the broad public support for an Alaska bill, the opponents' only real hope was to sabotage it in committee. They soon found a chink in Seiberling's armor. The three Democrats on the subcommittee most closely associated with organized labor were sensitive to accusations that the bill would cost the jobs of Alaskan workers. That group included two first-term representatives, Austin Murphy and Matthew F. McHugh (D-NY), neither of whom had taken a prominent role in the hearings, and a surprising leader, Lloyd Meeds, a veteran liberal, one of the drafters of ANCSA, who generally had supported wilderness legislation. Meeds was apparently swayed by criticism that he had not done enough for timber interests in his district and believed he had to protect union members who worked seasonally in Ketchikan and other southeast Alaska towns. Alaska Coalition leaders were concerned that he also reflected the concerns of western Washington business and labor leaders and of Sen. Henry M. Jackson, whose Senate Energy Committee would have to draw up and pass a similar bill. If they voted as a bloc, Meeds, Murphy, McHugh, plus Santini, who was closely allied with the miners, and the five Republicans could control the seventeen-member subcommittee.

Seiberling was determined to prevent Meeds and Young from taking over the subcommittee. When Meeds proposed a substitute bill that would have reduced the total acreage and eliminated most of the wilderness, Seiberling rallied his followers, prevailed upon Murphy and McHugh to join them, and won by a narrow victory. He defeated other emasculating amendments by one or two votes. Meeds became so frustrated that he boycotted the subcommittee sessions for several days. By early February, Seiberling was victorious, and the bill went to the full committee.

In the committee markup Seiberling had the assistance of Udall, Burton, and Tsongas. Murphy did not attend the sessions, and McHugh resigned from the committee, alleviating other potential problems. Still, there were several close votes. On March 1, when Meeds proposed an amendment that would have essentially opened the parks and refuges to economic activities, he lost by only three votes. To defeat another Meeds amendment that would have reduced the wilderness acreage by nearly two-thirds, Seiberling and Udall agreed to delete the 2.5-million-acre Misty Fjords Wilderness, the largest of the proposed Tongass wilderness areas. After the U.S. Geological Survey issued a positive report on the oil potential of parts of the Arctic National Wildlife Refuge coast, which was to be wilderness, the Republicans on the committee sought to delete the entire coastal region from the wilderness area. Seiberling countered with a proposal for additional study. He finally won by two votes. The committee approved the bill on March 21 by 32 to 12. It now included 98 million acres of parks and refuges and 75 million acres of wilderness.

The bill then went to a subcommittee of the Merchant Marine Committee, which had jurisdiction over wildlife refuges. Because Young served on that subcommittee too, Rep. Robert L. Leggett (D-CA), the chairman, negotiated an agreement to reduce the wilderness acreage in exchange for Young's pledge to cooperate. The subcommittee deleted 8 million acres of wilderness and then added the 26-million-acre national petroleum reserve, just west of Prudhoe Bay, as a wildlife refuge. The final bill, drafted by Seiberling and Leggett, included 43 million acres of national parks, 77 million acres of wildlife refuges, and 68 million acres of wilderness.

Once the bill had cleared the committees the only remaining question was the size of its victory margin. An overwhelming victory might influence the Senate, which had not yet acted. Udall and Seiberling and their staffs worked closely with the Alaska Coalition to produce the largest possible margin. The environmental groups mobilized a small army of lobbyists, volunteer coordinators, and media experts for what they called the "Land Conservation Vote of the Century." On May 19, 1978, the House defeated several amendments proposed by Young and Meeds (the most serious challenge, Meeds's amendment to reduce the total wilderness acreage to 33 million, lost 119 to 240) and voted 277 to 67 in favor of the bill, giving Seiberling and his allies the margin they sought. Representatives from the Northeast and Midwest voted overwhelmingly for the bill; representatives from the South and West were more evenly divided, especially on the Young and Meeds amendments. Apart from the California and Colorado delegations, a majority of westerners favored the amendments.[77]

Senator Jackson's committee began the markup of an Alaska bill in June. Jackson himself had long been a champion of environmental legislation but was less enthusiastic about Alaska. He derided the House bill, invited Alaska's senators to attend the committee's proceedings, and made it clear that he would not be influenced by the Alaska Coalition. His coolness apparently reflected his antipathy toward Carter, sensitivity to Washington state business and labor interests, and concerns about future energy supplies. Jackson also held the proxy votes of several senators who rarely attended, enabling him to outvote opponents on virtually any issue. Consequently, the committee meetings after mid-August typically consisted of Jackson, Alaska senator Stevens (Gravel refused to attend, pledging to filibuster any bill), and John P. Durkin (D-NH), the bill's nominal sponsor. The result was distressingly similar to what Meeds had proposed six months earlier. It provided for 93 million acres of parks, refuges, and other conservation units; 38 million acres of wilderness, a third Alaska national forest; and five BLM "conservation" areas that would be open to some economic activities. Jackson's bill also called for an eight-year study of the Arctic coast and placed most of the Tongass wilderness areas in a "pulp bank" to provide timber for the pulp mills if other supplies proved inadequate. The committee approved the bill on October 5, nine days before the end of the session.

Despite this setback, a compromise settlement remained a possibility, largely because it was known that President Carter planned to use the Antiquities Act and other administrative measures to set aside large areas of Alaska if Congress failed to act. On October 11, Jackson organized a meeting of interested senators, including Stevens and Gravel, plus Udall and Seiberling. Andrus also attended after Gravel dropped his threat to filibuster the bill. The meetings went on for several days, often lasting late into the evening, with the staff working for several hours afterward. "It was a very trying thing," Harry Crandell recalled.[78] By October 13 the group was close to a deal. The senators agreed to discard the new national forest and make the enlarged Arctic National Wildlife Refuge a wilderness, except for the Arctic coast. The House conferees agreed, in return, to adopt the less generous Senate boundaries for parks and refuges. Udall and Jackson ordered the staff to work through the night on a new bill that would incorporate the final compromises. At that point Gravel, who had said little, interrupted to demand additional transportation corridors through parks and wilderness areas. Jackson and Udall told the staff to take his demands into consideration, and the meeting adjourned. During the night Roy Jones and other staff members prepared a new bill that included 95 million acres of parks and refuges and 51 million acres of wilderness.

The informal committee met again at 9:00 A.M. on October 14, the last day of the session. Before any substantive discussions, Gravel complained that his demands had not been met and threatened to filibuster the bill. A senator questioned him: "I understand, Mike, that even if we accepted this [transportation corridors] you have a bunch of other killer amendments that you're going to offer." And Gravel said "That's right."[79] That ended the meeting and the possibility of an Alaska lands bill in 1978. Despite the effort that had gone into the legislation, most supporters were unhappy with the last-minute deals and preferred to rely on the president and the new Congress. Alaska Coalition leaders were actually relieved that the compromise legislation had stalled; Seiberling reluctantly agreed. Udall was confident that the Interior Committee and the House would act quickly in 1979, giving the Senate no excuse for additional delay. He joked that if Gravel filibustered, "it will be a 29-month filibuster and I want tickets for the front row."[80]

Seiberling suspected that the Alaskans might try to have the last word by adding a rider to an unrelated Senate bill prohibiting land withdrawals or other restrictions that would hamstring the president. That was possible because the House typically passed bills by unanimous consent at the end of the session. (A single negative vote would require a full-scale debate, which was impossible.) He therefore became a "watchdog" to make sure Stevens or Gravel "didn't slip something in some bill." He recalled that "as each bill came over to the House from the Senate, I would interrogate the manager of the bill as to whether there was anything in it dealing with public works or Alaska. I was on my feet 40 straight hours during that weekend."[81]

At 3:00 A.M. a rivers and harbors bill arrived with millions of dollars in Alaska projects. Gravel was the Senate manager, and he accompanied the bill to monitor its progress. When Seiberling objected, Gravel approached, asking for an explanation.

> I said, "Well, tit for tat. You stymied our effort to come up with a reasonable Alaska lands bill. Why should I agree to something with a lot of pork barrel stuff in it for Alaska. . . . You know that the President is going to put these all in national monument status anyway, but I think it would be better to avoid a confrontation. . . ." Gravel replied, "Well, I don't care if there is confrontation. You know I'm for secession."
>
> I said, "Well, Mike, all I can say is if you want to try secession, you better have a lot more than 400,000 people in your state." That was the end of that conversation.

Seiberling had shown, as he recalled, that he could be "just as big an s.o.b." as Gravel.[82]

The "Parks Barrel"

The dramatic story of the Alaska lands legislation was one indication of the new possibilities of the late 1970s. But there was another, equally compelling example. While Seiberling, Udall, and the Alaska Coalition were absorbed in the Alaska negotiations, Phil Burton, largely on his own, was shepherding an equally ambitious national parks bill through Congress. His success was testimony not only to his negotiating skills but also to the popularity of parks and wilderness. Together, the two campaigns marked the century's last great effort to insulate the most important remaining natural areas in the United States from commodity interests and urban sprawl.

As Udall explained, Burton's loss of the majority leader's post had "burned in his soul. . . . He decided he was going to go somewhere. The vehicle he chose was parks."[83] Taking over the national parks subcommittee in January 1977, he concluded, in his biographer's words, that "he could easily step into a leadership role in an environmental movement he saw as politically inept but potentially powerful."[84] Burton's first project was to rescue California's Redwood National Park, which had been created in 1968 amid great controversy. The park boundaries had been dictated by political rather than geographic considerations, and continued logging on the nearby hillsides had led to erosion and landslides, threatening to destroy the preserved area. To expand the park, Burton had to take on the timber companies, the timber workers' unions, and a hostile local congressman. A hearing in Eureka, California, in the spring, anticipated Seiberling's appearance in Sitka the following July. Burton refused to be intimidated, but he did add a half-billion-dollar plan to compensate laid-off workers. More maneuvers were required to mollify the AFL-CIO, but by January 1978, Burton had succeeded. Both houses passed Redwood bills. Burton dominated the conference committee, and Carter signed the legislation in March. Burton's efforts ended decades of controversy and showed that environmental groups and unions could work together productively.[85]

In the meantime Burton had begun work on an omnibus bill that answered his question, "Why not get something for everyone?" California projects topped his list. He added the Mineral King area to Sequoia National Park, a longtime Sierra Club goal; expanded Golden Gate NRA and Point Reyes National Seashore; and created the long-disputed Santa Monica NRA. To attract votes he added other pet projects. By May 1978 the bill included lands in forty-four states and two hundred congressional districts. It created eleven NPS sites; expanded twelve wilderness areas; authorized funds for thirty-four existing parks, including $29 million for land acquisitions in the CVNRA; extended eight wild and scenic rivers; and created four national trails. Seiberling called it the "national parks and recreation bill of the century."[86] Burton maneuvered it through the House but faced the same kinds of obstacles that Seiberling did in the Senate. By constantly adding and deleting provisions he was able to appeal to a large group of senators and thoroughly confuse the rest. Burton's bill passed the House by a six to one margin and, after the Senate had adopted a slightly different version by voice vote, passed the House again during the fateful night of October 14–15 by unanimous consent. Carter signed the legislation on November 10.

Burton's success, which would be duplicated in the following session on a lesser scale, was possible because of Udall's cooperation and the receptivity of Congress to preservationist legislation. But it was also a tribute to his skills as an intimidating and canny negotiator. His close relationship with organized labor, demonstrated in the Redwood campaign, eliminated one potential hurdle that the Alaska politicians were able to use effectively in attacking the Tongass wilderness designations. Burton was also able to sell parks as economic stimuli, a rationale that had limited appeal in Alaska. As a result, the opposition was limited to traditional conservatives and senators and representatives whose specific interests were not favored.

From the perspective of late 1978, the future looked bright indeed. An Alaska bill was almost certain to pass in the next session, and Udall, Burton, and Seiberling were ready to tackle other ambitious projects. With the Alaska deliberations nearing completion, and Teno Roncalio nearing retirement, Seiberling agreed to head the subcommittee on public lands, which had an ambitious agenda of wilderness legislation in 1979. But there were also reasons for caution. Growing opposition to the environmental movement, notably in the intermountain West where the commodity producers were strongest and where a handful of politicians had launched a "Sagebrush Rebellion," was troubling, but the performance of the Carter administration was an even greater concern. Apart from his personal goals, a major reason for Burton's aggressiveness had been his sense that Carter's ineptitude would lead to the election of a Republican in 1980. Whatever Seiberling and his allies decided to do might well have to be completed in two years, a short time by congressional standards.

❧[7]❧

New Challenges, 1978–80

Two and a half weeks after the collapse of the Alaska negotiations, Seiberling won a fifth term in the House, once again by a margin of more than
two to one. The 1978 campaign was low key and lackluster, both because
of Seiberling's absorption with Alaska and his unimpressive opponent,
Republican businessman Walter Vogel. Yet election day was one of the
last relatively calm moments Seiberling would enjoy for some time. Over
the next two years he would face a variety of unusually sensitive issues.
Some grew out of hometown problems: the emergence of the midwestern
Rust Belt, the trials of Akron's venerable manufacturers, and the stresses
of creating a new national park from mostly privately owned land. Others
were broader, such as the continuing challenge of Alaska and a host of
related problems that came with new congressional responsibilities.

The completion of the Alaska subcommittee's work left him with an
enhanced reputation, but no leadership post. Udall continued to chair
the energy and environment subcommittee, and the vacant chairmanship
of the mines and mining subcommittee was less appealing now that the
strip-mining bill had passed. Seiberling continued to work closely with
Burton on national parks, playing a key role in drafting and promoting the
landmark 1980 amendments to the Historic Preservation Act, for example.
But his most important decision was to accept the chairmanship of the
public lands subcommittee, which was available because of the retirement
of Teno Roncalio. Seiberling knew that public lands would have to address a growing controversy over wilderness, the result of another flawed
attempt by the Forest Service to respond to environmentalist pressures.

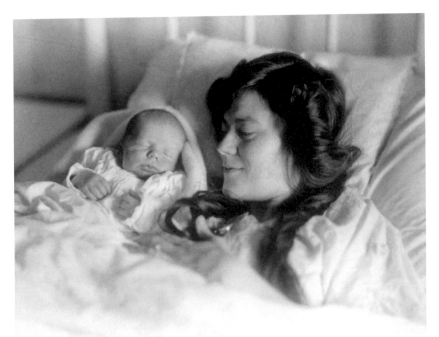

John F. Seiberling Jr. and his mother, Henrietta, shortly after his birth in September 1918. (Courtesy of Betty Seiberling.)

Stan Hywet Hall in December 1941. Photo by JFS. (Courtesy of Betty Seiberling.)

JFS at Mont Ste. Michel, Normandy, August 1944. (Courtesy of Betty Seiberling.)

JFS and colleagues at their office overlooking the Champs Élysées, October 1944. (Courtesy of Betty Seiberling.)

Fred Seiberling, JFS, and son John, Christmas 1951. (Courtesy of Betty Seiberling.)

JFS on vacation, Inyo National Forest, California, July 1967. (Courtesy of Betty Seiberling.)

JFS, Betty, and sons, 1970 campaign photo. (Courtesy of Betty Seiberling.)

JFS and Gerald Ford at Ford's confirmation hearing, 1973. (Courtesy of Betty Seiberling.)

JFS in his congressional office, 1970s. (Courtesy of Betty Seiberling.)

JFS and an Alaskan Native at Kotzebue, on the northwest coast, 1975. (Courtesy of Betty Seiberling.)

JFS and the Cuyahoga River, campaign photo, 1970s. (Courtesy of Betty Seiberling.)

JFS and his antagonist, Rep. Don Young (R-AK), during the Alaska subcommittee hearings, 1977. (Courtesy of Loretta Neumann/Akron Public Library.)

Anti-Seiberling demonstrators at the Alaska subcommittee hearing in Seattle, June 1977. (Courtesy of Loretta Neumann/Akron Public Library.)

The Alaska subcommittee hearing, 1977. Subcommittee members are on the dais (JFS in the middle, flanked by Don Young on the left and Morris Udall on the right). Subcommittee staff is below them. Harry Crandell is third from left; Loretta Neumann and Roy Jones are on right. (Courtesy of Loretta Neumann/Akron Public Library.)

Interior Secretary Cecil Andrus testifies on the Alaska legislation, 1977. Rupert Cutler, assistant secretary of agriculture, is on the left. (Courtesy of Loretta Neumann/Akron Public Library.)

JFS at Alaska Coalition reception, May 1979. (Courtesy of Loretta Neumann/Akron Public Library.)

JFS at his desk, ca. 1980. (Courtesy of Betty Seiberling.)

JFS and CVNRA sign, ca. 1980. (Courtesy of Betty Seiberling.)

Cartoon by Chuck Ayers, May 24, 1981. (© *Akron Beacon Journal.*)

John and Betty Seiberling at an event honoring Seiberling in the CVNRA, 1999. Rep. Ralph Regula is on the left; Rep. Tom Sawyer, his successor, is on the right. John Debo, park superintendent, is between Seiberling and Sawyer. (Courtesy of Loretta Neumann/Akron Public Library.)

JFS in the CVNRA, 1996. (Courtesy of Loretta Neumann/Akron Public Library.)

He did not anticipate the time and attention that would be required, or the complications that would arise. Over the next six years he would find himself deeply involved in more than a dozen state campaigns that recalled his Alaska experiences. And though the immediate stakes were not as great as they had been in Alaska, where parks, refuges, and other conservation issues were involved along with wilderness, the longer-term implications of the subcommittee's action were as great or greater. The wilderness bills that emerged during these years not only set aside large areas of the national forests but also ensured that additional wilderness lands could be created in the future. Seiberling would rightly look back on these events as a signal accomplishment.

Rust Belt Politics

The mid-1970s were disastrous for the midwestern economy, for industrial cities like Akron in particular. The severe recession of 1973–75, precipitated by the Arab oil embargo against the United States, was a devastating blow to the mature and energy-intensive industries such as steel, autos, and tires that dominated the Ohio economy. Since the 1940s, periodic recessions had resulted in large, temporary layoffs of industrial workers; the recession of 1973–75 led to large, permanent layoffs and plant closings. It came at a time when many of these plants were already in trouble, the results of old age, mismanagement, labor turmoil, and a shift in corporate spending to plants in the South or foreign countries. It thus accelerated a process that was already well advanced. As a consequence Seiberling and other midwestern politicians devoted much of their time in the years after 1975 to finding "solutions" to problems that they knew or strongly suspected had no happy solution.[1]

The situation was even more painful because the economic downturn coincided with the first meaningful national campaigns against air and water pollution. The pollution problem, exemplified by the burning of the Cuyahoga River, led to a series of federal regulatory measures and the creation of the Environmental Protection Agency (EPA).[2] The consequences included a rapid decline in the most easily corrected problems and mounting demands on industrial firms for modernization through new, less polluting technologies and improved management. The environmental gains benefited everyone; the costs were borne mostly by those firms that were responsible for the pollution, which in the Midwest meant old-line manufacturers and public utilities. Many tried to stall through appeals and lawsuits. Ohio firms were particularly uncooperative, in part because the new governor, James A. Rhodes, reelected in 1974, was closely allied with the state's coal producers and hostile to the regulatory effort. By the end of the decade Ohio had become a "symbol of recalcitrance," the "last outlaw."[3]

The delays meant that little was accomplished before the economic downturn, when layoffs and plant closings overshadowed everything else. It then became convenient for industrial leaders and their political allies to blame the new regulations and the EPA, suggesting that the public had a choice between environmental protection and prosperity. A corollary, which hostile politicians eagerly emphasized, was that the Carter administration, allied with the Sierra Club and other environmental groups, was working against its hitherto loyal supporters, industrial workers and organized labor.

Seiberling's response was to search for a way of defusing the conflict, which at this stage focused on air pollution. (The Cuyahoga River cleanup took much longer and resulted from the decline of Cleveland industry as well as regulatory measures.) His aide Suzanne Goulet summarized: "Seiberling does not want to see Summit County industries violate the Clean Air Act. He'd like to see industry stop using EPA regs as the whipping boy for industries leaving our area. However, we want to keep the jobs and other benefits those industries bring our area."[4] He encouraged negotiations and flexibility by the EPA. His political standing with the Carter administration, and especially with Barbara Blum, the deputy EPA administrator and a longtime environmental activist, ensured that his requests received serious consideration.

There were two distinct local problems, Akron's large firms—the tire plants, the local electric utility, Ohio Edison, and the large but antiquated PPG plant in nearby Barberton—all burned coal and were in violation of the new sulfur dioxide regulations; and a half-dozen small foundries were in violation of the limits on particulate emissions. All of them except Ohio Edison were economically precarious, and any additional financial burden might cause them to move or go out of business. In either case, the result would inevitably be blamed on overzealous government regulation. The issue came to a head in 1976 when the state's failure to adopt acceptable regulations forced the EPA to step in. Challenged in court, the EPA was unable to enforce limits for specific pollutants until early 1978.

In a final attempt to avoid the installation of "scrubbers," costly equipment that removed sulfur dioxide from coal smoke, the large firms proposed in late 1978 to spend as much as $1 million to conduct tests for sulfur dioxide pollution at various sites in Summit County. Their contention was that the EPA data, based on computer models, exaggerated the problem. EPA officials were skeptical, pointing out that local sampling did not address the acid rain problem in the Northeast. Nevertheless, the proposal was an indication that industry was ready to make some adjustments.

Seiberling seized on this concession to propose a meeting between EPA administrator Douglas Costle and representatives of Akron industry. His personal appeal persuaded Costle to attend. The meeting, on February 9, 1979, was largely a media event. Phil Leonard, president of the Akron Labor Council, told the group that excessively stringent enforcement measures would "be setting the stage for the largest ghost town in the United States." Akron mayor John S. Ballard, also a devotee of Old West metaphors, warned against the folly of "strapping on our six guns and facing each other down."[5] Amid the hyperbole, an understanding emerged: the EPA would work with the Akron industrialists to obtain the best possible data and use that data to devise appropriate measures. Goulet wrote that the meeting "was extremely successful in resolving the problems between the rubber companies and the U.S. EPA." She cited a letter from a B. F. Goodrich executive who reported that "for the first time, there is cause for optimism."[6] The subsequent studies showed that the EPA was right and that Akron residents, not just those in New York or New England, were suffering.[7]

The February meeting not only broke the impasse but also created divisions among the industrialists. The tire companies, which had more serious problems to address, were willing to deal once they were assured of EPA flexibility.[8] Ohio Edison was more wary because it had a larger stake in the pollution regulations; and PPG, which was preparing to close the Barberton plant, remained intransigent. The EPA and the tire companies soon reached agreements that brought the tire factories into compliance with the Clean Air Act. Ohio Edison, by closing two antiquated Akron area plants and using more low-sulfur coal, also resolved its problems. Thanks to Seiberling's persistence, the foundries were allowed to continue their operations as long as air quality generally did not suffer. PPG remained the notable holdout.[9] Apart from improvements in air quality, these developments clarified the politics of environmental regulation, at least in Summit County. The events of 1978–79 proved that there was a local health problem, that the EPA was not rigid and authoritarian, and that the culprits were not the EPA officers but the short-sighted industrial managers who had stalled and stalled until a full-blown crisis had emerged.

In contrast to the promising developments in Akron, the larger contest between the EPA and the state over sulfur dioxide controls became increasingly tangled. The obvious answer for Ohio utilities was to switch to low-sulfur coal from western states. But Ohio senator Metzenbaum had pushed through a controversial 1978 Clean Air Act amendment, designed to preserve the small and beleaguered Ohio coal industry, that banned changes in suppliers if the change would result in economic distress. His amendment and Governor Rhodes's continuing hostility ultimately persuaded the EPA to retreat, allowing two Cleveland power plants to burn Ohio coal without scrubbers. Environmentalists were outraged. Although the utilities would eventually have to conform, the delay was widely— and probably correctly—seen as a way to postpone the controversy until after the 1980 presidential election. Seiberling was not involved in these calculations and was not even informed of the eventual decision. "No wonder," he observed, that "Carter's in trouble with his own party."[10]

Two events of 1980 also affected these controversies. The first was the renewed energy crisis that accompanied the Iranian Revolution of 1979 and the onset of another severe recession.[11] Midwestern industry was again hard hit, with more plant closings and long-term unemployment. Barberton, with five major plant closings, including PPG and Seiberling Rubber (from which the last of the Seiberlings had retired in 1970), became a symbol of the region's plight.[12] Akron was less severely affected, mostly because of its earlier losses. The last remaining passenger- and truck-tire production ended in 1982, and the city began a long and difficult transition to a service-oriented economy. With the decline in manufacturing, air quality improved, though the utilities' continued reliance on coal limited even that benefit.

The second event of 1980 was the presidential election, won by Republican Ronald Reagan on a platform of deregulation and states rights. With new administrators dedicated to reducing the burdens on industry, the EPA became less aggressive, mired in scandal, and in many cases wholly ineffectual.

CVNRA in Turmoil

In contrast to the pollution problem, which had emerged over a long period and promised to generate controversy for many years, the CVNRA seemed about to fulfill its promise, especially after the 1978 park bill provided additional funding. In fact, it too became the subject of disputes that threatened to affect its future and, conceivably, Seiberling's. The history of the CVNRA in the late 1970s illustrated the inevitable problems in creating a park out of an area with substantial residential and commercial development. But it was also a case study of institutional and cultural conflict. An agency devoted largely to administering rural, mostly vacant lands in the West was now assigned to carve out a park from a largely urban area in the Midwest. Not surprisingly, the central point of contention was the National Park Service's (NPS) relations with the Valley's private landowners. That prospect had generated sporadic resistance before 1974; at the end of the decade, land acquisition conflicts became more threatening and significant. As Seiberling quickly discovered, the missteps of NPS officials provided a platform not only for critics of the CVNRA but also for opponents of environmental legislation in general.

The problems grew out of the very conditions that had encouraged the creation of the CVNRA. Rapidly rising land prices created a sense of urgency; they also led Seiberling and other park supporters to emphasize that much of the private land in the Valley would be subject only to easements, not outright purchase. In 1975–76, Superintendent Bill Birdsell was acutely aware of these pressures, but with only a small staff to aid him, he fell into the "familiar trap of *not* delegating, thereby handling all major aspects of the operation himself."[13] Moreover, as Betsy Cuthbertson, Seiberling's aide who handled CVNRA complaints, recalled, Birdsell was "really stubborn. . . . There was a real feeling I got from him of bureaucracy and inflexibility. . . . I think it was not the best match, unfortunately."[14] To speed the process of land acquisition, he borrowed five employees from the Army Corps of Engineers. Their customary approach was to give orders and move people out.

An example of the misunderstandings that arose from such an approach occurred in October 1977, when a number of Valley property owners, including Seiberling, received a letter from the Park Land Acquisition Office announcing that their property was about to be appraised. The letter also listed procedures for "those whose property is being acquired." Seiberling called Jim Jackson, president of the CVA, to see if he too had received such a letter. He had. "Jim and I then had a somewhat lengthy discussion," he recalled. Their concern was "the ineptitude of the Park Service in dealing with land owners and its apparent policy of buying fee title beyond its needs, usually where the owners desired to sell." They also discussed the impersonal and intimidating language in the letter.[15] On October 17, Jackson went to the park office to complain to land acquisition officer M. J. Sweeney, who had signed the letter. He was surprised to learn from Sweeney that the CVNRA planned to purchase his land and that of the others who had received letters. Jackson "had understood as did other [nearby] owners . . . that theirs would be a scenic easement acquisition" and that the letter "did not give the property owners all the information that they should have," such as the option of occupying their property after sale. Furthermore, "he had been in touch with Representative Seiberling and that Mr. Seiberling was furious." Sweeney replied that he had been told to buy the land.

Later that day Seiberling called Sweeney. He indicated that Jackson and others had contacted him, and "he was concerned that too many properties were being acquired in fee and few if any scenic easement interests were being acquired." He reminded Sweeney that Congress had intended to rely on easements "whenever possible."[16] "I then asked him to whom else they had sent the letter and he told me that they had simply sent the form letter to all of the people owning land . . . regardless of the type of ownership the Park Service might eventually wish to acquire. I told him I thought that was a very stupid thing to do and that the form of the letter was so bureaucratic that it was no wonder that the Park Service was getting a lot of flak from residents."

Later, Seiberling had "a long talk" with Birdsell and "told him frankly that . . . he had failed to exercise close enough supervision over the Land Acquisition Office." He also complained about the NPS's "continuing lack of sensitivity to the feelings of the residents of the Valley." Birdsell replied "that one of his problems was that he had inherited the personnel from the Corps of Engineers."[17]

By that time it was apparent that Birdsell himself was partly responsible for the complaints. The harried, overworked superintendent had been inundated by people wanting to sell their land, including many whose land had not been scheduled for fee purchase. Others wanted to build houses or otherwise develop their land before it was too late. The requests and complaints had become so overwhelming that Birdsell decided to postpone easement negotiations for two years in order to concentrate on purchases.[18] Under great stress, he often lost his temper when confronted by people whom he considered irresponsible, including the mayor of Valley View, who wanted CVNRA land for industrial development, and the trustees of Boston Township, who sought to rezone land to increase its sale price.[19]

Birdsell was also indifferent to the Valley's cultural and historical heritage. Seiberling recalled: "I went with him on a tour of the valley. . . . We passed several houses that were historic. . . . And I would say, 'Well, Bill, what are you doing about that house?' He would say, 'Oh, I guess it'll be torn down eventually.' And I'd say, 'No, if you'll read the Act, it says that the Park Service shall preserve the natural and historical character of the valley.'"[20] Such criticism had little effect. Houses that could not be used for park functions were boarded up to await demolition, creating a "ghost town" setting.

The missteps of the Land Acquisitions Office particularly aroused the ire of residents who had been opposed to or indifferent to the CVNRA from the beginning. A Homeowners and Residents Association, formed in early 1977, soon became strongly hostile to the NPS. For the next two years it circulated petitions, filed lawsuits, and organized protest meetings, with the goal of forcing the NPS to give landowners the option of an easement (if they wanted to stay) or an outright sale (if they decided to leave), regardless of the NPS's plans. The group was relatively small, with a core of 100 to 150, and perhaps 200 total supporters, but it succeeded in portraying itself as the defender of local residents against callous, insensitive government bureaucrats.[21]

The homeowners' activism in turn provoked the park's supporters, regardless of what they thought of Birdsell and his staff. Norman Godwin, one of the earliest champions of the CVNRA, spoke for many of them when he accused the homeowners' leaders of a strategy of intimidation designed to wring more money from the government. They were guilty of "gangsterism." That, he added, was "the kind of [organization] the homeowners association has turned into."[22]

He and most CVNRA supporters were particularly critical of Leonard Stein-Sapir, the most outspoken member of the Homeowners Association. A lawyer who had moved to Peninsula in 1974, Stein-Sapir had varied business interests. In mid-1975 he and his brother-in-law purchased seventy-two acres on Oak Hill Road, south of Peninsula, for $150,000. Stein-Sapir later claimed that he was merely seeking a rural retreat and was unaware of the park.[23] However, in the summer and fall of 1977 he and his brother-in-law divided the land into a six-acre section with a house and barn, which they valued at $15,000, and a sixty-six-acre section, which they divided into building lots. They also transferred the mineral rights to another firm they owned. To prevent development, the park bought the undeveloped land, appraised at $220,000, for $248,000. Stein-Sapir then spent about $85,000 to remodel the house and create a "party barn." This property was appraised at $180,000. Stein-Sapir demanded $500,000 and, after an extended dispute and a trial, sold the property to the park for $651,000. Seiberling's staff calculated his profit from the seventy-two acres at $664,000.[24]

During the same period Stein-Sapir became the most incendiary of the CVNRA critics. As he profited handsomely and had no interest in preserving the traditional character of the Valley, his motivation was unclear. He was a newcomer, "bright and articulate" according to David Cooper, editor of the *Akron Beacon Journal*, and yet willing and even eager to play the role of demagogue.[25] He portrayed himself as the champion of abused neighbors, but he made little effort to intercede with NPS officials on their behalf or to negotiate exceptions to the land acquisition plan.[26] Whatever his motives, Stein-Sapir was instrumental in giving the Homeowners Association its militant character and in introducing a new political phase to the protest movement.

Apart from exacting more money from the NPS, Stein-Sapir's lawsuits against the government failed; his propaganda swayed few local residents and even backfired as outraged members of the Cuyahoga Valley Park Federation and its supporting organizations became more insistent that the NPS not make concessions. Directly or indirectly, however, he soon attracted political extremists who sought to use the controversy to advance their antigovernment agendas and to discredit Seiberling.

In mid-July 1978, when the Homeowners Association held its first public rallies and Stein-Sapir emerged as its spokesperson, a Californian named Charles Cushman arrived on the scene and became prominently associated with the attack on the NPS. Cushman had been active in a group that called itself the National Park Inholders Association and consisted of people who owned land within Yosemite National Park. It opposed the plans of the NPS to buy out park inholders. The resourceful Cushman soon expanded to other parts of the country, changed the organization's name to National Inholders Association (NIA) in 1980, and became associated with various groups that had dealings with public land agencies. NIA soon became an advocacy group for commodity interests. Cushman insisted that he and his organization supported national parks, but they opposed most park policies, the Land and Water Conservation Fund (LWCF), and the creation of new parks. In the 1980s NIA became part of the so-called wise use movement, which sought to roll back much of the environmental legislation of the 1960s and 1970s.[27]

Cushman's appearance changed the character of the Cuyahoga Valley Homeowners Association's protests. Whereas the individual members had a variety of complaints, mostly directed at Birdsell and the NPS, Cushman's target was Seiberling. He repeatedly charged that Seiberling had received preferential treatment from the NPS, in particular that he had received an easement on his property while everyone else had been forced to sell out. Cushman evidently knew nothing about easements, park policies, or the history of the CVNRA. But the facts were irrelevant to his campaign. In response to a scurrilous piece he wrote for the Fairbanks, Alaska, *News-Miner,* in April 1979 (at the time when the Interior Committee was again debating the Alaska legislation), the CVNRA staff prepared a detailed rebuttal. To Cushman's charge that Seiberling had received an easement, it replied that "Rep. Seiberling had not received anything. He had *donated* a scenic easement to the Akron Metropolitan Park District in 1972. This was prior to the authorization of CVNRA in December, 1974. This easement is still held by the Akron Metropolitan Park District."[28]

Seiberling nevertheless took the charges seriously, and, as he recalled, "spent an entire evening recapitulating the appraisal, tax deductions, [and] resulting tax credits."[29] He showed that he not only had donated an easement on his property, preventing future development and greatly reducing its market value, but had also sold his undeveloped land to the Trust for Public Land, to be held for eventual resale to the CVNRA, at a loss of another $20,000. Yet rather than applauding his contributions, Cushman and his allies tried to portray them as preferential treatment. Seiberling became frustrated when several local papers, including the *Akron Beacon Journal,* mentioned Cushman's accusations without critical comment, implying that they might have substance.[30] He realized that something more was afoot when he was contacted by NBC television regarding a program it was preparing on government land acquisitions.

The program, called *Prime Time Sunday,* aired on December 16, 1979, and featured reporter Jessica Savitch interviewing NPS officials and individuals who owned land in several of the new parks, including the CVNRA. The program largely embraced the Cushman line. Sensing this bias, NPS director William Whalen had had a transcript made of his interview, which he distributed to members of Congress. Birdsell's efforts to explain the situation were reduced to a few seconds, and Seiberling's forty-five-minute interview was not used at all.[31] The brief segment on the CVNRA did not attack Seiberling directly; otherwise it was almost wholly devoted to the NPS's critics.

By that time there was little doubt that the Homeowners Association's complaints had given way to a wider counterattack against the public lands initiatives of the 1970s. Writing to Walter Sheppe, the chair of the local Sierra Club group, who had made this point in a letter to the *Akron Beacon Journal*, Seiberling noted that

> you are absolutely correct in perceiving that the attacks on the Park Service and on me personally are part of a nationwide ef-fort by the exploitive industries (oil, mining and timber) to grab huge chunks of the public domain in the name of states' rights and property rights. It certainly is a remarkable coincidence that the two areas chosen by NBC's Prime Time Sunday for this sleazy attack . . . were in the state represented by Senator Dale Bumpers [D-AR], chairman of the Senate subcommittee on National Parks and Public Lands [Buffalo National River, Arkansas] and the congressional district represented by me. . . . Senator Bumpers and I have refused to be intimidated or seduced by these self-seeking interests, and they have evidently decided to do what they can to embarrass us politically.

He concluded that it was "certainly time that the conservationists in the country are alerted to the nature of the assault."[32]

Other environmentalists had reached the same conclusion. The Park Federation and the Cuyahoga County League of Women Voters launched a letter-writing campaign to alert public officials to the "errors, sensationalism and distorted statements" of the homeowners group and its allies.[33] Representatives of the Sierra Club and the League of Women Voters picketed a theater in Cleveland Heights when it showed a documentary based on Cushman's charges. Jim Jackson, who wrote a weekly column for the *Akron Beacon Journal*, complained that the "one-sided reporting" of the NBC program "spreads public misunderstanding."[34] The paper's editors attacked Cushman's "warped sense of right and wrong."[35]

Seiberling asked the Government Accountability Office (GAO) to audit his financial dealings with the NPS, confident that such an investigation would "completely refute [Cushman's] baseless and, indeed, slanderous statements."[36] He and his allies also took the offensive. A February 7 column by the *Akron Beacon Journal*'s David Cooper urged the NPS to "move quickly to get things back on track."[37] Later Seiberling and Sen. Metzenbaum were more explicit, urging NPS director Whalen to "thoroughly reevaluate" the land acquisition program in the CVNRA and halt action against uncooperative landowners.[38]

Whalen had already received a confidential report on the CVNRA from a team of NPS officials that included Tedd McCann, one of the original park planners, and Lewis Albert, the superintendent of the Lowell National Historical Park in Massachusetts. They were highly critical of Birdsell's stewardship and recommended that he be "quietly eased out." The CVNRA's problems resulted from the lack of a "clear cut plan of action," a General Management Plan (completed in 1977) that was "too vague and general," and an approach that "displays a lack of intelligence, common sense, and flexibility." They called for the appointment of a professional planner, greatly increased "area and site planning," and settlements with the most vocal homeowners. "The park management is letting too many things drag on. . . . Frankly, the whole staff is overly 'hung up' on land acquisition. . . . Let John Seiberling deal with Stein Sopier [*sic*]." They urged the creation of a public relations office to mobilize public support, "use the Cleveland T. V. stations on positive park programs, avoid defense posture at all costs, go on the offensive across the board."[39]

One result of this critique was a conference that Seiberling hosted in Washington on May 22, 1980. Members of the CVNRA's advisory council presented its evaluations, McCann and Albert summarized their report, and Birdsell responded, but most of the daylong event was devoted to programs that would improve the park's effectiveness. Members of the CVNRA staff and specialists from the NPS discussed a variety of cultural activities.[40] Seiberling concluded that the group had "made great headway" in defining problems and, "more important, the outstanding opportunities that exist in the Cuyahoga Valley."[41]

Birdsell was subsequently "promoted" to a new position in Washington, and Lewis Albert, now well acquainted with the park and its problems, was appointed to succeed him. Sadly, in August, as Birdsell was about to leave for his new post, he suffered a second heart attack, this time fatal. Despite his history of heart trouble, he had seemed in good health. Presumably the strain of his job, especially during the previous two years, had contributed to his premature death.[42]

The events of the summer of 1980 essentially brought the tumultuous first phase of the CVNRA's history to an end. By the time of Albert's arrival, Stein-Sapir and one of his neighbors were the only landowners who had not settled their differences with the park, and one of Albert's first decisions was to halt additional purchases. He called the land acquisition program "unnecessarily detailed and rigid" and ordered his staff to purchase property only when faced with incompatible development. He specifically excluded agricultural land, defusing an emerging conflict over the proposed purchase of a Valley farm that sold corn and other vegetables to the public. "I am convinced," he added, "that the time had come to move CVNRA rapidly out of an almost all-consuming land acquisition posture and into an operating posture." To counteract the park's image as the "armpit" of the Midwest region, he sent each department manager to the regional office for several days to "develop an effective working relationship." His primary objective, however, was to multiply the number of activities and services. He proposed a visitor center, a youth hostel, an artist-in-residence program, and various landscaping projects. For the first time there would be signs at each entrance.[43]

Seiberling was relieved. A GAO report in August formally absolved him of any conflict of interest, and the criticism of Cushman and others had no apparent effect on his reelection campaign. In response to later reports that Stein-Sapir was still trying to stir up trouble, he wrote that "things have been so quiet lately on the Cuyahoga Park front that I assumed he had 'run out of steam.'"[44] Cushman proved to be more persistent. Though he moved on, the story of the Cuyahoga Valley outrages and Seiberling's preferential treatment remained part of his repertoire as he attempted to generate opposition to the NPS and its preservationist orientation.

Alaska Revisited

To supporters of the Alaska lands legislation, the failure of the House and Senate to come up with a satisfactory bill in the fall of 1978 was a temporary setback, comparable to Ford's veto of the strip-mining legislation in 1975. The Seiberling hearings had demonstrated a high level of public support; the basic features of the legislation—the number and location of parks and wildlife refuges, the need to address land transfers to Native corporations and subsistence rights—were not in dispute. The most heated controversies pitted environmentalists against commodity interests: the oil companies that wanted access to the entire Arctic coast; the timber industry and the Forest Service, which wanted to turn the Tongass National Forest into a tree farm; and the miners, who were most concerned about a potential molybdenum mine site in the proposed Misty Fjords Wilderness. For all of them the amount and location of wilderness areas were the keys. For Udall, Seiberling, and their allies, the challenge was to offer enough concessions to persuade the Senate to act. Two factors complicated this process. One was the absence of a powerful Senate sponsor; the second was the Alaska senators: Stevens, who wanted a weakened bill with as many loopholes as possible, and Gravel, who seemingly opposed everything.[45]

An added, increasingly important factor was the Carter administration. An Alaska lands bill remained at the top of its legislative list, and when the 1978 negotiations collapsed, Secretary Andrus urged the president to use his authority under the Antiquities Act to create a series of national monuments that would preserve the most critical areas. In December, as the d(2) withdrawals were about to expire, Carter set aside 56 million acres as monuments, and Andrus used his administrative authority to designate an additional 40 million acres as wildlife refuges. Despite the boldness of this action, unprecedented in scope, it was not the equivalent of a land law. The president could not create wilderness and would have to persuade Congress to appropriate money to manage the monuments. (The Arctic National Wildlife Range had had no appropriations in the 1960s because of the opposition of Alaska's senators.) Nor did Carter's actions address the other issues, such as subsistence rights, that had received so much attention in the hearings. The monuments were a starting point for the new campaign, a way to seize the initiative. Most observers predicted that both houses would quickly act and send the legislation to a conference committee where the real negotiations would take place. Given the new monuments and the continuing aggressiveness of the Alaska Coalition, the likely outcome would almost certainly be superior to the compromise package of October 1978.

In the House, Udall submitted a slightly revised version of HR 39 that provided for 114 million acres of parks and refuges and 85 million acres of wilderness, including 6 million acres of Tongass land and the entire coast of the Arctic National Wildlife Refuge. He took the bill to the full committee for action. The opposition was also prepared. Meeds had retired to work as a lobbyist for the state of Alaska, but most of his allies remained, and they could count on several additional Republican votes. They enlisted Jerry Huckaby (D-LA) to introduce an alternative to Udall's proposal; Huckaby's bill called for 97 million acres of parks and refuges but only 50 million acres of wilderness, several new multiple-use areas, and numerous prodevelopment loopholes. On February 28, 1979, Udall, Seiberling, and their allies were shocked when the committee voted 22 to 21 in favor of the Huckaby bill. All fifteen Republicans joined seven Democrats in voting against Udall. The most surprising vote was that of Austin Murphy, who had flirted with Meeds in the previous session but in the end had supported Seiberling. The legislation then went to the Merchant Marine Committee, where another bipartisan coalition voted to support a bill similar to Huckaby's.

The angry Udall quickly counterattacked. He revised his bill, reducing the wilderness areas to a total of 67 million acres; recruited several Republican cosponsors; worked with the Alaska Coalition and the administration to sway undecided representatives; and persuaded the Rules Committee to schedule a vote on his bill before the vote on the Huckaby bill. As Jack Hession, the Sierra Club's representative in Alaska, observed, "It shows you the power of an enraged committee chairman."[46] The vote in mid-May was a lopsided 268 to 157 in favor of the Udall bill, with strong support from the northeastern, midwestern, and Pacific coast delegations. The Republicans divided evenly.

Largely because of the opposition of the Alaska senators, the Senate Energy Committee did not take up the 1978 bill until October 1979, when it added a number of weakening amendments, producing a bill that Chuck Clusen of the Alaska Coalition condemned as "hopelessly shortsighted."[47] Because of Jackson's disinterest and the reluctance of other powerful senators to champion the Alaska Coalition's bill, the leader of the environmentalists was newly elected Paul Tsongas (D-MA), who had been an inactive member of Seiberling's committee in 1977–78. For several months he was unable to persuade the Senate leaders to schedule a vote in the face of Gravel's filibuster threats. Finally, in February 1980, Tsongas negotiated a deal with the Alaska senators to bring up the bill in mid-July, with limits on amendments and other restrictions. The Tsongas deal meant that the bill would not be considered until the end of the session, in the midst of the presidential campaign. The Alaska senators gloated; they had re-created the conditions of 1978.

For Seiberling the delay was unwelcome because of its implications for the Alaska legislation but also because it meant that critical negotiations between Senate and House leaders were likely to occur at the time he was shepherding a major historic preservation bill through the House. That bill, a response to complaints by state and local preservation groups about the ponderous NPS bureaucracy, which administered the program, and a tendency of federal agencies to disregard it altogether, also conflicted with a Carter administration effort to centralize control in Washington. Loretta Neumann did the background work, but Seiberling was the principal sponsor—Burton, who ordinarily would have played that role, was uninterested—and conducted a highly successful hearing in March. After that, there was little opposition. The final obstacle was a Republican effort to require written permission from private property owners before a structure could be added to the National Register of Historic Places. Seiberling negotiated a compromise that required the Interior Department to reconsider if the owner objected. The final legislation gave the states greater flexibility, created a mechanism for enlisting local groups in the preservation effort, and required federal agencies to give serious attention to historic structures. The 1980 amendments to the 1966 law "set the course" for historic preservation in the following decades.[48] Carter signed the final legislation in December.

Meanwhile, Seiberling and his allies were growing more anxious about the Alaska bill as the months passed. Once again the issue was whether supporters of the legislation could strengthen a weak Senate bill, either on the floor, in a conference committee, or in some type of ad hoc setting. With the help of the Alaska Coalition, Tsongas rallied support for a series of major amendments to the Energy Committee bill. When the first of these passed overwhelmingly, Stevens forced a series of delays and ultimately the creation of another ad hoc committee. For more than a week, Tsongas, Stevens, Jackson, and their staffs (including Roy Jones from the House Interior staff) negotiated. By July 29, Tsongas was satisfied that he had won a number of significant changes and recommended passage.

On July 30, Udall, Seiberling, Andrus, and leaders of the Alaska Coalition met to decide how to respond. They agreed that additional concessions were necessary but disagreed about how to proceed. On the one hand, Andrus and Seiberling believed that they had to win meaningful improvements by August 6, when Congress would adjourn for the

Democratic National Convention. After that, the political campaign would make additional negotiations almost impossible. Alaska Coalition leaders, on the other hand, insisted that they hold out, even beyond August 6. They recruited Phil Burton to "assert a calming and flowing influence on John Seiberling . . . and having John come to believe, with Phil's help, that getting more will not imperil the whole thing."[49] By that evening Andrus and Seiberling had agreed that significant concessions were essential, regardless of the timing.

Tsongas initially disagreed. He was eager to have the vote as soon as possible and had won major concessions from Stevens—eliminating the Tongass "pulp banks" and restoring the Misty Fjords Wilderness with the exception of the molybdenum mine site. Gravel, however, still promised to filibuster and ultimately forced the Senate leaders to postpone any action and schedule a cloture vote. On August 18, the Senate voted overwhelmingly for cloture and then passed the Alaska bill, 78 to 14. It was the first and only Senate vote on the Alaska legislation.

The House leaders were still not satisfied. Because there was little time, and Gravel, and possibly Stevens, could still mount a filibuster, their options were limited. Several members of Udall's and Seiberling's staffs met regularly with Stevens's staff to try to negotiate changes in the Senate bill. They made little progress because of the likely election of the Republican presidential candidate. Carter had been an invaluable ally in 1978; now, weakened by the new energy crisis, the deepening recession, and a hostage crisis in Iran, he was a liability. At one point Stevens contemptuously remarked to Seiberling: "I know Reagan's going to get elected. Why should I even be talking to you?"[50] The actual outcome was even worse than the environmentalists had feared. Reagan did win, and the Republicans, spearheaded by western senators who were closely allied with commodity interests, took control of the Senate. Acknowledging the new reality, Udall called for a vote on the Senate bill on November 13. It passed on a voice vote.

The drama of the legislative battle and its less than satisfying conclusion could not obscure the significance of what was at stake and what had been accomplished. ANILCA added 44 million acres to the national park system, 54 million acres to the wildlife refuge system, 3 million acres to the national forests, and 2 million acres to the emerging BLM land conservation system. It added twenty-five wild and scenic rivers and designated twelve other rivers for study, added 56 million acres to the Wilderness Preservation System, and facilitated land transfers to the state and to the Native corporations. ANILCA more than doubled the size of the national park system, tripled the acreage of the wildlife refuges, and quadrupled the amount of land in the Wilderness Preservation System. The ten new parks encompassed entire ecosystems; the vast wildlife refuges preserved the summer nesting grounds of a large percentage of America's migratory birds and the open spaces essential to the large mammals characteristic of Alaska. Some of the parks— Denali (the expanded Mt. McKinley), Katmai, Glacier Bay, and Kenai Fjords—were highly accessible and attractive to tourists and, indeed, helped to transform Alaska's economy in the following years. Others remained inaccessible to all but the most intrepid travelers; they were, at least in the twentieth century, de facto wildlife refuges.

The single most hotly contested provision of ANILCA, the Tongass wilderness designations, did not have the effect that either side had predicted. The 5 million acres of wilderness represented the first significant departure from Forest Service policy there and an apparent triumph for Alaska's environmentalists. Yet the following decade saw greatly accelerated logging in the Tongass, mostly because several of the Native corporations had been given selection rights to nearly a half-million acres of Tongass timber. In reaction to the continuing devastation and to another sustained political campaign, Congress passed the Tongass Timber Reform Act of 1990, which closed one of the most glaring ANILCA loopholes, a mandated subsidy to the timber industry, and preserved another million acres. By that time most of the old-growth timber was gone and the mills at Sitka and Ketchikan were under attack by various government agencies, including the Forest Service, for water and air pollution violations and bid-rigging on timber leases. When they finally closed in the early 1990s, the results were surprisingly modest; the rise of tourism in southeast Alaska more than compensated for the ill-starred timber program.[51]

Two other controversial provisions had no immediate ill effects. Despite a compliant Forest Service, administrative appeals and lawsuits by environmental groups delayed the development of the molybdenum mine site in Misty Fjords for several years. In the meantime, the effects of the recession on raw materials prices and the prospect of more legal wrangling persuaded the United States Borax Company to abandon the project. The concession remained, but there was no mine. The coast of the Arctic National Wildlife Refuge also remained a de facto wilderness, though it was the object of a prolonged political struggle. For twenty years Republican presidents and oil company lobbyists tried to persuade

Congress to open the coast to oil leasing, only to be thwarted first by the *Exxon Valdez* disaster of 1989, which generated a firestorm of public opposition to the oil companies, and then by the environmental organizations and their political allies, who succeeded in making the preservation of the Arctic National Wildlife Refuge coast a litmus test of environmental sensitivity.[52]

Seiberling looked back on ANILCA as his greatest single achievement. In the prolonged and often heated political battle, he had been instrumental in demonstrating public support for the Alaska Coalition bill and in pressuring the House to retain as many provisions of that bill as possible. The final legislation, though less generous, was a tribute to his persistence, negotiating skill, and ability to work with citizens groups. These were qualities he would put to good use as chairman of the public lands subcommittee at a critical juncture in the history of the wilderness movement.

The Public Lands Subcommittee

With the Alaska lands issue nearing resolution, Seiberling turned again to the national forests and a second Roadless Area Review and Evaluation (otherwise known as RARE II), as the U.S. Forest Service attempted to address the environmentalists' demands. This initiative proved to be no more successful than other Forest Service efforts to finesse the Wilderness Act. In this case, it also had unanticipated repercussions. By late 1979 it threatened to paralyze the operation of the national forests, with varying implications for commodity interests and political elites in many western states. They demanded immediate action by Congress, much as they had in 1975 when the clear-cutting controversy raised a similar specter. But wilderness legislation fell under the jurisdiction of the Interior Committee's public lands subcommittee, not the proindustry Agriculture Committee, which managed most national forest legislation.[53] And Seiberling, as the new subcommittee chair, was dead set against a quick fix. His methodical approach to policy issues made him skeptical of simple solutions, and his practical instincts, aided by his ties to the environmental community, suggested the possibility of a meaningful solution to the clashing interests that had given rise to RARE I, the 1971–72 evaluation, and RARE II in the first place. After a decade and a half of wilderness warfare, a peace accord might be possible.

To help him, Seiberling turned to the now veteran group that he had recruited for the Alaskan hearings. Crandell, Sloss, and Neumann transferred to the public lands subcommittee staff and would continue to work on lands issues for the rest of Seiberling's career. He also added Andrew Wiessner, a young attorney who had worked for Roncalio and was familiar with the RARE II investigations and the legislative options that were likely to emerge from them. Quiet and intense, Wiessner shared Seiberling's love of the outdoors and his conviction that in these matters the details were all-important. For the next six years he would serve as Seiberling's authority on the often esoteric distinctions that separated them from the commodity groups and as the subcommittee's principal contact with the ad hoc wilderness coalitions that formed in the wake of RARE II.

Seiberling planned to approach the wilderness issue exactly as he had approached the Alaska lands issue. He took the competing demands of environmentalists and industrial groups as the starting point, then personally inspected the lands at issue (ultimately visiting at least 150 of the 250 proposed areas), sought to find common ground between contending groups, established principles that would guide the ultimate settlements, and personally negotiated with the representatives whose districts were affected. Neumann, who accompanied him on several inspection trips, recalled how he "would have these breakfasts, or little gatherings . . . town meetings like we did in Alaska, and [Seiberling] always stressed that all sides had to be there. We had to include both the proponents and the opponents. If there was a local miner or off-road vehicle person, then the local Sierra Club person would be there too. . . . [The staff] at first thought . . . that it would end up in fights. Instead, because . . . under other circumstances the people were friends, they got along."[54] By carefully setting boundaries, they discovered that both sides could often achieve their objectives. This process frustrated the more extreme elements in both camps, but it resulted in a doubling of wilderness acreage in the lower forty-eight states, preserved the promise of more wilderness in the future, and provided a temporary respite from the conflicts that had been a feature of the political landscape since the passage of the Wilderness Act. Unlike the Alaska legislation, this activity attracted little attention nationally and virtually none in Ohio.

The post-1979 wilderness legislation had its origins in NEPA, the National Forest Management Act of 1976, and more generally in the ongoing campaign of the environmental organizations to force the Forest Service and other federal land management agencies to take their mandated responsibilities seriously. Few environmentalists opposed all commercial activities; their concern was the management agencies' preoccupation with those activities. The Wilderness Act and NEPA were expressions of their mistrust, and the multitude of lawsuits and grassroots campaigns against the government agencies were a gauge of their unhappiness with the status quo.

In 1977, as Congress again considered wilderness legislation that the Forest Service opposed—the eventual Endangered American Wilderness Act of 1978—M. Rupert Cutler, the new assistant secretary of agriculture, announced that the Forest Service would undertake another examination of its roadless lands in an effort to resolve the seemingly endless conflicts over potential wilderness designations. The proposed RARE II would provide a fuller accounting of national forest lands and divide those lands into three categories: wilderness, nonwilderness, and lands requiring further study. The Forest Service would recommend the first category to Congress for formal wilderness designations, continue to evaluate the lands in the third category for wilderness or nonwilderness recommendations, and implement the forest management plans (required by the 1976 Management Act) on lands in the nonwilderness category. The plans would preclude additional wilderness evaluations until new forest plans were drawn up in ten to fifteen years. Cutler apparently expected the noncontroversial lands to be allotted to the first and second categories, with the contested areas placed in further study. He did not adequately account for the agency's biases.[55]

In the process of formulating their recommendations, Forest Service officials held numerous public workshops in 1977 and invited public comments on their draft reports in 1978. Here is what a New Mexico state park official reported after attending most of the workshops in that state:

Cuba, July 12: " . . . disorganized and did not deal properly with the issues or the people's questions. I felt it was evasive and misleading. . . ."

Albuquerque, July 13: " . . . expressed a basic misunderstanding of the Forest Service process of gathering of criteria . . . workshop was unclear and ineffective."

Truth or Consequences, July 18: Ranchers thought RARE II "pushed through by the Sierra Club. . . . They felt it should be scenic or else not a wilderness." If the Forest Service had answered questions "it could have made the people less fearful and more open to wilderness."

Alamogordo, July 20: "This workshop was definitely unconstructive."

Santa Fe, Aug. 3: Forest Service officials explained the issue fully, "the first time this has been done at any workshop."[56]

Environmental leaders soon concluded that RARE II would be another "quick and dirty" study, like RARE I. An angry confrontation between leaders of several organizations and Cutler at a meeting in Roanoke, Virginia, in the spring of 1978 anticipated the "incredible storm" that accompanied the preliminary Forest Service report.[57] The environmentalists' unhappiness grew when they, and Cutler, discovered that the Forest Service had no intention of deferring judgment on the most controversial areas. The allocation of only 16 percent of roadless lands in California, Oregon, and Washington State to wilderness was particularly offensive. The final report in January 1979 called for 15 million acres of wilderness, one-third of which was the Tongass land already included in the ANILCA legislation. Thirty-six million acres were to be "released" for multiple-use management, and 11 million acres, including many areas with oil and gas potential and therefore unlikely to be recommended for wilderness designation at a future date, were allocated to further study. If the Tongass lands and the "wilderness study" lands that the agency had already been directed to evaluate were deleted from the totals, the Forest Service recommended only 8.9 million acres of wilderness and 6.5 million acres for "further planning."[58] A California example was illustrative. The RARE II report recommended 4 percent of the roadless national forest land in Trinity County, California, as wilderness. A citizens' committee, appointed by the county government and including representatives of the timber industry and other business groups, had recommended 48 percent.[59]

This was the situation, then, when Seiberling took over the public lands subcommittee. He immediately faced a host of issues related to the RARE II recommendations. Two were of particular importance and largely shaped his activities as subcommittee chairman over the next five years. The first was what to do about the proposed 15 million acres of wilderness. The timber industry and its allies wanted an omnibus bill that would include the recommended areas, but no more, ever—a once and for all bill that would end the debates over wilderness. The Carter administration backed the RARE II recommendations but, in deference to its environmentalist supporters, opposed an omnibus bill, as well as any restrictions on subsequent wilderness studies. The environmental groups considered the RARE II recommendations as a starting point for more realistic wilderness proposals, one more step in a process that began in 1964 and would continue as long as there were roadless areas in the national forests. To Seiberling this was an easy choice. "Learning from my experience with Alaska and Phil Burton," he recalled, "I decided we were going to do two things. One [was] to study the issues on a state-by-state basis . . . a sort of divide and rule basis. . . . It also made sense because there was such a huge amount of land that we couldn't begin to cover it all in one Congress." The second was to emphasize states where there was relatively little controversy, so "we could get some momentum going."[60] Rather than accepting the RARE II recommendations, which an omnibus bill implied, the subcommittee would work out the best possible arrangement for each state.

The other challenge, no less significant in the political debates that followed, was the fate of the roadless land that was *not* included in the wilderness bills. The nonwilderness lands were a large proportion of the total, and the best part, from the perspective of the commodity groups. Timber and other industrial interests wanted this land legislatively released and permanently available for logging and other multiple-use activities, meaning it would not be eligible for wilderness consideration when new forest plans were prepared in the future. In the jargon of that era, they wanted a "hard" release. Environmentalists favored a "soft" release, which meant that the land would be managed under existing forest plans during the next decade, but when new plans were drawn up, additional wilderness recommendations would be possible. In the interim nothing would prevent Congress from designating some or all of the roadless land as wilderness.

Seiberling was immediately challenged on these critical issues by Rep. Thomas M. Foley (D-WA), who headed the Agriculture Committee and was an ally of the timber industry. In early 1979 Foley sponsored a bill to release permanently all of the RARE II land that the Forest Service allotted to nonwilderness and to set deadlines for Congress to consider the lands recommended for wilderness and additional study. Foley later sought to make the bill more appealing by adding the RARE II wilderness recommendations, making it a proindustry omnibus bill. That raised red flags, and not just among environmentalists. As Andy Wiessner explained: "Introduction of an omnibus bill . . . would be politically embarrassing to several Democrats. . . . A Foley bill which would force them to take a public position on the President's proposals, raises the possibility that they would be exposed to severe criticism from both industry and conservationists."[61] One representative, for example, did not want any national forest bills that would affect his district "until I can get the next election behind me." Even Foley had to worry about "becoming a highly controversial figure, and perhaps a top environmental 'hit list' contender."[62] Foley grasped these problems and let his bill die, but the campaign for hard-release legislation continued and might have succeeded except for the opposition of Seiberling and the public lands subcommittee.

At first Seiberling adopted the position that no legislative release was necessary, because the president had already released the nonwilderness land in his RARE II report. Furthermore, releasing nonwilderness land via legislation would be "extremely complex," involving Congress "in nitty gritty management details." It would inevitably undermine Forest Service "morale" and the forest planning system.[63] A soft release could be achieved by including a statement in the report on each bill that the subcommittee had studied the land in question thoroughly and that, together with the Forest Service's RARE II evaluation, was "sufficient" to protect the decision from court challenge and allow the Forest Service to implement its forest plan. That way, the whole politically sensitive question could be handled quietly and effectively. He soon discovered that a quiet and effective approach was impossible and that more explicit language was essential.

In 1979 Seiberling had two choices for generating "momentum." One was to focus on California, which had the largest and best-organized environmental lobby and incomparable Phil Burton to orchestrate negotiations. But it also posed enormous challenges. The state's huge national forests were concentrated in the north, in congressional districts with Republican or conservative Democratic representatives, who were often uncooperative, even in the face of Burton's pressure tactics. The industry and environmental groups also had well-defined positions and were in no mood to compromise. The California battle was notable for both its length—five years—and intensity.

In the wake of the RARE II report, the two sides squared off. Rep. Harold "Bizz" Johnson, a friend of the timber industry, introduced a California wilderness bill that incorporated the Forest Service recommendations (1.3

million acres of wilderness) and a hard release of nonwilderness land; Burton introduced a competing bill that called for 5.1 million acres of wilderness and a soft release of nonwilderness lands. Seiberling visited northern California in July, held a hearing in Weed, praised the area's beauty—"If I ever moved to California, this is certainly the part I want to move to"—and made it clear that he had little regard for the RARE II recommendations.[64] At a Washington hearing in November, a coalition of California environmental groups left no doubt about their view of the Johnson bill. It was a "fraud," a "non-wilderness bill," a "timber industry scheme to pillage a major part of our remaining wild lands."[65] From that point the question was not whether the subcommittee would consider the Johnson bill, but what changes Burton would have to make to win the support of the northern California representatives. He spent the next six months negotiating with them and their allies. Seiberling helped him work out an accommodation with the ski industry, and Sierra Club activist Joe Fontaine took the lead in negotiating an acceptable compromise with Rep. William M. Thomas, an influential Republican.[66] By the summer of 1980 Johnson and his neighbor Rep. Don H. Clausen (R-CA) were the lone holdouts to a bill that designated more than 2 million acres of wilderness and provided a soft release of nonwilderness land.

In the meantime the state government had complicated the situation in unpredictable ways. California governor Edmund G. "Jerry" Brown strongly supported additional wilderness and was as unhappy as the Sierra Club with the RARE II report. He ordered his natural resources director to prepare a lawsuit attacking the Forest Service's environmental impact statement, which accompanied the RARE II recommendations. This prospect added "a sense of urgency" in the words of the Sierra Club's Tim Mahoney.[67] The environmentalists feared that a suit, if successful, would shut down the forests for an indefinite period and precipitate a congressional stampede to the Foley bill, the Johnson bill, or something similar. At first Huey Johnson, the natural resources director, agreed to delay any action, but as it became clear that there would be no immediate congressional action, he decided to sue. In January 1980 a federal judge agreed and issued an injunction covering forty-six California roadless areas. For the next four years the California injunction was an important consideration for both friends and foes of wilderness legislation. Environmentalists worried about a political backlash, while timber interests feared that if they were too inflexible additional lawsuits would paralyze the Forest Service in other states.[68] In the end, the California injunction proved to be a boon to Seiberling, but that effect could not be foreseen in 1980.

The California negotiations continued through the summer. The resolution of the release issue (see later discussion) made Bizz Johnson more amenable to a settlement, and Seiberling recalled how Burton dealt with Clausen, the last holdout: "Phil Burton wasn't getting anywhere with Don Clausen, and one day he said to me: 'After the House finishes its legislative business, I'd like you to come over to my office. I want you to meet Don Clausen. . . . ' At the meeting Phil had a couple of vodkas and then he really started to put the pressure on Don. He said, 'Now Don, you know you're crazy not to go along with the Trinity County wilderness proposals because everybody signed off on them.'"[69] The badgering continued until Clausen finally agreed to go along. Seiberling then asked Wiessner to work with Clausen's aides "to bring out a report in a form suitable to you and the minority members of the [Interior] Committee."[70]

Burton's "legislative miracle" passed the Interior Committee on July 30 and the House on August 18, despite a last-minute effort by the Forest Service to delay it.[71] The bill designated 2.1 million acres of national forest wilderness (plus 1.4 million of national park wilderness in Yosemite and Sequoia-Kings Canyon Parks), set aside an additional 120,000 acres for wilderness study, and declared the RARE II environmental impact statement and the Interior Committee's review "sufficient" to void the California suit and allow the Forest Service to manage the nonwilderness areas (580,000 acres plus 240,000 acres of wilderness study that had been covered by the injunction) until a new forest plan was prepared.[72]

With the end of the session approaching, the Senate had still not acted. Since California senator S. I. Hayakawa opposed the settlement and the members of the Energy Committee were ambivalent because of the soft release, the fate of the compromise package depended on the other California senator, Alan Cranston. Cranston was generally supportive but was running for reelection and was wary of offending the timber industry at a time when the Republicans seemed likely to make gains in Congress. In September, California Sierra Club lobbyist Russ Shay complained that the senator's staff was "becoming confused rather than decisive" because of the criticism of the timber interests and the Forest Service, as well as complaints by some environmentalists that the House bill gave away too much.[73] In October, Cranston pledged his support for a California wilderness bill, but not necessarily the Burton bill. Given Cranston's tepid endorsement and the opposition of the Energy Committee's Republicans, the Senate refused to act. The bill failed, and the injunction remained in effect. With the election of Reagan and a Republican Senate, "we can expect," as Shay observed in December, "to refight the battle on 'release language.'"[74]

The prolonged struggle in California left Colorado at the top of Seiberling's list. Colorado was not a leading timber producer and had a sympathetic Republican representative, James P. "Jim" Johnson, who was a member of the public lands subcommittee. A bill designating 1.4 million acres of national forest land as wilderness and an additional 650,000 acres as wilderness study (environmental groups had sought 5 million acres of wilderness), with no release language, easily passed the subcommittee, the Interior Committee, and the House. The legislation encountered more problems in the Senate after Rupert Cutler claimed, in hearing testimony, that explicit release language was necessary, and when the state's Republican senator, at the urging of ranchers, tried to include explicit language on grazing in wilderness areas. The Wilderness Act did not forbid grazing where it had been an established activity, but the proposed language guaranteed its indefinite continuation, creating an unacceptable precedent.[75] Despite the warnings of Udall and Seiberling that the grazing provision could lead to the bill's defeat in the House, the senators did not drop it until the last minute and even then insisted on motorized access to existing grazing areas. The Colorado law thus created an opening for special interest provisions that would become an enduring challenge for wilderness proponents. The Alaska legislation and a few of the earlier wilderness laws had had such provisos, but Alaska was considered sui generis, and the others had little impact. More than any other wilderness legislation, the Colorado act introduced the era of congressional micromanagement.[76]

In the meantime Wiessner and his Senate counterparts worked out a formula that became the standard for other wilderness legislation. It included "sufficiency" language to block California-type lawsuits (they had to excise the word *release* in order to avoid involving the Agriculture Committee); a soft release for nonwilderness lands in the current round of forest planning; and a prohibition on additional comprehensive (RARE III) studies. In effect, the formula allowed the Forest Service to do its work without new restrictions and permitted environmental groups to continue to agitate for additional wilderness designations in future forest planning cycles. The inclusion of the soft-release formula in the Colorado bill (it was also added to ANILCA to apply to the Tongass and Chugach forests), and Seiberling's determination to adhere to it in the future, had far-reaching effects in the following years.

A potentially serious threat to the Seiberling approach came as the Colorado legislation was nearing completion. Sen. Frank F. Church (D-ID), a leading Senate liberal, proposed a 2.2-million-acre central Idaho, or "River-of-No-Return," wilderness that covered parts of several national forests with no release or sufficiency statement. The Senate passed the bill in late 1979. Church was running for reelection in 1980, and his opponent, Rep. Steven D. Symms (R-ID), sought to turn the bill into a campaign issue. He prepared a competing bill, proposing only 1.4 million acres and excluding areas that the timber and mining industries sought. He also included a hard release for the state's RARE II nonwilderness lands. Symms won the support of the Republicans and several western Democrats on the public lands subcommittee and appeared to be able to derail the standardized state-by-state approach and embarrass Seiberling. But Seiberling, Udall, and Church successfully pressured the Democrats to change their positions, and a bill similar to Church's won on a party line vote, 9 to 7. Symms described the result as "outrageous" and a "lock up." He tried again in the Interior Committee and on the House floor (by that time he had raised his wilderness total to 1.8 million acres) with no greater success. The final legislation, which included the major provisions of the Senate bill, was one of the great triumphs of the wilderness movement. The River-of-No-Return Wilderness (renamed the Frank Church River-of-No-Return Wilderness after Church's death) was the largest single wilderness area outside Alaska and an affirmation of the Seiberling approach. But it had been a close call and became an excuse for Idaho politicians to oppose a state wilderness bill in the following years.[77]

In the meantime, the public lands subcommittee was devoting considerable attention to other RARE II bills. Apart from the release issue, Wiessner and the other staff members paid close attention to boundaries, having discovered that the Forest Service's proposed wilderness boundaries were often poorly drawn and were an invitation to conflict. They were careful to include areas of scenic value or significance for wildlife, as well as lands essential to preserving particular ecosystems. With equal care they excluded areas of commercial potential, such as mine sites. Public hearings helped to identify conflicting interests and controversial areas. The single most important step in the formulation of most bills was Seiberling's personal visit, which typically featured an aerial tour, usually by helicopter, inspections of areas of unusual importance or controversy, informal meetings with interest groups and knowledgeable local people, and a day or two of hiking, horseback riding, or other outdoor activity.

Seiberling's first such expedition, in May 1979, was to the Allegheny National Forest north of Pittsburgh. He, Rep. Peter Kostmayer (D-PA), Wiessner, and Neumann, together with a Forest Service representative from Washington, D.C., flew by Forest Service plane to Bradford, Pennsylvania. A reception and dinner at the local Holiday Inn enabled them to meet interest group representatives, including Sierra Club members from northeast Ohio, who Seiberling insisted be included, and a local congressional representative. The following morning they flew over the forest, visited a roadless area that had been the subject of much controversy, and had a picnic lunch and a hike. During the afternoon they toured parts of the forest where oil and gas exploration was occurring and possible wilderness areas before returning to Bradford and then to Washington.[78] A month later Seiberling devoted a week to northern California and southern Oregon, where he conducted a hearing and took several helicopter tours of proposed wilderness areas. He also enjoyed an overnight stay at a mountain camp and joined other politicians for a barbecue at Redwood National Park. A month later Betty joined him for two weeks in Colorado, Wyoming, Montana, Idaho, Washington, and Oregon. Personal highlights included an overnight hike into Brewster Lake in Wyoming's Gros Ventre roadless area and a reception for Alaska activists at the home of Jim Whittaker in Seattle. At the end of the official tour, the Seiberlings drove a rental car from Portland to San Francisco.[79]

Sometimes it was impossible, or nearly impossible, to adhere to this regimen. During the summer of 1980, at the time of the heated Alaska negotiations, Sen. Pete V. Domenici (R-NM) tried to attach a "consensus" New Mexico wilderness bill to the Colorado legislation. Domenici's bill had received scant consideration in the Senate and none whatever in the House. The senator made no effort to consult the state's environmentalists and included less wilderness land than the Forest Service had in its RARE II report. All other New Mexico roadless areas would be permanently released to the Forest Service. Moreover, if the final legislation included the controversial Colorado grazing language, both states would be covered.[80] Seiberling demanded major changes, including a separate New Mexico bill, more wilderness land, and the standard release language.

He scheduled an inspection trip to New Mexico for early November, just after the election. Wiessner and Neumann joined him, and Sen. Harrison Schmitt (R-NM) and Rep. Manuel Lujan (R-NM) traveled with them for several days. They scheduled a half-dozen community meetings. Seiberling recalled that "at the end of each of these sessions I would take a poll . . . and ask them whether they thought this particular area ought to be a wilderness. More and more of the people . . . voted [yes]. They said . . . they did want to protect this area." One incident proved to be especially important. When they reached the Apache Kid area in the Apache National Forest,

> A rancher was there [who] was a personal friend of Congressman Lujan, and he asked if he could come around with us in our helicopter flight over this proposed area. I said, "Yes, we'd love to have you." He said, "I'll show you where the Forest Service has drawn the boundaries wrong and where they ought to be."
>
> So we flew over, and he showed me. . . .
>
> So I said, "You know, I agree with you. They've got the boundaries wrong, and we'll try to correct them." As a result, he became a supporter. . . . I think that helped convince Congressman Lujan and Senator Schmitt. Their eyes were opened by the response that we got as we went around . . . at the end. Manny Lujan said . . ."I think we've resolved this. I think we can get this thing done." And Manny said, "Let's pass this in the lame duck session before the new Republican Congressman from southern New Mexico comes in because we'll have to educate him all over again."[81]

A final New Mexico wilderness bill passed at the end of the session, creating twelve wilderness and six wilderness study areas totaling more than 700,000 acres.

If New Mexico proved to be a pleasant surprise, serious, seemingly implacable conflicts were more often the rule. In the East and South, opponents often questioned the desirability of any wilderness. Congress passed "consensus" bills creating small wilderness areas in South Dakota, South Carolina, Louisiana, and Missouri, but it did not act on more controversial proposals. Those included state bills for Pennsylvania, where opinions on the future of the Allegheny National Forest were highly polarized; Indiana, where Seiberling and Rep. Lee H. Hamilton (D-IN), who represented the prospective wilderness area, agreed that there should be no public hearings—"delicate matters such as wilderness are best discussed in other than the confrontation climate" of the hearing room; and Illinois, where Rep. Paul M. Simon pleaded for inaction because opponents were so well-organized.[82] Major conflicts over acreage, boundaries, and release language also made a statewide Montana act impossible, though one small (33,000-acre) noncontroversial wilderness area was created.

Despite the many unresolved issues, the immediate legacy of RARE II was impressive. In 1979–80, the first term that Seiberling headed the public lands subcommittee, Congress created 4.4 million acres of national forest wilderness outside Alaska and designated another 600,000 acres for wilderness study. That raised the total in the lower forty-eight states from 9 percent to nearly 12 percent of all national forest land.[83] If the 5 million acres of Tongass wilderness are added, the significance of Seiberling's work becomes even more obvious. That impact was likely to grow in the following years, as more than 7 million acres of RARE II–recommended wilderness remained to be considered, not to mention the much larger areas that environmentalists proposed. Still, nothing was assured, and the advent of the Reagan administration promised to raise existing hurdles and to create additional ones for Seiberling and his subcommittee.

❧ 8 ❧

Confronting Adversity, 1981–84

For Seiberling and most of his colleagues, the early 1980s were an un-welcome replay of the events of 1973–76. The most severe recession since the 1930s devastated the industrial Midwest. Akron's tire industry, which had been in continuous decline since the mid-1970s, now virtu-ally disappeared; by 1983 only the headquarters offices of the largest firms remained. Seiberling described the situation as an "economic Pearl Harbor."[1] Wrenching changes in the political arena exacerbated the eco-nomic crisis. The election of Ronald Reagan on a platform of tax cuts for the wealthy and reduced domestic spending added to the plight of industrial workers, particularly those in older cities like Akron. Reagan differed from Nixon in one respect, however. Aloof from day-to-day affairs, the new president delegated most domestic policy initiatives to the right-wing activists and industry lobbyists who took over most of those positions in the new administration. The new secretary of the interior, James G. Watt, and the new assistant secretary of agriculture, John B. Crowell, were notable examples.[2]

Largely because of their experiences during the last years of the Nixon administration, Seiberling and his colleagues were better equipped to oppose the people and policies they now confronted. Though the Repub-licans had captured the U.S. Senate in 1980 and held it through 1986, the president's appointees were notably unsuccessful in the legislative arena. On environmental issues they now faced a greatly enlarged environmental movement with a powerful Washington lobby and experienced legislators such as Seiberling. By mid-1982, Watt and the other outspoken Reagan

appointees had become political liabilities, and after the midterm elections, which added to the Democratic total in the House and reduced
the Republican majority in the Senate, they were gradually jettisoned.

Reagan's rise had no effect on Seiberling's personal situation—his election margins in 1980, 1982, and 1984 were virtually unchanged from the
1970s—but the new administration did have a major impact on his congressional responsibilities. Apart from frequent confrontations with Watt
and the other Reagan officeholders, the most important changes resulted
from Seiberling's close relationship with Phil Burton. In order to devote
more time to the administration's labor and social welfare initiatives,
Burton asked Seiberling to add national parks to his portfolio. Seiberling
agreed, making him the principal defender of parks *and* wilderness areas.
But Burton also wanted him to take charge of the Pacific trust territories,
which had been Burton's special interest. A surprised Seiberling replied
that he didn't know anything about Micronesia. Burton was unimpressed:
"That doesn't matter, you're the only guy on this committee that I can
trust to see that those people get justice." "Boy," Seiberling responded,
"you sure know how to make it hard to say no."[3]

Seiberling versus Watt

"If Jim Watt did not exist," a knowledgeable Colorado journalist wrote
in 1981, "Ronald Reagan would have had to invent him." Watt was
"everything" Reagan wanted at the Interior Department.[4] When the
president-elect interviewed Watt, they had agreed on five points: opening
more public lands to multiple use, reducing the country's dependence
on foreign oil, establishing a strategic minerals policy, giving conces-
sionaires a larger voice in the management of the national parks, and
marginalizing the environmental organizations and other activists who
had been influential under Carter.[5] In effect, the president-elect approved
a systematic effort to reverse virtually all the public lands initiatives of
the previous twenty years. Seiberling and his allies had had many disputes with Interior Department administrators over specific proposals
and expenditure levels; they had yet to confront officials who rejected
their basic assumptions about the goals of public policy.

The man chosen for this ambitious assignment had little in common
with Rogers Morton or Cecil Andrus. A graduate of the University of
Wyoming and its law school, Watt identified publicly and professionally

with the rural West and the conservative values of its business establishment. He had worked as an aide to Sen. Millard Simpson (R-WY), as a lobbyist for the U.S. Chamber of Commerce, and as a midlevel Interior Department official during the Nixon years. Morton had promoted him to head the malfunctioning Bureau of Outdoor Recreation (BOR) in 1972, and he had served in that position during the debates over the CVNRA, favorably impressing at least some proponents of urban parks and Land and Water Conservation Fund (LWCF) expenditures. Cleve Pinnix, who served on the staff of the national parks subcommittee at the time, recalled, "Watt was the guy who helped us. . . . He was giving us data from the Interior Department about all the investment generated by the federal grants at the state level. . . . There was no crazy religious stuff. . . . We almost felt like this guy was a mole inside the administration."[6] However he may have appeared to park activists, he became a controversial figure in the Interior Department. A member of a fundamentalist church, he held prayer meetings in his office, demoted BOR employees who did not share his outlook, and opposed spending for wild and scenic rivers. There were also questionable financial dealings.[7] By 1975, Morton had had enough. Given Watt's ties to the Republican right wing, firing him meant "promoting" him to the Federal Power Commission, an obscure regulatory agency, where he became an outspoken proponent of deregulating natural gas prices. When Carter took office, Watt was among the first to be asked to leave.

The Sagebrush Rebellion, the late 1970s opposition to federal management of public lands in the intermountain West, offered new opportunities. Orchestrated by public officials in Nevada, the premier public land state, it soon spread to other states with large Bureau of Land Management (BLM) holdings. Reminiscent of the earlier upheavals, the Sagebrush Rebellion was a protest against the growing assertiveness of the BLM, in the wake of the Federal Land Policy and Management Act.[8] In response, five legislatures passed bills calling for the state takeover of federal public lands. By 1980 the "rebellion" had attracted commodity interests that opposed any change in the rural status quo and had become potent politically in the Rocky Mountain states. As a candidate Reagan had endorsed the "rebellion." As president-elect he looked for appointees who could deal sympathetically but effectively with it.

In the meantime various business interests, stung by the successes of the Sierra Club and other environmental groups in the courts, had created a series of organizations to fight the environmentalists' litigation strategy. In 1976, Joseph Coors, a wealthy Colorado brewer and one of the principal financial backers of this effort, formed the Mountain States Legal Foundation (MSLF) and was searching for a director. Watt was available, ideologically acceptable, and enthusiastically confrontational. Under his aegis the MSLF became "anticonsumer and [anti]feminist, antigovernment, antiblack, and above all, antienvironmentalist."[9] In the meantime, Reagan had increasingly fallen under the influence of men like Coors. Lou Cannon, his biographer, writes that the president-elect "essentially relinquished environmental policy to Coors and his allies."[10] In 1980, after Reagan's first choice for interior secretary declined and no other well-known westerner stepped forward, Watt was chosen. Coors supposedly said, "I got him this job."[11] Environmental groups strongly opposed Watt, but he was cautious and circumspect at his confirmation hearing, and the new Republican-dominated Senate approved him.

Watt immediately made waves. He fired all the Carter appointees on his first day, surrounded himself with men of similar backgrounds and outlook, and made a point of having no contacts with the department's civil servants. He told a sympathetic audience in March 1982 that he would "get rid" of uncooperative employees.[12] He wanted to prohibit individual memberships in environmental organizations but backed down after protests.[13] In early 1982, he banned contacts between Interior employees and congressional committees. He told a reporter that he wanted to "rein in" the House Interior Committee.[14]

He was no less aggressive in his attacks on public land policies. Watt abolished the BOR's successor agency and tried to divert LWCF money from land purchases to park operations, shrink the national park system, undermine the Wilderness Preservation System, and increase the powers of ranchers with grazing leases. He encouraged oil, gas, and minerals leasing.[15] His calls for cooperation with local governments placated many western "rebels." Watt wrote the president that "the Sagebrush Rebellion is over, and America has won."[16]

ANILCA was a predictable target, given the opposition of Alaska's political establishment to many provisions of the act. The law gave the secretary of the interior discretionary authority in implementing many of its provisions, and Watt used that authority to try to nullify parts of the legislation. He named the more proindustry U.S. Geological Survey, rather than the Fish and Wildlife Service (FWS), to conduct studies of the Arctic coast (a federal court later reversed this decision); halted BLM wilderness studies in Alaska; stopped park and wildlife agencies from cooperating with their Canadian counterparts; encouraged oil and minerals leasing wherever possible; and authorized a variety of land trades with Native corporations to open areas—including some wilderness areas and the Arctic National Wildlife Refuge coast—to oil drilling. He also used his budgetary authority to starve the agencies' Alaska operations.

Outside of Alaska, Watt's attacks on wilderness generated the greatest controversy. He tried to eliminate the BLM wilderness studies and encouraged new mineral claims in wilderness areas before a 1984 cutoff date. In his first appearance before a congressional committee, in March 1981, he called for opening wilderness areas to economic activity. Shortly afterward he announced that he would process mineral claims in the Bob Marshall Wilderness in Montana (the Interior Department had routinely refused to process claims in wilderness areas as the deadline approached), forcing the House Interior Committee to invoke an emergency provision of the BLM organic act to stop him. Although Watt agreed to desist, he encouraged the MSLF to sue, with the goal of forcing him to proceed. In December the BLM approved oil leases on land adjacent to national forest wilderness lands in New Mexico. The leases permitted immediate directional drilling under the wilderness with potential access to the surface.[17] Several months later Watt proposed, supposedly as a "compromise," a leasing ban on wilderness lands until 2000. Seiberling condemned the Watt "compromise" as an effort to "gut the nation's wilderness system." It was "deficient and unacceptable in every major respect."[18] Burton called it a "fraud and deception."[19] Even the Republicans on the Interior Committee who reluctantly sponsored the Watt plan, Manuel Lujan (R-NM) and Richard B. "Dick" Cheney (R-WY), considered it unacceptable. Cheney reported an avalanche of protest letters. "I'm not just talking about environmentalists," he explained. "I'm talking about ranchers, farmers, snowmobile advocates, hunting and fishing guys."[20] Watt soon abandoned his plan. In the fall of 1982 the House passed a bill formally closing wilderness areas to leasing. A majority of senators also supported the ban, but the Republican-controlled Energy Committee prevented it from coming to a vote. Riders on budget bills nevertheless tied Watt's hands.

· It had long been apparent that Watt's initiatives were designed primarily to attract headlines. After reviewing his initial comments, Andy Wiessner observed that he "is more concerned with appearances and discrediting the environmental movement than with policy." He was "lending support to . . . an ongoing campaign by industry to incorrectly identify wilderness in the public mind as the prime cause of virtually all environmental delay." His goal was to "breed public contempt for the environmental movement" in order to "weaken various environmental protection laws and promote accelerated development of all kinds."[21]

Watt's management of the national parks was consistent with this analysis. He asked Russell Dickenson, a Carter appointee, to remain as director of the National Park Service (NPS), supposedly to ensure continuity, but at the same time attacked the "terrible deterioration" of park visitor facilities and pledged to err "on the side of public use versus preservation." In one of many quips that came back to haunt him, he noted, "I don't like to paddle and I don't like to walk."[22] His affinity for Dickenson presumably reflected his perception of the director as a dutiful subordinate who would follow orders. In any case, Watt and his inner circle of advisors—in particular Ray Arnett, the assistant secretary—made the important decisions.

On April 20, 1981, Watt sent Seiberling a copy of an editorial that had appeared in the *Washington Post* on April 11. Although the editorial was critical of Watt, it included a sentence suggesting that if Watt was unhappy with the park system he should "recommend to Congress which parks should be deauthorized." Watt maintained that he had no plan "for deauthorizing any of the parks" but insisted that it would be "irresponsible" of him and Congress not to pay attention to the advice of the national parks advisory board (an appointed group), which had reached a "consensus opinion that there had been too many recent additions to the National Park System, which did not have national significance." There were, in Watt's language, "city parks . . . in the federal system." He reported that he had then asked the advisory board for advice on "preserving those nationally unique areas of critical importance."[23]

Three days after Watt's memo to Seiberling, Arnett ordered Dickenson to find out "what is necessary for divestiture of Cuyahoga Valley NRA to state ownership." Arnett wanted similar information about the Santa Monica NRA and a meeting with the superintendent of that park "to discuss political activities in the area and his assistance in an accelerated divestiture program."[24] The memo was soon leaked, and Watt and Arnett were grilled about it at a hearing of the House Interior appropriations subcommittee. Watt denied that he planned to "deauthorize" any of the parks, and Arnett insisted, despite overwhelming evidence to the contrary, that the memo had never been sent. Seiberling told reporters that he was "absolutely stunned" when he saw the memo. He immediately called Dickenson "and asked him what was going on . . . and then I read the memo to him. He said he had seen it and that it had been passed on down the line." Seiberling added, "There isn't going to be any deauthorization as long as I'm chairman of the (House Interior) public lands subcommittee—and that's exactly what I told Watt even before this memo surfaced." At the appropriations subcommittee hearings Rep. Ralph Regula, the senior Republican, was hardly less critical, reminding Watt that Congress determined the number and size of national parks. Aides to Ohio governor James Rhodes insisted that the state's budgetary problems made a takeover of the CVNRA an impossibility.[25]

Having failed to win Republican support for "deauthorization," Watt announced in early May a moratorium on land acquisitions and called for legislation to allow the use of LWCF money for park operations. He later explained that the LWCF "could cause an abuse to the concept of private ownership of property" and had certainly resulted in "the establishment and acquisition of areas of less than outstanding national significance."[26] This proved to be the first skirmish in a continuing political battle over land acquisitions and park appropriations, a battle that Watt and his successors eventually lost. The costs, in terms of park planning and operations, and NPS morale, were substantial.

Watt's other efforts to discredit Seiberling were more personal. Seiberling recalled: "Jim Watt called me one day [in May 1981] and said, 'I have heard there are criminal activities going on in the Cuyahoga Valley National Recreation Area.' And I said, 'Well, I'll tell you this, Jim, if you think that's the case, you send your inspector general out there immediately and have him turn the place upside down. I don't think you'll find anything, but that's what you should do.' Watt said, 'Okay. That's what I'm going to do,' and he did."[27] From the beginning the "investigation" was suspect. Loretta Neumann described it as a "cover-your-bottom action by Watt to explain away the so-called hit list." The secretary refused to explain how he had learned about the "criminal activities," but it was widely assumed that the source was Charles Cushman, whom Watt had appointed to the NPS's advisory board in August, much to Seiberling's disgust. In any case, Watt apparently did not have much confidence in the accusations, as he did not bother to contact Dickenson or order the records sealed.[28]

The investigation targeted four urban parks (CVNRA, Santa Monica, Indiana Dunes, and Fire Island National Seashore) and Sleeping Bear Dunes National Lakeshore, all associated with the park campaigns of the 1960s and 1970s. Watt said his goal was "to see why park boundaries have been drawn the way they have been, to see whose properties have been protected and whose have been taken."[29] The investigation focused on CVNRA and Santa Monica NRA and continued for nearly a year. Seiberling recalled that "the National Park Service was putting all kinds of pressure on [Supt.] Lew [Albert] to try to find out things that went wrong for the park, but Lew just steadfastly resisted all these pressures."[30] The inspector general's report, in April 1982, concluded that there had been no irregularities in either case and that Watt's suspicions had been baseless.[31]

Several days before the report was released Watt spoke to a Republican fund-raising dinner in Canton, Ohio. Proclaiming himself a defender of the environment, he attacked Seiberling and insisted that he, Watt, had supported CVNRA "all along." He also disputed Seiberling's association with the park: "It's really Congressman Regula's park," he told the local Republicans. Regula was not so easily flattered, telling reporters that Congress would appropriate money for land acquisitions regardless of what Watt did. Watt responded lamely that he would act "aggressively . . . as soon as our economic recovery is in place."[32]

Seven weeks later an editorial titled "The Silent Scandal" appeared in the *Wall Street Journal*. Repeating Cushman's familiar charges of preferential treatment for Seiberling and of heartless bureaucrats exploiting "little property owners," it was part of a media campaign that featured another Jessica Savitch television exposé, this time on the Public Broadcasting Service's *Frontline* series. The *Wall Street Journal* belatedly published an edited version of Seiberling's protest letter, but there was no way to refute charges that already had been repeatedly investigated and found to be false. On June 7, the *Akron Beacon Journal* reprinted the *Wall Street Journal* editorial together with a systematic assessment of each of the accusations. It concluded that the charges were based on numerous misstatements of facts and produced "a gross distortion of the reality we have seen here."[33] Cushman continued to make his charges and to show the *Frontline* report to anyone who would pay attention and even attempted to raise funds for Seiberling's Republican opponent in 1984. But with only the complaints from the 1970s to back his arguments, his appeal diminished quickly.

Wiessner, Crandell, and other staff members with close ties to the environmental movement had long urged Seiberling to be more aggressive. Watt "needs to be provoked," Wiessner wrote. "We need to expose his programs for the overreactionary proposals they are, and we can't do that by being gentle with him."[34] Seiberling, following his own inclinations as well as Udall's advice to "give Watt a bit more rope," at first refused to attack directly.[35] He wrote, for example, that the national park system was so popular "that I do not think even Mr. Watt can do it any fundamental damage, though his actions are damaging to the morale of the Park Service and will result in some temporary delays in completing some of the newer parks."[36] As Watt's intentions became clearer, Seiberling's criticism became more pointed, but he did not follow Udall's example and publicly call for Watt's resignation or dismissal.[37]

By 1982 it was not necessary to attack Watt directly. His heavy-handed efforts to turn back the clock, together with insensitive public comments on a range of subjects, had produced a strong backlash. The environmental movement eagerly exploited his record with a variety of news releases and publications. The Sierra Club, his old nemesis, enjoyed a boom in memberships and financial contributions, its budget more than doubling during the Watt years and quadrupling in the 1980s, as it solidified its position as a national organization.[38] Other groups enjoyed similar gains. By mid-1982 Watt realized what was happening and attempted to soften his image. Traveling widely, mostly in the West, he portrayed himself as a responsible moderate, even making minor concessions on controversial oil proposals. But it was too late. Republican leaders blamed Democratic gains in the congressional elections partly on Watt's exaggerated behavior, and he became a political liability. At first the president stubbornly resisted his advisors' advice to fire Watt. Yet by the summer of 1983, even Reagan acknowledged that Watt "has an important way of putting his foot in his mouth. . . . He knows he can no longer be effective with Congress."[39] In one of Watt's last appearances before the House Interior Committee, Udall, Seiberling, and Burton conspired to embarrass him. Udall recognized Burton, who immediately surrendered his time to Seiberling, who in turn devoted the entire period to an extended and blistering recital of Watt's stewardship. The secretary had no opportunity to reply.[40]

If Watt failed rather dramatically in the political arena, he did succeed in slowing public land acquisitions. Largely because of his influence, Congress did not authorize a single addition to the national park system between 1981 and 1983 and only two trails and a single historical site during Reagan's first term. In addition, the Interior Department refused to spend money that Congress appropriated, attempted to prevent land deals with the Trust for Public Land and other private land conservancies, and tried to centralize land purchase authority in Washington. Most of these efforts failed or were only temporarily successful. The result, however, was that the NPS purchased less land in 1981–82 than in any year since 1966, and in 1983 the total was lower still. As Seiberling noted, the effect was greatest in the newer parks such as CVNRA, where Watt's policies led to "lengthy and needless hardships" as willing sellers had to endure extended delays.[41]

Regulating Coal

The other policy area where Watt had a substantial impact was the implementation of the landmark Surface Mining Control and Reclamation Act of 1977 (SMCRA), Seiberling's principal interest aside from public lands. Like most of those who had been active in the campaign to regulate strip-mining, Seiberling believed that there were two essentials: tough uniform nationwide regulations and effective reclamation, including a fund to reclaim abandoned sites. Both were controversial because conditions varied so widely and because profitability in many cases depended precisely on the activities reformers sought to curb. An additional consideration in the 1970s, a time of high inflation, was the impact of regulation on production costs and consumer prices. The final legislation was thus a patchwork, "a series of small victories for proponents and opponents" of federal regulation.[42] The law satisfied no one, and several of the leading reform groups had even called on President Carter to veto it.

Carter appointed Walter Heine, a mining engineer who had worked for the Pennsylvania mine regulatory authority and was favored by environmental groups, to head the new federal office, the Office of Surface Mining (OSM). Heine's job was to implement the law, guide the states in assuming their responsibilities, and simultaneously deal with critics on both sides. Heine's agents began to enforce the law in mid-1978, before the OSM had approved the state enforcement plans or had staffed its regional offices. The result was widespread confusion and resistance from miners who opposed any regulation. Numerous lawsuits attacking the constitutionality of the law (which the Supreme Court rejected in 1981) added to the uncertainty. Heine came under growing pressure to be more flexible and accommodating to the states and, indirectly, the industry.

By 1979 the focus of the controversy was the rules that were to govern the state programs. Two apparent concessions riled environmentalists. The draft rules included a "state window" that permitted variations from the federal standards and did not explicitly permit citizens with complaints to accompany the state inspectors on their rounds, as the law provided. In a widely cited letter to Heine, Seiberling warned that the state window would permit states "to continue the very practices and enforcement patterns" that led Congress to act.[43] At an oversight hearing in March 1979, Heine refused to respond directly to this criticism, promising a written statement at a later date. "The mere fact that you cannot give a ready answer to that heightens my concern," Seiberling told the OSM chief and reiterated his belief that the "state window" was a serious error.[44] Heine later insisted that he would uphold the federal standards, and the final rules did include a provision for citizen access.

In the meantime Heine's problems worsened when the U.S. Senate embraced the so-called Rockefeller plan, sponsored by West Virginia's governor, which allowed each state to interpret the law without regard to OSM rules. By a 68–26 vote, with several prominent Democratic senators taking the lead, the Senate passed a Rockefeller plan rider in September 1979. Udall refused to act on it, but the Senate vote was a measure of the power of the mining industry and the continuing hostility of much of that industry to federal regulation.

At the time Carter left office, the OSM was still embroiled in conflict. The western states and several important Appalachian states (West Virginia and Virginia) had adopted satisfactory enforcement plans, but other mining states, including Ohio, remained in limbo. OSM, moreover, had become an issue in the presidential campaign, with Reagan attacking it as an example of heavy-handed regulation. In his first public comment on proposed changes at the Interior Department, Watt singled out the OSM as a prime example of "excessive and counterproductive regulatory activity." His appointees to the agency, James Harris of Indiana and J. Steven Griles of Virginia, had been leading opponents of federal regulation.[45] Their goal was to turn the program over to the states as quickly and completely as possible. Strip-mining reformers and sympathetic politicians such as Seiberling had argued for years that state regulation was hopelessly ineffectual. Yet, in a notable statement to the House Interior Committee, Harris said, "The only question at this point is: do you trust the states? Our answer is 'yes.'"[46]

Harris soon began a sweeping reorganization of OSM, reducing the role of the Washington headquarters, slashing its staff and budget, firing or transferring virtually every top administrator, and shifting responsibility to the states, which were given greater flexibility in interpreting the law. The number of federal inspectors declined, and those who remained became more accommodating. One researcher reported an OSM manager's comment: "There's a possibility of some policeman-type mentality being maintained by the inspectors, but it's something we're aware of and going to change."[47] Environmental groups responded with lawsuits and attacks on Watt and Harris. In the coal fields a new generation of grassroots organizations emerged to continue the campaign against strip-mining.[48]

Seiberling did what he could to defend SMCRA and the federal regulatory effort. As one who "fought in the trenches," he told a hearing in July 1981, "I am not going to sit here . . . and let it be dismantled."[49] The following September he told Harris, "When I read in the paper that Mr. Watt said that we have to change the requirement [that] . . . 'the approximate original contour must be restored'—the hackles went up on my neck. That is the guts of the act, restoration of the approximate original contour. For Mr. Watt to say we have to get rid of that showed to me he intended to make an assault on the very heart of this act."[50] Seiberling went on to attack virtually all the changes Harris had introduced. He predicted "another period of confusion. . . . The operators are going to push for watering down various requirements . . . and the people who are opposed to that, the conservationists and others, are going to be fighting that. . . . Things are going to be in another state of flux, I would say, for many, many months."[51]

He was no less critical in subsequent encounters with Harris and no more successful in pressuring the beleaguered director to enforce the law. He could be more positive, he noted, if he "felt that the OSM was really trying to carry out the act in every detail, instead of trying to come up with clever interpretations to avoid some of the clear requirements of the act."[52] Seiberling did accompany Harris on a June 1983 inspection trip of strip-mining operations in Pennsylvania and West Virginia. The tour, designed to highlight good and poor examples of reclamation, emphasized how little had been accomplished since 1977.[53]

Harris outlasted Watt by only a few months and was followed by a succession of Reagan appointees who were only marginally more successful than Heine and Harris in placating Congress or in imposing uniform standards on the industry. The insistent opposition of the Appalachian mining companies made their jobs difficult; their own ambivalence about regulation left OSM in a "comatose state," in the words of Ed Grandis, a reformer and Seiberling confidant.[54] Still, there was progress. Because the "extreme pro-industry stance" had only generated turmoil and criticism, as one scholar notes, "the new agency strategy was to try competence." By 1984, OSM "began to implement the law."[55] When Seiberling retired from Congress in 1987, nearly a decade after SMCRA, the federal and state reclamation programs were in operation, and strip-mining, on the whole, was less destructive. Yet a loophole in the 1977 law, permitting so-called mountaintop removal, had become as great a threat as the less dramatic forms of strip-mining that had so agitated Seiberling and a generation of activists.

Wilderness: Continuing Progress

The advent of the Reagan administration also raised doubts about the fate of the remaining RARE II bills. If existing wilderness areas were to be opened to oil drilling or mineral exploration, what was the point of additional legislation? Why go to the trouble of creating wilderness, when wilderness meant so little? The Watt strategy thus had the potential to bring the wilderness movement to a halt and, in the simultaneous campaign for hard-release legislation, to end it permanently, at least as far as the national forests were concerned. The legislative battles of the early 1980s, which revolved around obscure legal distinctions and received virtually no systematic media coverage, were in effect battles over the future of American conservation. Would the country go back to the time before the 1960s, when public lands were viewed largely as repositories of raw materials, or would it continue the pattern of the 1960s and 1970s that had emphasized genuine multiple use? Seiberling and the public lands subcommittee were at the center of this conflict.

　　The arrival of a hostile national administration also meant that the wilderness campaign required closer cooperation between Congress and the outside groups that rallied public opinion and lobbied representatives and senators. Seiberling had long relied on the Sierra Club, Wilderness Society, National Audubon Society, and others to provide information and public support (as well as to provide knowledgeable recruits for his staff). During the four-year campaign that followed, they cooperated more closely than ever. The unexpected deaths of Phil Burton (April 1983) and

Sen. Henry M. Jackson (September 1983), earlier champions of wilderness legislation, made this partnership more important than ever.

During the 1981–82 congressional term, when Watt was most assertive and enthusiasm for the Reagan program of deregulation and reduced domestic spending was at its peak, Seiberling and his staff spent more time responding to Watt than they did formulating legislation. The legislative surge, which had culminated in 1979–80, came to an abrupt halt, and Seiberling's subcommittee managed no major park initiatives and only a handful of wilderness bills.

The first test of 1981 was the Helms-Hayakawa National RARE II Release bill. Written by timber industry lobbyists, the Hayakawa bill was the most extreme of the hard-release bills. Unlike the Foley bill of 1979–80, it did not combine wilderness designations with the release of other lands; it simply released nonwilderness and "further study" lands immediately and RARE II wilderness lands if Congress did not act on the recommendations for the eastern forests by 1983, and the western forests by 1985. It also repealed the wilderness legislation of 1980 and the provision in the 1976 National Forest Management Act that required the Forest Service to consider wilderness in preparing its forest plans.[56] If passed, it would have effectively abolished the wilderness movement. In earlier years it would not have been taken seriously, but with Republican control of the Senate and Sen. James P. McClure (R-ID), a reliable industry ally, in charge of the Energy Committee, the Hayakawa bill was at least viable. In August, Sierra Club lobbyist Tim Mahoney wrote that Senator Jackson had held the committee's Democrats in line, and they, together with a handful of moderate Republicans, had prevented McClure from acting.[57] Although a similar House bill, sponsored by Jerry Huckaby and Don Young, had no chance, Senate action would have emboldened the industry to insist on some form of hard release in the next group of state wilderness bills.

A second, related test came in late 1982, when John Crowell, the assistant secretary of agriculture and former timber industry lobbyist, proposed a new study of roadless areas, in effect a RARE III. Because the California injunction remained in effect, the status of the roadless areas remained uncertain, and, according to Crowell, a new evaluation was warranted. Environmentalists were incensed. They interpreted his proposal as an effort to reduce the amount of wilderness that had been recommended in RARE II and build support for an omnibus bill, presumably with a hard-release provision. Seiberling and his staff pointed out that there had been no additional lawsuits, that the state-by-state approach was working smoothly in most cases, and that they were addressing the remaining issues through other state bills. Seiberling castigated Crowell's plan as "a clumsy attempt to revive the moribund effort for nationwide release legislation" that had "zero chance" of passage.[58] Crowell's trial balloon coincided with the president's veto of a Florida wilderness act, the first veto of a wilderness bill, and Watt's decision to curtail wilderness studies of BLM lands. Like most environmentalists, Seiberling saw these events as "part of an Administration-wide broadside assault on the nation's wilderness heritage."[59] He knew, though, that the Forest Service strongly opposed a RARE III because of the costs and uncertainties that were likely to arise and was only using it as a way to encourage hard-release legislation.[60] As Mahoney and a Sierra Club colleague explained, "Crowell's carefully designed 'crisis' contains the seeds of its own failure because Crowell had to admit that the *one* formula which has actually worked is the state-by-state approach."[61]

While Seiberling and his staff devoted most of their attention to these attacks, they could claim a handful of legislative successes. Non-controversial Indiana, Missouri, and Florida state bills (Reagan vetoed the Florida law because of an unrelated spending provision; he signed a similar Florida bill in 1984); California and Alabama state bills that later died in the Senate; and above all, an important West Virginia bill were all enacted in 1982.

The Eastern Wilderness Areas Act of 1975 had created two wilderness areas and a wilderness study area, the Cranberry backcountry, in the picturesque Monongahela National Forest of eastern West Virginia. The Cranberry area, encompassing 35,600 acres, was high, rugged, and remote and had long been prized for hunting, fishing, and backcountry hiking. It was an archetypal wilderness area, and the RARE II report recommended a wilderness designation. One major obstacle remained. The CSX Railroad Company owned the rights to coal that underlay much of the Cranberry. Pressured by environmentalists and hunters, the state legislature passed a law in 1978 that made it impossible for CSX to mine the area and in 1979 called for an exchange of the CSX holdings for other federal coal lands. In 1980 the U.S. House passed a West Virginia wilderness bill that called for an exchange of the CSX rights and included the Colorado release language, which was not an issue. Presumably a similar RARE II bill would pass in the next session with little or no controversy.

The Reagan Forest Service appointees viewed the situation differently. Apart from opposing wilderness in principle, they objected to the proposed arrangement with CSX and to several smaller areas included in the bill, which were potential natural gas fields. They also opposed the Colorado release language. Seiberling's job, then, was to maneuver the bill through the House in the face of a hostile administration. He had an ally in Rep. Cleveland K. Benedict (R-WVA), who represented the area, strongly favored the land exchange with CSX, and supported the soft-release language. Working with Benedict, Seiberling persuaded the subcommittee's Democrats to adopt the Colorado language, preserving the soft-release formula, and won the cooperation of CSX, which was eager to extricate itself from Cranberry.[62] The remaining issue was the hostility of the Westvaco Company, a paper manufacturer in nearby Covington, Virginia. Westvaco feared that a wilderness designation would lead to more stringent air pollution regulations for the Covington area, which might threaten its operations. Similar complaints had stalled a Virginia wilderness bill for more than a year.[63] Although Seiberling refused to include air quality restrictions in the bill, the subcommittee report provided reassurances to the company. The final bill passed the House and Senate overwhelmingly, creating the second largest wilderness area in the East. CSX later settled for a cash payment of $15 million.

The California Wilderness Act

However valuable the eastern wilderness acts might be to people who lived nearby, the California bill was the critical test of the health of the wilderness movement in the Reagan era. The state's size and many national forests, the strength of the environmental movement there, the 1980 injunction, and the influence of California on other states were all indicators of its importance. California was also central to the Sierra Club's "leapfrog" strategy for the Pacific Coast states. A California House bill would be first. "Then," as Tim Mahoney explained, "as California bogs down in the Senate," the environmental lobby would try to move the Washington bill through both House and Senate. "If Washington goes through, the odds on Oregon increase. The success of all three are interrelated, and if any of them fail badly, it hurts the others and our overall campaign."[64]

Seiberling's role in the California campaign was that of facilitator and ally, first to Burton and then, after his death and House passage of the California bill, to Sen. Alan Cranston, who led the prowilderness effort in the Senate. In 1980 the House had passed an impressive California wilderness bill, only to see it die in the Senate because of the opposition of Senator Hayakawa and other western Republicans. Hayakawa's successor, Sen. Pete Wilson, was a Republican moderate who sought the support of the environmental community. His efforts to reconcile the competing interests of his constituents would ultimately dictate the outcome of the California campaign.

The election of 1980 had brought one other important change to the California delegation, the defeat of the veteran Democrat Harold "Bizz" Johnson by Eugene A. Chappie, who had campaigned as an opponent of wilderness. To emphasize the degree of hostility in his district, which included Trinity County, the center of the northern California timber industry, Chappie asked the public lands subcommittee to hold a public hearing in Weaverville, the Trinity County seat. On May 22, 1981, the small town experienced a "traffic jam bigger than any in [its] history" as environmental activists, mobilized by the local Trinity Wilderness Coalition, and employees of local lumber mills jammed the school gymnasium. The orange armbands of the timber workers and the green shirts, buttons, and balloons of the environmentalists—"Wilderness is multiple use"—made the scene reminiscent of the 1977 hearings in Sitka and Ketchikan.[65] Seiberling's request for testimony had elicited 357 volunteers, about four to one (estimated by the subcommittee staff, through telephone calls) in favor of the new Burton bill, which called for several times as much northern California wilderness as the RARE II report. The subcommittee staff winnowed the witness list to 163, two to one in favor of the Burton bill.

At the beginning of the hearing Seiberling demanded the removal of all signs and balloons and prohibited demonstrations. "That's no way to conduct a hearing," he lectured the crowd of more than 1,500. For nearly nine hours he and the northern California representatives listened to the procession of witnesses, most of whom enthusiastically backed the Burton bill. There were several dramatic moments. Seiberling, for example, asked one timber executive if his industry "should profit at the expense of the fishing industry," which depended on rivers that originated in the area. A lumber plant manager called on Congress to "forget the demands of marijuana growers and food stamp users and listen instead to the people who care about our economic growth."[66] And an official from nearby Humboldt County engaged in a shouting match with Rep. Jim Weaver, an outspoken wilderness advocate. But these were exceptions. As the Sierra Club's Russ Shay reported, "We outnumbered wilderness opponents, presented far better prepared testimony, and offered an impressive diversity of interests."[67] When a leader of the timber trade association later protested at the "obvious manipulation of the witness list and blatant favoritism," Seiberling replied that the "confrontational atmosphere" promoted by the industry had become "a bit tiresome." In fact the industry had simply been "outworked or 'outhustled' by conservationists."[68]

Representative Chappie said little during or after the hearing and remained publicly uncommitted, a victory for the environmentalists. He would later join the other Republicans in opposing the Burton bill, but his reticence was an indication of their defensiveness and fear of Burton.[69]

Since the Burton bill was almost identical to the one the House had passed in 1980, and the deals with the various congressmen and women remained in effect, Seiberling's job was simple. He had a Washington hearing in mid-May, and the subcommittee reported the bill out on Tuesday, July 14, after minimal discussion. Burton then took over. The full committee reported the bill on July 15, and the House passed it by a voice vote on Friday, July 17. One observer estimated that the three votes took a total of nine minutes. Everything happened so quickly that the timber trade association's hotline was still urging callers to contact their representatives on Friday afternoon, after the final vote.[70] There was no debate on the 1980 release language, even as Watt, Crowell, and the Senate Republicans were promoting the Hayakawa bill and other hard-release formulas. "It is significant," wrote Mahoney, that the Interior Committee Republicans "did not indicate unalterable opposition to our release compromise." Their "wishy-washy attitude" augured well for later wilderness bills.[71]

The Burton bill once again died in the Senate, when Energy Committee chairman James McClure and Senator Hayakawa refused to act. No other western wilderness bill passed in the 1981–82 session, and the California injunction remained in effect. The whole process began again in 1983, when the political atmosphere had become more favorable. By that time several western Republican senators, notably Oregon's Mark O. Hatfield (R-OR), who had deferred initially to McClure, were eager to insulate their states against California-style injunctions. Hayakawa's retirement also improved the prospects of the California legislation. An aide to Sen. Pete Wilson quoted him to a Sierra Club official: "There will be a California Wilderness Bill."[72]

The improved outlook was reflected in the House debates, where the timber industry's allies mounted a more aggressive effort. At a hearing in early March 1983, Seiberling and Burton were challenged by Rep. Larry E. Craig (R-ID) and by the California Republicans, supposedly to Seiberling's surprise.[73] At the full committee markup on March 16, the Republicans, led by Don Young, attempted to reduce the wilderness acreage to 1.3 million, as recommended in the RARE II report. After several hours of debate the committee approved the Burton bill without significant changes by a party-line vote. It designated 2.3 million acres of California national forest as wilderness, released nonwilderness lands for the duration of the current forest plan, protected the Forest Service from court challenges based on RARE II, and presumably would lead to a lifting of the injunction. Thanks to Burton's finagling, a final vote was scheduled for an early date, Tuesday, April 12.

On Friday, April 8, Seiberling heard that Burton was ill, at home in San Francisco, and called: "Phil, if you're not feeling well, I'll be glad to postpone the bill." Burton insisted that the vote take place whether or not he was there.[74] The next day Burton suffered a massive, fatal heart attack. On Tuesday, Seiberling and Udall acted as floor managers. Some opponents wanted to delay the vote, supposedly out of respect for Burton. But Seiberling reminded them of Burton's last wish, and they proceeded. A motion to substitute the RARE II acreage lost 157 to 163; the final vote was 297 to 96. Seiberling was happy that the Republicans split evenly for and against the bill. "If Phil had known he was going to die," he observed wryly, "he would have put a lot *more* wilderness in this bill."[75]

For the following year, Seiberling was involved, at times directly, at times tangentially, in the effort to break the deadlock over wilderness legislation that continued to paralyze the Senate. The principal points of contention were the soft-release language, the wilderness acreage totals, and the boundaries of specific areas. With the arrival of Senator Wilson, California became the pivotal state in this fight. Unlike Hayakawa, Wilson accepted the soft-release formula. But to preserve his ties to the industry, he also held out for a substantial reduction in the Burton bill's 2.3 million acres. Environmental leaders became frustrated at his preoccupation. "These are not raw acres to be traded like poker chips," scoffed the Sierra Club's Doug Scott at one Wilson proposal.[76] Given the political climate of California, a reduced total in 1984 would not necessarily mean much; subsequent bills were likely to make up the difference and more. But the reduced total would send a message to wilderness opponents in other states, reinforcing the message that Assistant Secretary Crowell and other Reagan appointees were trying to convey.

Wilson sought to win enough concessions from the environmentalists to please the industry without compromising his image as a friend of the environment. He also wanted a deal that Seiberling would accept without a conference committee. At the end of a Senate subcommittee hearing on the California bill in late July 1983, subcommittee chair Malcolm Wallop (R-WY) urged Wilson and Cranston to negotiate a settlement, and they agreed. Each of the senators, and Seiberling, assigned a staff member to confer. When the staffers came back with a proposal for 1.9 million acres—the product of "enormous concessions"—in mid-September, Wilson rejected it as too generous.[77] Subsequent meetings over the next three months were inconclusive. In February 1984, Wilson unilaterally released his own plan, which called for 1.69 million acres of wilderness, plus a wild and scenic river designation for the Tuolumne River, an unrelated local issue that had divided Democratic representatives.[78] Environmentalists were outraged, and Cranston, Seiberling, and Sala G. Burton, Phil's widow and his successor, agreed that Wilson's plan was unacceptable. When the senator refused to return his calls, Seiberling went to his office, resolving to wait until Wilson saw him. An embarrassed Wilson soon emerged and explained that the timber companies adamantly opposed a more generous settlement. "They're stringin' you, Pete," Seiberling replied, "they don't care about acreage, all they care about is board feet, and 85 percent of all the board feet . . . [are] outside this bill. They're just being hoggish and want it all." Wilson promised to reconsider.[79]

In the meantime several other developments worked in Cranston's and Seiberling's favor. The Washington congressional delegation approved a consensus bill that provided for a million acres of wilderness, three times the RARE II recommendation. In early May 1984, McClure finally agreed to the soft-release language in a "compromise" brokered by Seiberling and Wiessner. "Seiberling agreed to wording changes so that McClure could concede the major points and still declare victory," observed one environmentalist.[80] McClure's agreement, mostly a response to Hatfield's success in winning the support of the Energy Committee for an Oregon bill with a soft-release provision, meant that the threat of a congressional backlash had greatly diminished and that environmentalists could again threaten lawsuits. Finally, at a hearing on Wilson's Tuolumne proposal, Seiberling indicated that he would not act until the wilderness bill had passed.[81]

On June 28, Cranston and Wilson announced a settlement of their differences. They called for 1.8 million acres of wilderness, the designation of the Tuolumne as a wild and scenic river, and the creation of a Mono Lake Scenic Area (another issue that was high on the environmentalists' agenda). Seiberling, also present, pledged to support the package in the House without amendment.[82] Wilson subsequently persuaded McClure to schedule a vote by the Energy Committee, which passed it on August 1 without changes. The Senate approved it by voice vote on August 9.

As promised, Seiberling brought up the Senate bill in early September, after the congressional recess. A vote to prohibit amendments passed, 295–112, and the final vote on September 12, by a margin of 368–41. Afterward Cranston presented a red rose to Sala Burton.[83] Reagan reluctantly agreed to sign the bill.

The California Act was a far cry from what Burton had originally proposed or what California's environmentalists wanted. Apart from the 1.8 million acres of wilderness, it released 1.3 million roadless acres for multiple-use planning and approved the creation or expansion of ten ski resorts and other commercial projects.[84] Activist George Whitmore summarized the sentiments of many Californians when he told reporters that he was not "wildly enthusiastic as it is a compromise."[85] Yet it was the most ambitious of the wilderness measures of the early 1980s and by far the most important symbolically. Seiberling described the final House vote as the "conservation vote of the 88th Congress."[86] As he implied, it was only one step in a longer progression for California, but a giant stride for his subcommittee.

Other Wilderness Legislation, 1983–84

The latter phases of the California struggle coincided with the generally successful conclusion to the RARE II negotiations. The role of the public lands subcommittee in reconciling the environmentalists' wish lists with the minimalist approach of the Forest Service and its industry allies and the continuing pressure of the environmental organizations were decisive factors. Seiberling urged the interest groups to come together and negotiate a mutually satisfactory agreement, but that happened in only a handful of states. As a result he and the public lands staff had to work out the details of most of the bills.

One anecdote from the Wyoming campaign, one of the most bitterly fought of all the RARE II efforts, captured the dynamics of this process. Wyoming environmentalists proposed 2.4 million acres of wilderness, while the state's economic leaders and elected officials insisted that a half-million acres was about right. Any legislation was bound to disappoint one, and probably both, of the groups. One day folk singer Carole King, now an Idaho resident and environmental activist, came to Seiberling's office to plead for the larger amount. Seiberling, long a fan of King's music, responded by singing a few lines from one of her best-known songs: "Sometimes you win, sometimes you lose," he crooned, as a way of emphasizing that the result was likely to be more modest.[87] Still, King and most of the environmentalists realized that the subcommittee's role guaranteed a genuine compromise and not simply what the state's elected officials were willing to concede.

That role required a heavy workload and incessant travel for Seiberling and Wiessner. The wilderness legislation required five trips of two to five days in 1980, three in 1982, four in 1983, and one in 1984. (There were an equal number of trips in those years to inspect NPS sites, including a nine-day visit to Alaska in 1983 and extended foreign sojourns in 1982 and 1983.) The itineraries typically included aerial inspections, meetings with local officials and interest group representatives, and a public hearing. From consultations with environmental groups, Wiessner gathered detailed information about proposed areas and boundaries, and from local officials and industry representatives, objections and counterproposals. As his experience increased, Wiessner became known, and feared, as the Capitol's foremost student of wilderness. In the extended Wyoming negotiations, the state's elected leaders refused at one stage to deal with him because of his encyclopedic knowledge and aggressive defense of the environmentalists' demands.[88]

This activity was frequently successful because of the continuing threat of legal challenges that would halt Forest Service activity in roadless areas. Although the Sierra Club and Wilderness Society remained wary of lawsuits because of a possible congressional backlash, many local environmental groups did base administrative challenges to Forest Service initiatives on the inadequacy of the RARE II environmental impact statement.[89] But the threat itself was often sufficient. The likelihood of legal action persuaded Sen. Mark Hatfield (R-OR) to end the

long-running stalemate between the Oregon Wilderness Coalition and
the timber industry, regardless of the intransigence of the Republicans
who dominated the Senate Energy Committee.[90] More than anything else,
his action convinced Senator McClure and his allies that their efforts to
win hard-release language, either in a single national bill or in the state
legislation, were futile.

Given this setting, some state groups were able to reach consensus. The
Florida bill passed again in early 1984 without the offensive provisions of
the 1982 measure. A Wisconsin wilderness bill passed both houses with
no opposition. A half-dozen other eastern and midwestern state bills
added modestly to the totals. Above all, the Washington bill demonstrated
the possibilities of a low-key campaign that did not polarize the state.
In other cases, notably Arkansas and Missouri, opposition came from
an individual representative from the district where the wilderness area
was located. Rep. Norvell W. "Bill" Emerson (R-MO), at the urging of
a local lead-mining company, insisted that the Irish Wilderness in the
Mark Twain National Forest be limited to 15,000 acres, despite the fact
that an additional 2,000 acres included important scenic and wildlife
areas. Emerson prevailed in the House, but the Senate bill, sponsored
by Sen. John C. Danforth (R-MO), called for 17,000 acres. When the
conference committee met, Seiberling suggested to Danforth that they
split the difference, and he agreed. Emerson was furious and appealed
to the president—without success—to veto the bill.[91]

In other cases there was consensus except on one or two seemingly
minor issues, usually related to some existing activity in the proposed
wilderness. Often the environmental groups were willing to approve
special provisions in order to placate opponents, despite the fact that such
concessions encouraged additional demands for tailor-made wilderness
laws. As Wiessner explained: "I think that if we allow the ball to roll
much further, we won't be able to stop it. . . . The 'third system' is the
easy way out for timid politicians. It allows them to seek a mixture of
language and protective classifications that will *substitute for wilderness* in an effort to offend as few groups and interests as possible. . . . I
believe the only effective way to dissuade this is to take a hard and fast
stand against *any* type of third system."[92] He argued specifically against
a Vermont bill that permitted snowmobile travel in a wilderness area.
There were many other proposals, seemingly innocuous, that had the
potential to undermine the Wilderness Act and create administrative
nightmares for the Forest Service and other conservation agencies.

Seiberling agreed that they must hold the line. A critical test was the battle over the Utah bill, in which he confronted prickly Sen. Edward J. "Jake" Garn, a defender of local prerogatives. Garn antagonized Seiberling by first insisting on an unrelated provision that would have given local ranchers lifetime rights to graze cattle in Capitol Reef National Park, and then by letting the Ohioan know that he was compiling a list of bills that Seiberling had sponsored or cosponsored for possible reprisals.[93] Garn called him at home in Akron one morning to threaten the CVNRA appropriation if he did not agree to the grazing proposal. Seiberling refused to back down.[94] Their final dispute was over Garn's defense of helicopter skiing in a proposed wilderness area. The conflict was finally resolved by changing the wilderness boundaries to exclude the ski area in exchange for other lands.

If Seiberling routinely and successfully resisted pleas for "third systems," he understood the persuasiveness of constituent pressures. He approved the Utah boundary changes and similar alterations in other cases, as long as they did not compromise the legislation or the Wilderness Act. The most common concession was a wilderness study designation for a controversial area, provided that it also included an all-important addendum, "until Congress determines otherwise." Wilderness study effectively banned any activity that altered the wilderness character of the land but permitted other activities (snowmobile use was the most common example) that had no permanent effect. If the wilderness study was not restricted, the Forest Service would later transfer the land to multiple use, but with the addendum the area would have to remain as de facto wilderness until Congress once again considered wilderness legislation. Many of the wilderness areas created in the early 1980s had been earlier wilderness study areas.

All of these factors were involved in the Wyoming campaign, the climactic wilderness battle of the early 1980s. Wyoming's national forests had huge roadless areas, mostly in the mountainous regions south and east of Grand Teton National Park. The state's environmentalists had organized a Wyoming Wilderness Coalition at the time of the RARE II study and had lobbied effectively for an ambitious plan totaling 2.4 million acres. They also postponed plans to pressure the NPS for wilderness recommendations for Yellowstone and Grand Teton parks on the grounds that opponents would cite the park acreage as an excuse to reduce the national forest total.[95] They had two major political advantages, the 1.5 million acres that were already in wilderness study or other temporary restrictive classifications, and the 2 to 3 million acres that would be released if a wilderness bill passed. The most important obstacles were the state's increasingly conservative political climate and the prominence of the oil, coal, timber, and other extractive industries. In 1979, Representative Roncalio, a friend of wilderness, was succeeded by Dick Cheney, a Republican who as President Ford's chief of staff had strongly opposed environmental legislation, and who now identified closely with Wyoming industry.

Wyoming was high on Seiberling's list of states with wilderness potential. When he visited in 1979, he had been guided on an overnight horseback trip to the proposed Gros Ventre wilderness by Philip Hocker, the chair of the Wyoming chapter of the Sierra Club. Afterward, Hocker wrote to Wiessner: "'You know, [he recalled remarking to a friend,] we've had six weeks of beautiful weather: if it started to rain just now, with Seiberling coming I might have had to admit that the Creator didn't intend for there to be a Gros Ventre Wilderness. . . . But in fact the weather was perfect, and didn't start to turn until a few hours after you helicoptered away."[96] The setting had the desired effect. At one point, when they had come to a ridgetop, Seiberling turned to Hocker: "Doesn't this remind you of a Mozart piano concerto?"[97] Seiberling returned in August 1981, on another inspection trip, and was similarly impressed. He was also optimistic about the prospects for a wilderness bill. "There is little overlap" of the proposed wilderness and lands with the greatest economic potential, he assured Senator Wallop.[98]

Still, nothing happened until 1982, when industry pressures to release the roadless areas led the Wyoming delegation (Cheney and Senators Wallop and Alan Simpson) to propose a bill that directly challenged the Wilderness Coalition. Originally it included only 480,000 acres, mostly rock and ice, and a hard release. In response to environmentalists' protests, the delegation added 200,000 acres and softened the release to allow the Forest Service to consider additional wilderness designations after 2000. Because the second round of national forest plans was scheduled for the mid-1990s, the 2000 date effectively eliminated any consideration of wilderness until the following round, probably after 2010. The Senate passed the Wyoming bill in early 1983.

Seiberling flatly refused to consider the Senate bill. Wiessner told a reporter from the *Caspar Star Tribune*, the state's leading newspaper, that the subcommittee was "upset because they've already got 1.5 million acres protected, and this bill would protect half of that and open the rest up for development. Seiberling believes that if the conservationists aren't on board, the bill will get stalled in the House . . . the conservationists want three or four times what is in it." The release language was another large hurdle. "Under the Senate version, the Forest Service couldn't even look at it for wilderness consideration until after 2000. That's beef No. 1." He concluded that "there are just too many people complaining."[99] If Seiberling accepted the Wyoming release language, or some variation of it, he would be unable to insist on the conventional release language for Utah, Idaho, and other states where wilderness opponents held sway.[100]

The stalemate continued for almost a year, as Congress wrestled with the release issue, and Wallop, who headed the Senate subcommittee on public lands, held up other state wilderness bills to pressure Seiberling. In the meantime Wiessner worked on a compromise that would split the difference between the Senate bill and the Wilderness Coalition's plan. He believed that 1.1 million acres of wilderness, coupled with a soft release, was the minimum acceptable. Otherwise, he saw "little hope of crafting a bill that anyone can live with."[101] Seiberling and Cheney went over the proposal on September 22, 1983, and Cheney agreed to recommend it to Wallop. Afterward Seiberling reported that "Cheney seemed fairly reasonable, but Wallop['s] a big question."[102]

In early November Cheney and Wallop submitted a counteroffer, together with a detailed critique of Wiessner's plan. They agreed to add 175,000 acres to their bill, but as "third system" reserves, not wilderness, that would be open to oil and gas exploration and snowmobiling. They also agreed to cosmetic changes in the release language. Cheney complained that Seiberling "doesn't have any understanding of living in a public lands state. . . . He doesn't believe in multiple use." Wallop added that his tactic of holding up other wilderness bills had made Seiberling more flexible. The remaining "stumbling block" was Wiessner. "We can deal with Seiberling. . . . We could do a lot better if we could get his staff out of the picture."[103]

In February 1984, Seiberling formally rejected the Wyoming counteroffer, explaining that he had "personally spent a great deal of time reviewing" it, "with special attention to release language and third systems." He insisted that they resolve these "threshold issues" before considering specific boundaries. Assuming agreement on these points, he was optimistic that they could resolve their differences on specific areas.[104] At a press conference, Wallop attacked Seiberling's letter as "a peculiar piece of arrogance." He added that "if that's his idea of negotiation, he had brought to a halt all wilderness consideration in this Congress." He suggested that the Wyoming bill might be attached to another wilderness bill. "One way or the other we will get that bill considered." He was "not in despair," he concluded. "I'm just a little aggravated that the man could be so cussed."[105]

Two months later Seiberling wrote to Hocker: "We are still getting nowhere in negotiations with Dick Cheney and Malcolm Wallop, but we are now engaged in negotiations with Jim McClure on release language. The positions are still so divergent that I am not optimistic that anything will come of them. In the meantime, however, pressure is building from other senators who want their bills moved and see nothing wrong with the standard release language."[106]

During the spring and summer of 1984 the negotiations continued, with Seiberling gradually gaining the upper hand. McClure's acquiescence on the release issue removed one major obstacle. There was also growing evidence of friction between Cheney and Wallop, with Cheney adopting a more pragmatic stance. One Wyoming Republican leader wrote that Cheney "has come so far that Sen. Wallop is probably having him investigated."[107] The decision of the Wyoming Wildlife Federation to name Seiberling as "conservation Legislator of the Year," as well as the prowilderness editorials of several Wyoming papers, raised doubts about the claims of Cheney and Wallop that they reflected local opinion. By August the negotiations over specific areas and boundaries had produced a compromise plan that Seiberling approved. It called for 888,000 acres of wilderness and 243,000 acres of wilderness study to satisfy "third system" proponents.[108] The total was almost identical to Seiberling's proposal of September 1983 and included all of the environmentalists' priority areas. Last-minute changes reduced the wilderness study total to 180,000 acres and affirmed the state's right to water that flowed through the wilderness areas—the basis of the Wyoming politicians' later claims that they had gotten what they really wanted. The final legislation passed in October.

Seiberling later wrote that "it was a tough battle, in which I had to negotiate single-handedly with Wyoming's three man Republican delegation. I will say one thing for them, they are 'tough cookies.' The bill was not everything I would have liked but certainly a lot better than what we started out with."[109] Sixteen years later, when Cheney was running for vice-president, he boasted that he had supported wilderness legislation as part of a "balanced" approach to public land management. Hearing this claim, Seiberling called Wiessner, now a Colorado attorney, to ask if Cheney's claims squared with his memory of the events of 1983–84. "Well," Wiessner replied, "after you twisted his arm off, yes he supported it."[110]

By the time the Wyoming legislation was passed, Congress had created more than 6 million acres of wilderness in eighteen states, the largest total (apart from ANILCA) for any session since 1964. It was a notable achievement, particularly in view of the hostility of the Reagan administration and the Forest Service. The key to this seemingly paradoxical outcome was another related statistic. Together with 6.6 million acres of wilderness, the 1984 legislation released 13.6 million roadless acres for multiple use. Some of this land would be consigned to timber sales or other commodity uses; much of it, however, would be reevaluated again in the 1990s. Seiberling and his subcommittee staff had good reason for satisfaction and optimism.

The intense negotiations over wilderness boundaries and release language tended to obscure the larger achievement of the early 1980s. In 1979, when Seiberling took over the chairmanship of the public lands subcommittee, the Wilderness Preservation System had been a relatively little known "overlay" that restricted management prerogatives in small, mostly remote and mountainous areas of the national forests, national parks, and wildlife refuges. In the following years it emerged as a prominent feature of public land policy. The Alaska legislation had the greatest impact on the statistical totals and on public awareness of the wilderness system. But the Alaska lands were mostly wilderness in the classic sense: undeveloped and largely undisturbed. The RARE II legislation and the other wilderness legislation of the early 1980s dealt with land that was less remote, more accessible, more visible, and not far from cities and industrial developments. It called attention to the existence of roadless lands in many states, including many eastern states, and to the many activities that threatened such areas in the absence of restrictive measures. Most people at the time, including Seiberling, equated preservation first and foremost with visually and aesthetically appealing natural landscapes, such as mountainous terrain. But as time passed the value of wilderness for maintaining biological diversity, preserving habitat for plants and animals, conserving water supplies, and buffering the effects of climate-changing pollutants received greater attention. Wilderness was no longer seen—as its original critics had argued—as a taxpayer-supported gift to artists and backpackers. It had become an inexpensive and useful antidote to some of society's most intractable problems. Seiberling lived long enough to enjoy this belated appreciation of his handiwork.

By the end of 1984 Seiberling could look back on the first Reagan term with a certain grim satisfaction. He and his allies had not only survived the political reaction but in many respects had triumphed. James Watt was a discredited memory and the Reagan administration had become more circumspect. By 1984, the president and his advisors had effectively relegated the Interior Department to the policy periphery, and the impetus in land conservation had shifted to other federal and state agencies, and especially to the private land trust movement.[111] There would be few administration initiatives in the following years, and the legacy of the environmental movement of the 1960s and 1970s—the antipollution laws, the parks, and wilderness areas—remained secure. The notable exception was strip-mining, where the spread of mountaintop removal soon overshadowed the regulatory effort. Balancing that setback was the wilderness legislation of the early 1980s, which represented a major step toward an evenhanded multiple-use policy. Despite the inflamed rhetoric and best efforts of Watt and his acolytes, there was more continuity than change in the political developments of the early 1980s.

⊕ 9 ⊕

Retirement

In April 1984, at the height of the RARE II negotiations and the controversy over the Wyoming bill, Seiberling encountered Sen. Malcolm Wallop in the Capitol. "I asked how things were in Wyoming," he recalled. Wallop replied that Wyoming was "wonderful" and added, "You ought to retire and come out here and enjoy life." Seiberling responded that he was "not about to retire as long as Ronald Reagan is on the scene in Washington."[1] A few months later Reagan's reelection ensured that the president would remain "on the scene" for another four years. Seiberling's reelection, by one of his largest margins (75 percent vs. 25 percent for Jean Bender, a little-known corporate attorney), suggested that he too would remain "on the scene" for as long as Reagan or as long as he chose.

There were other reasons for Seiberling to be optimistic about his future. His handling of the RARE II legislation had strengthened his reputation as a careful, systematic, and relentless legislator. Although he readily identified with the environmental movement and other liberal causes, he enjoyed good personal relations with political enemies such as Don Young and Senator Wallop. His cautious manner and avoidance of ad hominem attacks served him well, especially in confrontations with more flamboyant political figures such as James Watt. Now that Watt was gone, his successors were more circumspect, and the president had signed all but one of the wilderness bills and had approved the Florida bill after it had been revised. Despite Seiberling's personal disdain for Washington, he had shown that he could get things done in good times and bad.

By 1985 he also knew that he would have greater opportunities in the future. He was second in seniority among Democrats on the Interior Committee, and Mo Udall had begun to experience the symptoms of Parkinson's disease, the neurological illness that would force his retirement in 1989 and take his life nine years later. Seiberling had assembled an excellent staff that could be trusted to write bills, transact committee business, keep abreast of developments in the Congress and Washington generally, and serve effectively in the new positions that would open with Udall's departure. In Harry Crandell, Seiberling had an astute Washington veteran who effectively managed the subcommittee staff.

Nor was there any shortage of challenges. The Idaho RARE II bill had stalled at the end of the congressional session, and the Nevada legislation had never gotten close to resolution. Several other state bills as well as other national forest and Bureau of Land Management (BLM) wilderness proposals remained to be addressed. Dissatisfaction with the Tongass provisions of ANILCA would soon generate another national forest campaign on a subject close to Seiberling's heart. On the horizon, moreover, were a large number of BLM wilderness recommendations, which were certain to be at least as challenging as the RARE proposals. Only aggressive congressional leadership would ensure that these lands, many of national park quality, would not be overlooked. If a more accommodating administration took over in 1989, the possibilities would multiply.

Despite all of these reasons for continuing, Seiberling decided to retire at the end of his eighth term, in 1987. The most obvious reason was his health. He had had a prostate operation in 1981 and would have a second operation, for prostate cancer, in early 1985. He told the editor of *Sierra* magazine a year later: "At 68, I realize that I don't have the energy I used to have. I went through a major operation last year, and that makes you think about the fact that you're mortal."[2] In fact, he recovered fully from the cancer and at the time of his retirement was probably in better physical condition than the majority of his colleagues. (Based on family history, his prospects were also favorable: his Seiberling relatives were notoriously durable, and his mother lived to ninety-one.) A Cleveland reporter described him in 1986: "His voice is scratchy now and his walk slowed, but Seiberling still looks almost boyish at times, with his hands stuffed in his pockets and his head cocked up a little."[3]

More important than his health was the grueling pace he had maintained over the nine years he had served in the House leadership. To

take advantage of the many opportunities that lay ahead, he would have
to maintain or even increase his workload. As he explained, "I see the
challenges ahead of us as being very big and difficult ones that are going
to require a lot of attention and work for a long time. That's a job for
a person who's young enough to stick it out and who has the energy
to carry on the fight."[4] Conversely, it might be too great a burden for a
man who was attentive to every detail, who disliked Washington, who
had long believed that (as he had said in 1973) younger members would
"contribute to the rebirth of Congress as a vital, vigorous institution of
government," and had once sponsored legislation to make retirement
mandatory at the customary age at the time, sixty-five.[5]

An additional factor for Seiberling was his positive feelings about the
people who were likely to succeed him. Bruce F. Vento of Minnesota,
who had worked closely with him on the Alaska and RARE II legislation
and was a personal friend, was in line to head the public lands subcommittee, and George Miller (D-CA), a protégé of Burton's, was next in line
to succeed Udall. Both of them saw eye-to-eye with Seiberling on most
public lands issues and had good relations with the environmental organizations. At home, the young, new mayor of Akron, Thomas C. Sawyer,
had indicated an interest in succeeding him, and Seiberling approved. In
typical fashion, he explained, "I've got to retire from this place sometime.
It seemed to me that the [election] year in between the presidential elections was a good time to try to get a good person elected in my place, and
I think we're going to succeed in that."[6]

Last Assignments

As Seiberling noted, the challenges facing the public lands subcommittee
after 1984 were "big and difficult." Since RARE II, the subcommittee
had had its hands full with wilderness legislation. The remaining states
were similar to Wyoming, with hostile interest groups and/or squab-
bling politicians to confront, and little likelihood of rapid progress or
acceptable deals in the near future. The experience of 1984 was not
likely to be repeated any time soon. Andy Wiessner resigned in 1985 to
begin a legal career in Colorado. Seiberling found a capable replacement
in Russ Shay, who had previously headed the Sierra Club's wilderness
campaign in California, but he could not match Wiessner's encyclopedic
knowledge and contacts.

Still, there were successes. A modest Michigan wilderness bill passed the House, although the timidity of the state's senators would delay final passage for another year. A more significant breakthrough occurred in Nevada, where Rep. Harry Reid, representing the southern, rapidly urbanizing part of the state, worked closely with Nevada's environmentalists. Opposition came from ranchers, the former "sagebrush rebels," and miners, who wanted to preserve as many options for exploration and development as possible. Seiberling conducted a field inspection during the summer of 1985. As Wiessner explained, the "wilderness proposals consist of islands of high terrain in the midst of the surrounding 'desert' type lands, and therefore offer some of the state's only opportunities for quality hunting, fishing, and primitive recreation."[7] Seiberling supported the environmentalists' pleas for 1.5 million acres of wilderness; Reid, who was running for the Senate in 1986 and wanted to avoid antagonizing potential supporters, called for half that total, and the state's Republican representative, and Reid's 1986 opponent, proposed a mere 130,000 acres. As Shay wrote in 1986, "We have always kept well to the left of Harry to protect him."[8] Reid's final bill designated 600,000 acres of national forest land as wilderness and created a 174,000-acre Great Basin National Park and Preserve. The park was created in 1986 and became the state's first national park; a separate wilderness bill passed three years later. Less than a decade after the Sagebrush Rebellion, Nevada had taken a major step toward embracing the new regime in federal land policy.

The other notable development of Seiberling's last term was his willingness to consider a proposed national park site called Steam Town USA, near Scranton, Pennsylvania, devoted to nineteenth-century transportation. The product of lobbying by veteran representative Joseph McDade (R-PA), it was, to National Park Service (NPS) administrators as well as to many observers, another expensive, superfluous project—indeed, it was often cited in later years as the most egregious example of the "park barrel" approach. Seiberling, who probably could have sabotaged the project, disagreed: "It seemed to me to be an opportunity to create a kind of a public museum of a very important epoch in our nation's transportation history. Being an old member of the Transportation Corps . . . and coming from a town whose existence was created by the automobile, I thought that it was something worthy of looking into. . . . I became convinced that this was a worthwhile expenditure of federal money."[9] Steam Town reminded him of the Lowell, Massachusetts, Historical Park, which he had supported in the early 1970s. Like the Lowell park, it would provide a realistic, practical introduction to the country's heritage that contrasted favorably with the image conveyed by the many presidential homes and battlefields that the NPS maintained. Seiberling agreed to McDade's request for a hearing, and the crafty Pennsylvanian later used that exposure, plus his influence with the Appropriations Committee, to make Steam Town a reality. Confounding the critics, Steam Town became a popular tourist attraction, though the "park barrel" aura remained and contributed to a growing reluctance among many members of Congress to consider additions to the national park system.

The subcommittee's responsibility for the Pacific trust territories created other unusual opportunities. In early 1982, Seiberling and a half-dozen other subcommittee members, plus Burton, made an extensive inspection tour, starting in Hawaii and moving on to Guam, Saipan, Samoa, Fiji, and several of the small islands under American trusteeship. This experience was helpful during the following years as the subcommittee prepared legislation to create an independent federation of island states. After Burton's death, Seiberling became the principal defender of the island residents, often in opposition to the State and Defense departments and their allies in the Congress. He was adamant on the creation of a $150 million trust fund to clean up the atolls that had been used as atomic bomb test sites in the 1940s and early 1950s. "It's very simple, gentlemen," he recalled telling the representatives of the Defense Department, "you want military bases and permanent agreements on Palau and Kwajalein, etc., and I'm not going to let the legislation out of this subcommittee unless you are willing to accept this." On another occasion he told the Foreign Affairs Committee that his insistence on the trust fund reflected "a pledge I made to the late Philip Burton . . . and I'm going to do everything I can to carry it out."[10] His persistence ultimately paid off.

Seiberling's aggressiveness on this issue reflected more than loyalty to Burton's memory. His entry into electoral politics had resulted from his opposition to the Vietnam War and the assumptions about the role of military power that lay behind that intervention. He had fought Nixon and Ford over the war and a variety of related issues, opposed Carter's plans for missile defenses, and was appalled at Reagan's military buildup, neglect of disarmament negotiations, and willingness to intervene in Third World conflicts. Despite the turmoil of the preceding fifteen years, the fundamental issue remained the same. As he told a reporter in 1986, "We assume the only thing [the Soviet Union] responds to is military threats. . . . As far as I can see, our military threats produce military threats from them and their military threats produce military threats from us."[11] In 1970, Seiberling had believed that the nation's public lands were being mismanaged and had done something about it. Despite his efforts and those of like-minded politicians, there had been no commensurate progress in foreign affairs. To his mind, the Reagan administration, with its devotion to increased military spending and anti-Communist zealotry, represented a backward step. The problem was that he had far fewer opportunities to influence foreign policy than he did to foil James Watt.

For Seiberling, the result was a sense of frustration but also a renewed determination to change the ways that the U.S. government operated on the world stage. Employing the methods that he applied to public lands issues, he began a low-key, methodical attack on the administration's foreign and military policies. In early 1981, Seiberling went to Peter Rodino, the chair of the Judiciary Committee, to explain that he wanted to transfer to the Foreign Relations Committee in order to confront the Reagan people more directly. Rodino protested and promised a new assignment if he would stay. Seiberling reluctantly agreed. That promise led to his appointment to the bipartisan U.S. delegation to the U.S. European Parliamentary Exchange, which met twice each year, once in the United States and once in a major European city.

The experiences themselves were fascinating and often illuminating. Seiberling joined his colleagues on extended European trips in January 1983, 1984, and 1986. They visited a half-dozen countries each year, had briefings by ambassadors, discussions with European parliamentary leaders, and traveled to historical and cultural sites. These were enviable experiences, but their practical value was less certain. Seiberling's recollections suggest that the discussions were often perfunctory and that Reagan and his foreign policy advisors had little interest in the impressions or reactions of Seiberling and his congressional colleagues.

One incident emphasized that point. During the January 1984 tour, Seiberling and his colleagues discovered that they would be at the Rome airport at the same time as Donald H. Rumsfeld, Reagan's special envoy to the Middle East. Rumsfeld was returning from Lebanon, where a recent terrorist attack had killed more than two hundred American soldiers stationed there as peacekeepers. A brief meeting ensued. Asked about the possibility of a U.S. withdrawal from Lebanon, Rumsfeld replied flippantly that "if that happened, the Soviet Union would take over the entire Middle East." Seiberling's response was that "if he really believed that, then he should get the 'Great Communicator' [Reagan] to go on TV and explain to the American people how 200 marines in Lebanon would stop the Soviet Union from taking over the Middle East."[12] Shortly afterward Reagan did withdraw the remaining troops from Lebanon with little notice to Congress and few, if any, consequences for U.S.-Soviet relations.

Seiberling's other effort to promote a more realistic approach to international issues was the Congressional Roundtable on U.S.-Soviet Relations, which he helped to create through the Peace through Law Education Fund, an offshoot of the Members of Congress for Peace through Law. The roundtable consisted of periodic dinners for members of Congress followed by discussions that featured distinguished scholars and experts in international relations. The first session was in November 1983, and the meetings continued until 1994. The objective, in Seiberling's words, was "to help create a more balanced, humane, and objective attitude toward our 'cold war' adversaries."[13] But the dinners, like the parliamentary exchanges, did not attract the people who were most responsible for foreign policy, and the results were uncertain. In any case, Seiberling later admitted to a reporter that "the crudity of our understanding of the Soviets is absolutely appalling."[14]

His comments on international affairs on the eve of his retirement were strikingly similar to his comments in 1946 when he was active in the Akron United Nations Council. "One mistake, or one madman," he told a reporter in 1986, "can cause the world to blow itself up. How we can tolerate that is just beyond my comprehension." Still, he had not given up hope. "There is still a chance of getting some meaningful arms reduction. Otherwise," he added, "I would be totally depressed."[15]

Seiberling's most satisfying foreign trips had more limited goals. In August 1983, he joined Udall in leading a large Interior Committee delegation on a nine-day trip to Alaska. Officially their purpose was to observe the implementation of ANILCA—more specifically it was to warn Watt's associates that Congress was keeping an eye on them and to foster, in Seiberling's words, "a shared understanding of the wonderful nature of the public lands of Alaska."[16] The delegation visited most of the new parks and refuges and received a warm welcome from Gov. William S. "Bill" Sheffield and Sen. Ted Stevens, though Don Young discovered "other commitments" and left the group shortly after its arrival.[17]

A year later Seiberling agreed to serve as the congressional delegate to a UN environmental conference on deforestation in Nairobi, Kenya, where he helped draw up the final recommendations for preserving the world's forests.[18] In September 1985 he joined a delegation of Interior Committee colleagues and staff members on a weeklong tour of Siberia. The goal was to inspect Soviet activities there and to lay the groundwork for greater cooperation on environmental issues. The most distinctive feature of the trip was the Soviets' new willingness to accommodate American requests for access, including a flight from Japan directly to a Siberian city, and visits to formerly closed areas. Seiberling, Udall, and others who participated understood the novelty of their venture and believed that it contributed to later agreements to share information on environmental conditions and to exchange experts on environmental affairs. Seiberling was delighted with the results.[19]

Finally, in early 1986, he organized a subcommittee trip to Costa Rica and Panama to focus on the problems of tropical forests. The subcommittee and Interior Committee subsequently approved a bill requiring U.S. aid agencies to make environmental impact analyses of the projects they financed in Central America. The legislation ultimately failed because of opposition from the State Department and other agencies that would have to conduct the studies.

Transitions

As the 1986 congressional elections approached, acquaintances often asked Seiberling what he intended to do in retirement. Washington friends in particular assumed he would stay in the area and become a lobbyist or consultant. His response was unequivocal: "Heck no, I'm moving back to Akron. It happens to be a very nice place and that's where my roots are."[20] He elaborated: "I don't like the life here," referring to Washington. "Never have; never will. I'm not like a lot of other Congressmen. When I get out of Congress I am going to get out of Washington."[21] In this regard, at least, little had changed since 1970. He remained ambivalent about the federal government, hostile to the political culture of Washington, and enthusiastic about and often uncritical of his hometown.

One last dramatic event, however, symbolized the potential of government. Though Seiberling remained as attentive to constituent complaints and requests as ever, and did what he could to help resolve community problems such as the dispute between the EPA and Akron industry, he had no easy answers to the city's continuing economic crisis. Like his neighbors, he could only watch as the factories closed and the jobs disappeared. Yet there was one mildly redeeming feature to this process.

The manufacturing operations closed and the jobs disappeared, but the headquarters operations and most of the research and technical departments remained. For a brief period, Akron seemed to be on the cusp of becoming what its establishment had long wanted: a community based on services and scientific research, with large numbers of highly paid professional workers.

But this possibility proved to be as fleeting as the promises of new tire factories. In the 1980s, B. F. Goodrich, Firestone, and General Tire all disappeared, a result of mergers with more aggressive foreign firms, and it became obvious that the industry's problems had been deeper and more intractable than the greedy unions and antiquated buildings cited in most press accounts. Management had also been poor and, in the case of Firestone, disastrous.[22] The one survivor, Goodyear, remained reasonably profitable and identified with Akron. But it too was weakened by the turmoil in the domestic industry and by a failed diversification effort. In mid-1986 its depressed stock price attracted a flamboyant British corporate raider, Sir James M. Goldsmith, who began to buy Goodyear stock with the goal of breaking up the company and selling its various divisions. If he succeeded, Goodyear would go the way of the other rubber companies.

Because the threat was so obvious and so dramatic, the Goldsmith raid soon took on political overtones. Local officials condemned Goldsmith, 36,000 Akron residents signed antitakeover petitions, and many people bought Goodyear stock in order to oppose Goldsmith's campaign. As a longtime critic of corporate abuses, Seiberling followed these developments closely. As the conflict neared a climax, he arranged for the House Judiciary Committee's subcommittee on monopolies and commercial law to hold a hearing on Goldsmith's plan. The hearing, on November 18, 1986, in the Rayburn House Office Building, attracted a crowd of reporters and a live broadcast by an Akron radio station. In his testimony, Goldsmith portrayed himself as the stockholders' champion against an entrenched and dysfunctional bureaucracy, personified by Goodyear chief executive Robert Mercer, who was seated next to him. Arguing that the parts of the company were worth more than the whole, he described his plan to reorganize Goodyear and sell off many of the divisions. Seiberling listened with increasing amazement. During the question period he quoted Goldsmith's earlier statement that he knew nothing about the tire business: "Now you are saying that you do know more about the tire business than those who have been in it for many years." And in the most notable statement of the hearing, one that evoked memories of earlier contests with Bill Ayres and James Watt, he added, "My question is: Who the hell are you?"[23] The crowd erupted in cheers and applause. Goldsmith, he recalled later, was a "selfish ruthless individual," whose challenge had far-reaching implications for Seiberling's family heritage, his former employer, and his hometown.[24]

Seiberling's statement captured the mood of the community and made Goldsmith realize, if he had not done so already, that he faced a long and difficult and probably financially enervating struggle. Mercer, and several local figures, including the Goodyear union leaders, followed Goldsmith and were no less outspoken. At the end of the hearing a less confident Goldsmith approached Mercer and proposed a settlement. The company subsequently bought his shares, and other shares, at a premium price, ending the takeover threat. Goldsmith earned a handsome $91 million, and Goodyear remained intact, though deeply indebted and shorn of its largest subsidiaries. It continued to be Akron's largest private employer and an important link to the past.

In the meantime, Loretta Neumann, Don Mansfield, and several other longtime staffers were planning a gala retirement party—gala at least by the standards of the Seiberling household and the environmental movement, which, as Neumann observed, had not had an occasion for a big Washington celebration since 1980. Her idea was to keep the costs low so "workers," the members of the committee staffs, together with representatives of the various environmental groups and their families, could attend. It would be a "great opportunity for the environmental field." To help with the arrangements she recruited Larry Rockefeller of the Natural Resources Defense Council.[25] The event was scheduled for November 17 at the National Building Museum.

The party brought together Seiberling's colleagues and assistants and leaders of the environmental groups that had been most active in promoting parks and wilderness. Teno Roncalio served as master of ceremonies; Mo Udall spoke; and Thomas Sawyer, Seiberling's newly elected successor, and Robert Mercer of Goodyear added their greetings. A skit featuring Chuck Clusen, Brock Evans, Rockefeller, and Andy Wiessner was another highlight. Seiberling's typically understated remarks and thanks followed. Then the crowd joined in singing Neumann's adaptation of the song "I Remember It Well" from the film *Gigi*. It went in part:

John preserved Wilderness for us all to see,
Saved old buildings and Archeology,

For Akron too, he did aspire
To save our jobs and Goodyear Tire,
   Ah yes, we remember it well.
When Nixon tried our laws to breach,
John stood and cried impeach, impeach,
   Ah yes, we remember it well.
He wasn't tense to cut defense, and
Wall Street's urge to merge he purged.
   Ah yes, we remember it well.
He saved Alaska's lands from oil companies
Took those photographs for us to see.
And later when things went to pot,
He helped defeat James Gaines Watt.
   Ah yes, we remember it well.[26]

In the following months the Seiberlings sold their modest Washington home, moved back to Martin Road, and resumed the life they had known before 1970. Seiberling accepted an appointment at the University of Akron Law School where he introduced a course titled "The Legislative Process," featuring case studies of the ANILCA campaign, the fight to regulate strip-mining, the Nixon impeachment, and the creation of the CVNRA.[27] In later years he also headed the university's Peace Studies program. Added to a congressional pension of $42,500, Seiberling's university salary of $30,000 afforded a life of middle-class comforts. The part-time nature of the work (especially in comparison to the hectic pace of the preceding decade and a half) left time for local charity fund drives, occasional political activities, photography, Stan Hywet, and the CVNRA. The Seiberlings' middle son, David, remained in the Akron area; the others settled in Washington and North Carolina.

In addition, Seiberling soon emerged as an elder statesman of the environmental movement. His dedication, consistent support, and close relations with the environmental organizations during his years in Congress were major qualifications, but so too were Udall's declining health and the slim ranks of retired politicians who had made the environment a priority. Adding to Seiberling's appeal was a growing appreciation of the significance of ANILCA and the national parks and wilderness areas created in the 1970s and 1980s. Seiberling welcomed this role as an extension of his congressional work.

His first major contribution came in 1990–91, when the national environmental organizations staged an elaborate celebration to mark the tenth anniversary of ANILCA. Their goal was to revive interest in Alaska's lands and mobilize opposition to the Bush administration's anticipated effort to open the coast of the Arctic National Wildlife Refuge to oil exploration. Udall served as honorary chairman of the organizing committee, and Seiberling agreed to be a featured speaker. The first event was on December 2, 1990, when they and other luminaries of the Alaska campaign joined former president Carter in an official observance of the signing. This was followed in early February by a Washington conference titled "Celebrate Wild Alaska," which was to draw up a new environmental agenda for the state. Chuck Clusen headed the steering committee, and Loretta Neumann took charge of the Washington arrangements. The official conference program featured one of Seiberling's photographs on the cover and a poem titled "Discovery" that Betty Seiberling had written about her experiences in Alaska. Other Seiberling photos were displayed at a reception in the Cannon Office Building Caucus Room.[28]

Seiberling was the first speaker on a panel that included a leader of Alaska's environmental community and Sen. Frank H. Murkowski (R-AK), Gravel's successor. Seiberling's speech captured the mood of the conference. "Despite ten years of mismanagement, non-management, understaffing, misinterpretation, and just plain violation of the statute by the Reagan and Bush Administrations, ANILCA has preserved much of the Great Land, *so far*." He listed the "unfinished business" that the conference was to address. However, he concluded, "oil development in the Arctic Wildlife Refuge . . . is where we draw the line." He cited the potential of alternative energy and the need for "credibility" in negotiating with Third World countries to save rain forests and curb carbon dioxide emissions. "I am sometimes asked," he added, "why is someone from Ohio concerning himself about Alaska land? I respond by pointing out that our environmental ethic did not come from nowhere. Rather, it is the natural outgrowth of the inner spirit, of reverence for life, and also the realization that in nature, all things are connected."[29]

Over the next decade Seiberling would be called upon for speeches, press conference appearances, appeals to Congress, and other statements opposing the opening of the Arctic Refuge, urging the preservation of the remaining old-growth timber in the Tongass, and defending wilderness. By the turn of the twenty-first century he was probably as closely identified with the American wilderness as any other individual.

In 1995 he received the Sierra Club's John Muir Award, the organization's highest honor, and in 1999, the Presidential Citizens Medal. These and other honors from virtually every national environmental group attested to the continuing relevance of the causes he had addressed and the effectiveness of his role as legislator and defender of the public interest in public lands.

Legacy

In 2004, at the urging of friends, Seiberling prepared a brief memoir of his life and congressional career that he called "To Make a Difference." That title nicely captured his motive for running for Congress in 1970 and for staying there as long as he did. Contemporary observers agreed that he was not venal, power hungry, or ambitious for higher office. In terms of personal style, his approach was best summarized by the union publication cited earlier: "No backslapping, no braggadocio." His friend and colleague Ralph Regula may have said it best when he referred to Seiberling's "total sincerity. . . . He believes totally in those positions and people respect him for that. . . . John doesn't indulge in political posturing. He is trying to do what he thinks is right and that is refreshing."[30] Seiberling was, then, a different type of politician, independent and at times iconoclastic—the kind of politician the voters profess to want but rarely vote for—but the question remains: Was the title of his memoir correct? Did he make a difference?

Seiberling had gone to Congress to help stop the war in Vietnam; to promote the new environmental activism that demanded, among many specific goals, a cleaner Cuyahoga River and a Valley park; and to make Congress more transparent and responsive. In a general way he contributed to the end of the war and to the exposure of some of its less savory domestic repercussions. Despite continuing efforts, he had little impact on foreign and defense policies in the 1970s, and even less with the arrival of Reagan. In this case "total sincerity" was no match for the posturing that reversed the more cautionary approach of the post-Vietnam years.

His efforts to reform Congress from within had a similar fate. Seiberling and others committed to change enjoyed a number of victories in the 1970s, victories that sometimes had unpleasant aftershocks, as when the newly empowered members of the House Interior Committee nearly derailed the ANILCA legislation in 1979. But it is less clear that Congress became more open or accountable in the following years. Procedural changes certainly made a difference, but they were often overshadowed by the bitter partisan rivalries that characterized the years after 1980.

Seiberling devoted most of his time and energy to environmental issues, and it is appropriate to measure his impact largely by what he accomplished in that arena. In the early 1970s he rode a wave of concern about the fate of the natural world that was both widespread and, initially at least, bipartisan. His support for the attack on pollution was an outgrowth of his identification with that concern. Yet Seiberling's personal interest was in the parallel movement for new parks and new ways of managing public lands. He aggressively sought a position on the Interior Committee in order to fulfill his dream and his promise of a Cuyahoga Valley park. By the time the park was a reality he had become committed to a variety of related causes, and from that time he worked consistently to extend the national park system and to preserve the most desirable remaining natural areas. How successful was he?

Between the mid-1960s and mid-1990s, the share of federal lands devoted to conservation (i.e., national parks, wildlife refuges, wilderness and wilderness study, wild and scenic rivers, and other classifications with a substantial or exclusive emphasis on preservation) rose from 10 percent to 40 percent.[31] The most important changes occurred in the 1970s and early 1980s and were associated with the wholesale transfer of public lands from the jurisdiction of the BLM, the agency that had been the classic example of a government department captured by interest groups, in this case ranchers and other western rural interests. In the 1960s and especially the 1970s, as the accompanying table demonstrates, the BLM surrendered one-third of its former domain to the federal conservation

PUBLIC LAND MANAGEMENT

Agency	(% of total lands)		Gains/Losses (millions of acres)
	1970	1983	
BLM	66	49	-132
Forest Service	26	28	+6
Nat'l. Parks	3	10	+48
Fish & Wild.	4	12	+57

Source: BLM, *Public Land Statistics, 1970, 1983* (Washington, D.C.: GPO, 1971, 1984)

agencies, the NPS, the Fish and Wildlife Service (FWS), and to a lesser degree, the Forest Service. With the Federal Land Policy and Management Act of 1976, the BLM became in part a conservation agency itself, so the shift documented in the table understates the actual change.

The transfer of public lands to agencies that were more responsive to the interests of the urban population, and to the growing community of scientists, wildlife experts, and others who emphasized the intrinsic value of natural areas, was only part of the story. Thanks to the two dramatic policy initiatives of 1964, the creation of the Land and Water Conservation Fund (LWCF) and the Wilderness Preservation System, the changes went much further. The LWCF paid for most of the park land that was purchased from private owners, a key step in the creation of the small urban national parks—mostly national recreation areas and national lakeshores—and the many state and local parks that became a hallmark of the era. The CVNRA would fit into a tiny corner of Wrangell–St. Elias National Park, the largest of the ANILCA parks (33,000 acres vs. 13,200,000 acres), but CVNRA typically had hundreds of visitors for every one who made his or her way to east central Alaska. Which park had the greater impact? That depends, of course, on what is being measured, but they both were potent symbols of the new order in public land management and the contributions of John Seiberling.

The wilderness system was equally important to an appreciation of what happened. It was an affirmation of the value of nature, based on aesthetic, scientific, spiritual, or, as in Seiberling's case, a combination of those concerns, but also of a conviction that the U.S. government had embraced policies that were terribly wrong. The Forest Service had become a logging agency; the NPS a road-building and resort-operating adjunct to the recreation industry; the FWS an ally of hunters; and the BLM was so hopeless that it was not even mentioned in the Wilderness Act. They had succumbed to the rampant commercialism of American society. With the Wilderness Act, Congress called a halt to this process and insisted that the agencies leave some of their lands undisturbed. This seemingly simple directive was so revolutionary to the agency bureaucrats of the 1960s and 1970s that they often fought it as vigorously as the commodity interests did.

Seiberling was involved in each of these changes and was instrumental in shaping the form they took. He did not start the movement for a Cuyahoga Valley park, but he came to the rescue when the campaign seemed on the verge of collapse and decided that a national park was the only satisfactory solution. He continued to be a friend of urban parks and the enlargement of the LWCF, which helped to finance them. He was one of a handful of congressional representatives who helped to make the BLM a permanent land management agency with a conservation mandate.

Seiberling's ideas about public lands and his methods of operation were probably most evident in his work on Alaska. The battle over the Valdez pipeline had been his baptism into national environmental politics. In the following years he closely followed the movement for an Alaska "national interest" land law and the work of the Alaska environmental groups. By virtue of his personal inspections, he soon knew as much about the proposed parks and refuges as anyone in Congress. His contribution after 1976 was to manage the legislation drafted by the Alaska Coalition, orchestrate the public support essential to its success, and lay the foundations for the overwhelming House votes that forced the Senate to take the d(2) withdrawals seriously. In his absence it is not clear who could or would have played his role or played it so well. In the years after 1980 he was among those public officials who fought to make sure that the victory of 1980 was not sabotaged by the commodity interests and their political allies.

A few months before the final ANILCA negotiations, Seiberling received a protest letter from an official of a forest products company in Redding, California, complaining that pending wilderness legislation would be the "biggest single reason" future generations of Americans would not be able to "afford a wood house (maybe housing of any nature)." This argument, Seiberling replied "is so fantastic—so divorced from reality that it boggles the mind."[32] He went on to explain how little impact wilderness legislation had on the forest products industry or lumber prices. Yet he could not deny that wilderness legislation generated more hostility and exaggerated claims, such as the Californian's letter, than national parks, wildlife refuges, or any other type of conservation initiative. The ANILCA battle and the debates over wilderness bills that followed RARE II provided abundant examples. Wilderness obviously had the potential to reduce the supply of timber, coal, petroleum, and minerals, but in reality the economic costs were slight, often nonexistent. The threat was as much psychological as economic. Wilderness signified a rejection of the status quo and the assumptions about prosperity and social prominence that had prevailed in the rural West and Alaska since the first settlements.

Seiberling's personal contribution to the wilderness debates was considerable. First, he sought to minimize actual losses through systematic studies and inspections and to diffuse the conflicts by working out compromises that allowed everyone to claim victory. Second, he emphasized the dynamic character of the environmentalists' demands. A satisfactory deal, circa 1982 or 1984, might not be satisfactory in 1995. Therefore wilderness advocates had to be afforded the opportunity to reopen the debate at a later date. The so-called soft releases that were written into the wilderness acts of the early 1980s were examples of this perspective.

That Seiberling was often portrayed in timber industry publications as a wild-eyed radical was an indication of how biased government policy had been in the past. He only succeeded in his role as umpire and mediator, however, where there was an active and politically assertive environmental movement, able to counter the political clout of the commodity interests. Thus he was highly successful in West Virginia and California, less so in Wyoming, and unable to push through statewide bills for Montana and Idaho. But even these limited achievements were sufficient to nearly double the amount of wilderness lands in the lower forty-eight states between 1979 and 1985.

Seiberling thus left his stamp on American government, on the character of public land management, the opportunities available to the public at large to share the kinds of outdoor experiences he had known as a boy, and the options available to new generations of environmental activists. He had been repeatedly energized by his exposure to "ordinary people who are approaching something not from the standpoint of selfish profit but of what is in the public interest." Yet, as he cautioned in his 2004 memoir, "there are 'no final victories.' The same interests who opposed wilderness protection are still trying to reverse these decisions. Whether they succeed will depend on how well we, the people, continue to use our power as citizens to preserve our wonderful land."[33]

Notes

1. John F. Seiberling and His Times

1. *Cleveland Plain Dealer,* June 23, 24, 1969.
2. "The Cities: The Price of Optimism," *Time,* Aug. 1, 1969, 41. Also see David Stradling and Richard Stradling, "Perceptions of the Burning River: Deindustrialization and Cleveland's Cuyahoga River," *Environmental History* 13 (July 2008): 515–31. For urban pollution problems, Martin V. Melosi, *Garbage in the Cities: Refuse, Reform, and the Environment,* rev. ed. (Pittsburgh, Pa.: Univ. of Pittsburgh Press, 2005), 190–226.
3. See Richard N. L. Andrews, *Managing the Environment, Managing Ourselves: A History of American Environmental Policy* (New Haven, Ct.: Yale Univ. Press, 1999), 227–54; Samuel P. Hays, *A History of Environmental Politics since 1945* (Pittsburgh, Pa.: Univ. of Pittsburgh Press, 2000), chaps. 5–7, 10; Paul Charles Milazzo, *Unlikely Environmentalists: Congress and Clean Water, 1945–1972* (Lawrence: Univ. Press of Kansas, 2005).
4. Ron Cockrell, *"A Green Shrouded Miracle": The Administrative History of the Cuyahoga Valley National Recreation Area, Ohio* (Omaha, Neb.: National Park Service, 1992).
5. John Frederick Seiberling Jr. [hereafter JFS] to Mario DiFederico, Dec. 8, 1975, John F. Seiberling Papers, Denver Public Library, Box 55 [hereafter Seiberling-Denver Papers].
6. JFS to J. Penfield Seiberling, Dec. 15, 1975, Seiberling-Denver Papers, Box 55.
7. JFS interview, Oct. 2, 2006, author's files.
8. U.S. House of Representatives, Hearings before the Subcommittee on General Oversight and Alaska Lands of the Committee on Interior and Insular Affairs, 95th Cong., 1st sess., pt. 6 (Washington, D.C.: GPO, 1977), 178–79.
9. Jeanne Nienaber Clarke and Kurt Angersbach, "The Federal Four," in *Western Public Lands and Environmental Politics,* ed. Charles Davis (Boulder, Colo.: Westview, 2001), 38.

2. *Origins*

1. JFS to J. Penfield Seiberling, Apr. 21, 1946, J. Penfield Seiberling Papers, Ohio Historical Society, Box 18.
2. See Samuel A. Lane, *Fifty Years and Over of Akron and Summit County* (Akron, Ohio: Akron Beacon Job Department, 1892), 467; Introduction, Catalogue, Frank A. Seiberling Papers, Ohio Historical Society.
3. Introduction, Catalogue, Frank A. Seiberling Papers.
4. E.g., Frank A. Seiberling income tax returns for 1916, Frank A. Seiberling Papers, Box 36.
5. Steve Love, *Stan Hywet Hall and Gardens* (Akron, Ohio: Univ. of Akron Press, 2000), 84.
6. Marlene Ginevan, *Not for Us Alone* (Akron, Ohio: Stan Hywet Hall Foundation, 1985), 57; JFS to Grace Seiberling, Aug. 2, 1978, J. Penfield Seiberling Papers, Box 58; J. Penfield Seiberling to Michael J. Osogwin, Mar. 28, 1945, J. Penfield Seiberling Papers, Box 16; J. Penfield Seiberling to Mr. and Mrs. Milton Harrison, July 8, 1946, J. Penfield Seiberling Papers, Box 18.
7. Love, *Stan Hywet*, 8–14.
8. Ginevan, *Not for Us Alone,* 12, 18.
9. John Frederick Seiberling to Frank A. Seiberling, Nov. 28, 1917, Frank A. Seiberling Papers, Box 36. Also see *Akron Beacon Journal* [*ABJ*], July 16, 1962.
10. Frank A. Seiberling to John Frederick Seiberling, July 13, 1917; Frank A. Seiberling to John Frederick Seiberling, July 31, 1917; John Frederick Seiberling to Frank A. Seiberling, Aug. 1, 1917, Frank A. Seiberling Papers, Box 36.
11. John Frederick Seiberling to Frank A. Seiberling, July 12, 1917, Frank A. Seiberling Papers, Box 36.
12. Frank A. Seiberling to John Frederick Seiberling, July 31, 1917, Frank A. Seiberling Papers, Box 36.
13. Henrietta Buckler Seiberling to Frank A. Seiberling, n.d. [November 1917], Frank A. Seiberling Papers, Box 36.
14. Frank A. Seiberling to Henrietta Buckler Seiberling, Dec. 18, 1917, Frank A. Seiberling Papers, Box 36.
15. See Charles P. Kindleberger, *The World in Depression, 1929–1939* (Berkeley and Los Angeles: Univ. of California Press, 1973), 32–33.
16. Daniel Nelson, *American Rubber Workers and Organized Labor, 1900–1941* (Princeton, N.J.: Princeton Univ. Press, 1988), 78–79.
17. Michael French, "Structure, Personality and Business Strategy in the U. S. Tire Industry: The Seiberling Rubber Company," *Business History Review* 67 (Summer 1993): 246–78.
18. Ibid., 251; Coverdale and Colpitts, Report on Seiberling Rubber Company, Apr. 25, 1939, J. Penfield Seiberling Papers, Box 8.
19. French, "Structure, Personality," 250–51.
20. J. Penfield Seiberling to Frank A. Seiberling Jr., Dec. 7, 1948, J. Penfield Seiberling Papers, Box 22.

21. Frank A. Seiberling to John Frederick Seiberling, Dec. 10, 1921, Frank A. Seiberling Papers, Box 46.

22. Laurence R. Gustin, *Bill Durant: Creator of General Motors* (Grand Rapids, Mich.: William B. Eerdmans, 1973), 235–46.

23. The semifictional account by Ruth McKenny, *Industrial Valley* (Ithaca, N.Y.: ILR Press, 1992), is the best-known source. Nelson, *Rubber Workers,* 111–42. The classic study of class conflict in Akron at the end of the decade is Alfred Winslow Jones, *Life, Liberty and Property: A Story of Conflict and a Measurement of Conflicting Rights,* ed. Daniel Nelson (Akron, Ohio: Univ. of Akron Press, 1999).

24. J. Penfield Seiberling to John Frederick Seiberling, July 17, 1933, J. Penfield Seiberling Papers, Box 1.

25. J. Penfield Seiberling to L. A. Joel, July 17, 1933, J. Penfield Seiberling Papers, Box 3.

26. L. A. Joel to J. Penfield Seiberling, Nov. 1, 1933, J. Penfield Seiberling Papers, Box 3.

27. J. Penfield Seiberling to Aillard D. England, Sept. 12, 1962; Harry Johnson to J. Penfield Seiberling, Sept. 28, 1962, J. Penfield Seiberling Papers, Box 39.

28. Interview, JFS, Oct. 11, 1998. This is one of a series of interviews conducted by Loretta Neumann in the mid- to late 1990s. The interview material is included in the Loretta Neumann Papers, University of Akron Archives [hereafter Neumann Papers].

29. JFS, foreword, in Love, *Stan Hywet,* xii.

30. Ibid., xv.

31. JFS interview, May 5, 1998, Neumann Papers.

32. Love, *Stan Hywet,* 52–53; *ABJ,* Dec. 27, 1934.

33. See JFS to Sigurd S. Olson, Nov. 13, 1973, JFS office files, University of Akron Archives, A331; "History of the Akron Metropolitan District," n.d., Neumann Papers. One of John Seiberling's favorite family anecdotes was of his grandfather in the 1940s driving through Sand Run Park with his nurse. The nurse observed that he might have had substantial dividends if he had sold the land instead of donating it to the park district. "You see that family having a picnic? You see those children playing?" Frank Seiberling supposedly replied. "Those are my dividends." JFS interview, Apr. 26, 1997, Neumann Papers.

34. Dick B., *The Akron Genesis of Alcoholics Anonymous* (Seattle, Wash.: Glen Abbey Books, 1992), 8, 20, 28–29, 32–33.

35. *ABJ,* Jan. 21, 1933.

36. The Oxford Group was an example of what Reinhold Neibuhr dismissed as "naïve" and "sentimental" religion in *Moral Man and Immoral Society* (New York: Charles Scribner's Sons, 1932).

37. *ABJ,* Jan. 21, 1933.

38. Ibid.

39. Dick B., *Akron Genesis,* 83.

40. Ibid., 90.

41. Ibid., 100.
42. Henrietta B. Seiberling, "Origins of Alcoholics Anonymous," [1971], 1, Neumann Papers.
43. Ibid., 3.
44. Dick B., *Akron Genesis*, 104.
45. Ibid., 91.
46. JFS interview, Aug. 19–20, 1997, Neumann Papers.
47. Mark J. Orr, "SMA School History," Staunton Military Academy Alumni Association Web site.
48. Henrietta Seiberling to JFS, Sept. 23, 1936, JFS personal papers (privately held).
49. JFS interview, Aug. 19–20, 1997, Neumann Papers.
50. Ibid., Aug. 5, 1998.
51. Ibid., May 19–20, 1997.
52. Theodore H. White, *In Search of History: A Personal Adventure* (New York: Harper and Row, 1978), 42. Also see the account of another history major of that era, Arthur M. Schlesinger Jr., *A Life in the Twentieth Century: Innocent Beginnings, 1917–1950* (Boston: Houghton Mifflin, 2000), chaps. 7, 9.
53. White, *In Search of History*, 42–51; JFS interview, Oct. 2, 2006, author's files.
54. JFS interview, Oct. 2, 2006, author's files.
55. Penfield Seiberling's correspondence of the late 1940s includes many statements about faculties at elite universities.
56. JFS interview, Oct. 2, 2006, author's files.
57. JFS interview, Aug. 19–20, 1997, Neumann Papers.
58. Ibid., Apr. 26, 1997.
59. Joseph Bykofsky and Harold Larson, *The Technical Services: The Transportation Corps; Operations Overseas; U.S. Army in World War II* (Washington, D.C.: Office of the Chief of Military History, 1957), 129, 285. Also Russell F. Weigley, *Eisenhower's Lieutenants: The Campaign of France and Germany, 1944–1945* (Bloomington: Indiana Univ. Press, 1981), 269–71.
60. Bykofsky and Larson, *Transportation Corps*, 330.
61. JFS interview, Aug. 19–20, 1997, Neumann Papers.
62. Bykofsky and Larson, *Transportation Corps*, 302.
63. Ibid., 340.
64. J. Penfield Seiberling to JFS, June 2, 1945, J. Penfield Seiberling Papers, Box 16.
65. JFS interview, Aug. 19–20, 1997, Neumann Papers.
66. JFS interview, Mar. 30, 2006, author's files.
67. Henrietta Seiberling to J. Penfield Seiberling, Mar. 24, 1947, J. Penfield Seiberling Papers, Box 20.
68. JFS interview, Aug. 19–20, 1997, Neumann Papers.
69. Ibid., Oct. 11, 1998.
70. See Kathleen L. Endres, *Rosie the Rubber Worker: Women Workers in Akron's Rubber Factories during World War II* (Kent, Ohio: Kent State

Univ. Press, 2000); George W. Knepper, *Ohio and Its People* (Kent, Ohio: Kent State Univ. Press, 1989), 383–402.

71. J. Penfield Seiberling to Mary Seiberling, Oct. 7, 1947, J. Penfield Seiberling Papers, Box 20.
72. "Proposal, Program for Disbursing Surplus Cash, Midland Continental Railroad," [1948], J. Penfield Seiberling Papers, Box 22.
73. J. Penfield Seiberling to Mary Seiberling, Oct. 7, 1947, J. Penfield Seiberling Papers, Box 20.
74. Love, *Stan Hywet,* 4–5.
75. JFS to Michael L. Ainslie, May 19, 1984, JFS office files, A55.
76. JFS to Betty Seiberling, Mar. 19, 1962, JFS Papers.
77. JFS to Henrietta Seiberling, June 7, 1961, JFS Papers.
78. JFS to Betty Seiberling, Nov. 27, 1961, JFS Papers.
79. JFS to Betty Seiberling, Nov. 27, 1961, JFS Papers.
80. JFS to Henrietta Seiberling, Nov. 11, 1957, JFS Papers.
81. JFS to Henrietta Seiberling, Aug. 15, 1964, JFS Papers.

3. A Political Career

1. *Kent (Ohio) Record Courier,* Oct. 21, 1972.
2. *Local 2 News,* October 1972, 1.
3. Transcript of Remarks, November 4, 1970, JFS office files, A13.
4. *North Summit [Ohio] Times,* Nov. 1, 1963.
5. See Robert Bordner to Robert L. Hunker, June 26, 1962, Robert L. Hunker Papers, Robert L. Hunker Foundation, Peninsula, Ohio [hereafter Hunker Papers].
6. Robert Bishop, memorandum, Sept. 29, 1962, Hunker Papers.
7. Henry P. Saalfield to Robert L. Hunker, Apr. 14, 1965, Hunker Papers.
8. Cockrell, "*Green Shrouded Miracle,*" 34.
9. "Conference with Fred Morr," Aug. 31, 1965, Neumann Papers.
10. John F. Seiberling, "To Make a Difference: Memoirs of Former Congressman John F. Seiberling . . . Preserving the Cuyahoga Valley" (unpublished manuscript, 2004), 5, JFS Papers.
11. Ibid., 6.
12. Director, Bureau of Outdoor Recreation (BOR), and Director, National Park Service (NPS), to Secretary of the Interior, Jan. 25, 1966, Neumann Papers.
13. Assistant, Division of State Grants to Regional Director, Lake Central Region, BOR, Mar. 18, 1969, Neumann Papers.
14. Ben Maidenburg to James A. Rhodes, Jan. 5, 1967, Neumann Papers.
15. Cockrell, "*Green Shrouded Miracle,*" 47–48.
16. JFS, "To Make a Difference . . . Preserving the Cuyahoga Valley," 6.
17. *ABJ,* May 22, 1968.
18. *ABJ,* June 6, 1968.
19. Ibid.

20. JFS, "To Make a Difference . . . Preserving the Cuyahoga Valley," 7.
21. Robert L. Hunker to Edwin J. Thomas, Apr. 23, June 28, 1969, Hunker Papers.
22. Robert L. Hunker to James A. Rhodes, Apr. 23, 1969; Hunker to John S. Knight, May 28, 1969, Hunker Papers.
23. John S. Knight to Hunker, June 4, 1969, Hunker Papers.
24. See, e.g., Robert Dallek, *Nixon and Kissinger: Partners in Power* (New York: HarperCollins, 2007), chaps. 5–7.
25. JFS interview, Apr. 25, 2006, author's notes.
26. JFS, "To Make a Difference . . . Commitment to Service, 1942–1970," 12.
27. JFS interview, Aug. 19–20, 1997, Neumann Papers.
28. Quoted in JFS, "To Make a Difference . . . Commitment to Service," 10.
29. Ibid., 11–12.
30. Ibid., 12–13.
31. "Expenditures for the Primary Campaign," JFS office files, A13.
32. Press release, Jan. 15, 1970, Ronald Marmaduke Papers (privately held).
33. JFS, "To Make a Difference . . . Commitment to Service," 20–21; *ABJ*, Oct. 10, 1970.
34. Press release, Apr. 26, 1970; *The Reporter*, n.d., JFS office files, A13.
35. "Summary of Seiberling Performance," JFS office files, A12.
36. "JFS Speech to Student Rally, May 6, 1970," JFS office files, A13.
37. *Buchtelite*, May 13, 1970.
38. Press release, Sept. 13, 1970, JFS office files, A13.
39. *ABJ*, June 20, July 2, July 8, 1970.
40. *Village Sun*, Dec. 17, 1970.
41. Draft, May 19, 1970, JFS office files, A13.
42. Apple article reprinted in *ABJ*, Aug. 20, 1970.
43. *ABJ*, Aug. 21, 1970; Press release, Aug. 26, 1979, JFS office files, A13.
44. *ABJ*, Sept. 3, Oct. 4, 1970.
45. *ABJ*, Oct. 10, 1970.
46. *ABJ*, Oct. 24, 1970.
47. *ABJ*, Oct. 11, 1970.
48. JFS interview, Aug. 6–7, 1997, Neumann Papers.
49. "Seiberling Campaign Ad," n.d., JFS office files, A13. Also *ABJ*, Oct. 29, 1970.
50. *ABJ*, Oct. 25, 1970; Draft letter, n.d., JFS office files, A13.
51. Press release, Oct. 19, 1970, JFS office files, A13.
52. *ABJ*, Oct. 29, 30, Nov. 1, 1970.
53. *ABJ*, Oct. 11, 1970.
54. *ABJ*, Oct. 22, 1970.
55. JFS interview, Apr. 23, 2006, author's notes.
56. *Wall Street Journal*, Oct. 26, 1970.
57. *New York Times*, Oct. 28, 1970. Also see *Cleveland Plain Dealer*, Oct. 5, 1970.
58. *ABJ*, Nov. 4, 1970.
59. JFS interview, Aug. 6–7, 1997, Neumann Papers.

60. "The Final Election Results, 14th Cong. District," JFS office files, A12.
61. J. Penfield Seiberling to Mr. and Mrs. W. C. Seiberling, Dec. 8, 1970, J. Penfield Seiberling Papers, Box 50.
62. *ABJ*, Dec. 9, 1970.
63. See "Keep Seiberling in Congress Committee," 1972, JFS office files, A12.
64. *ABJ*, Nov. 8, 1970.
65. JFS interview, Oct. 11, 1998, Neumann Papers.
66. JFS interview, Oct. 2, 2006, author's notes.
67. *ABJ*, Sept.10, 1972; Feb. 17, 1974.
68. *Falls News*, Sept. 14, 1972.
69. Nelson W. Polsby, *How Congress Evolves: Social Bases of Institutional Change* (New York: Oxford Univ. Press, 2004), 63–64; Thomas E. Mann and Norman J. Ornstein, *The Broken Branch: How Congress Is Failing America and How to Get It Back on Track* (New York: Oxford Univ. Press, 2006), 47–64.
70. *ABJ*, Feb. 17, 1974; Polsby, *How Congress Evolves*, 59–60.
71. *ABJ*, Sept. 10, 1972.
72. *ABJ*, Nov. 15, 1970.
73. JFS to John Daily, Jan. 26, 1971, JFS office files, A308.
74. Donald W. Carson and James W. Johnson, *MO: The Life and Times of Morris K. Udall* (Tucson: Univ. of Arizona Press, 2001), chaps. 19–20.
75. JFS interview, Apr. 26–27, 1997, Neumann Papers.
76. *ABJ*, June 11, 1972.
77. *ABJ*, June 10, Mar. 18, 1972.
78. *ABJ*, June 1, 1972.
79. *ABJ*, June 27, 1972.
80. *ABJ*, Apr. 19, 1972.
81. *ABJ*, Nov. 4, 1972.
82. *ABJ*, June 27, 1972.
83. JFS, "To Make a Difference . . . The Battle to Curb Strip Mining," 1.
84. Ibid.; JFS interview, Apr. 26, Aug. 6–7, 1997, Neumann Papers; *ABJ*, Mar. 3, 1972.
85. JFS Testimony (handwritten addition), Sept. 20, 1971, JFS office files, A281.
86. Chad Montrie, *To Save the Land and People: A History of Opposition to Surface Coal Mining in Appalachia* (Chapel Hill: Univ. of North Carolina Press, 2003), 41–129.
87. *ABJ*, June 25, 1972.
88. *Washington Post*, Apr. 30, 1972.
89. *ABJ*, Apr. 15, 1972.
90. *Falls News*, Sept. 14, 1972.
91. Staff to JFS, Apr. 22, 2972, JFS office files, A308.
92. *Washington Post*, Apr. 30, 1972.
93. Transcript of Election Night Tape, Nov. 7, 1972, JFS office files, A13.
94. "Public Opinion Survey," JFS office files, A13.
95. *ABJ*, Apr. 28, 1972.
96. *ABJ*, Nov. 8, 1972.
97. *ABJ*, Sept. 30, 1972.

4. The Cuyahoga Valley Park, 1971–74

1. *Wall Street Journal,* June 26, 1974.

2. See William E. Shands, "The Lands Nobody Wanted: The Legacy of the Eastern National Forests," in *Origins of the National Forests: A Centennial Symposium,* ed. Harold Steen (Durham, N.C.: Forest History Society, 1992), 19–44.

3. Stephen Fox, *The American Conservation Movement: John Muir and His Legacy* (Madison: Univ. of Wisconsin Press, 1985) is a good introduction. Pinchot's most recent biographer is Char Miller, *Gifford Pinchot and the Making of Modern Environmentalism* (Washington, D.C.: Island Press, 2000). Herbert Kaufman, *The Forest Ranger: A Study in Administration Behavior* (Baltimore, Md.: Resources for the Future, 2006) emphasizes Forest Service professionalism.

4. See William Voight Jr., *Public Grazing Lands: Use and Misuse by Industry and Government* (New Brunswick, N.J.: Rutgers Univ. Press, 1976), 299–303, for Clawson's role. Paul J. Culhane, *Public Lands Politics: Interest Group Influences on the Forest Service and the Bureau of Land Management* (Baltimore, Md.: Resources for the Future, 1981) compares the two agencies. Also Wesley Calef, *Private Grazing and Public Lands: Studies of the Local Management of the Taylor Grazing Act* (Chicago: Univ. of Chicago Press, 1960), 56–80.

5. See Alfred Runte, *National Parks: The American Experience,* 3d ed. (Lincoln: Univ. of Nebraska Press, 1987). Richard W. Sellers, *Preserving Nature in National Parks: A History* (New Haven, Conn.: Yale Univ. Press, 1997), and Theodore Catton, *Inhabited Wilderness: Indians, Eskimos, and the National Parks in Alaska* (Albuquerque: Univ. of New Mexico Press, 1997) examine major flaws in park management.

6. See Thomas R. Dunlap, *Saving America's Wildlife* (Princeton, N.J.: Princeton Univ. Press, 1988); Eric Jay Dolin, *Smithsonian Book of National Wildlife Refuges* (Washington, D.C.: Smithsonian Institute Press, 2003); Robert L. Fischman, *National Wildlife Refuges: Coordinating a Conservation System through Law* (Washington, D.C.: Island Press, 2003).

7. See Sally K. Fairfax, Lauren Gwin, Mary Ann King, Leigh Raymond, and Laura A. Watt, *Buying Nature: The Limits of Land Acquisition as a Conservation Strategy, 1780–2004* (Cambridge, Mass.: MIT Press, 2005), chap. 6; Ronald A. Foresta, *America's National Parks and Their Keepers* (Washington, D.C.: Resources for the Future, 1984); Culhane, *Public Lands Politics;* Richard Allan Baker, *Conservation Politics: The Senate Career of Clinton P. Anderson* (Albuquerque: Univ. of New Mexico Press, 1985).

8. Roderick Nash, *Wilderness and the American Mind,* 4th ed. (New Haven, Conn.: Yale Univ. Press, 2001) provides background; Mark Harvey, *Wilderness Forever: Howard Zahniser and the Path to the Wilderness Act* (Seattle: Univ. of Washington Press, 2005), and Steven C. Schulte, *Wayne Aspinall and the Shaping of the American West* (Boulder: Univ. Press of Colorado, 2003) examine the maneuvering that led to the 1964 act; Craig W. Allin,

The Politics of Wilderness Preservation (Westport, Conn.: Greenwood Press, 1982) discusses its aftermath.

9. See Doug Scott, *The Enduring Wilderness* (Golden, Colo.: Fulcrum, 2004) on the theory and application; Michael McCloskey, *In the Thick of It: My Life in the Sierra Club* (Washington, D.C.: Island Press, 2005) emphasizes wilderness as a response to management policy.

10. In addition to Scott and McCloskey (see n. 9, this chapter), see Dennis M. Roth, *The Wilderness Movement and the National Forests* (College Station, Tex.: Intaglio Press, 1988), and Allin, *Politics of Wilderness Preservation*.

11. Mark W. T. Harvey, *A Symbol of Wilderness: Echo Park and the American Conservation Movement* (Albuquerque: Univ. of New Mexico Press, 1994).

12. See Glenn O. Robinson, *The Forest Service: A Study in Public Land Management* (Baltimore, Md.: Johns Hopkins Univ. Press, 1975); David A. Clary, *Timber and the Forest Service* (Lawrence: Univ. Press of Kansas, 1986); and Paul W. Hirt, *A Conspiracy of Optimism: Management of National Forests since World War II* (Lincoln: Univ. of Nebraska Press, 1994).

13. Roth, *Wilderness Movement*, 16–19; Scott, *Enduring Wilderness*, 60–61.

14. Roth, *Wilderness Movement*, 21.

15. Ibid., chaps. 3–4; Allin, *Politics of Wilderness Preservation*, 150–59.

16. Roth, *Wilderness Movement*, 51.

17. Ibid., 37–38.

18. Ibid., 40.

19. Ibid., 38–45.

20. Jeanne Nienaber Clarke and Daniel McCool, *Staking Out the Terrain: Power Differentials among Natural Resource Management Agencies* (Albany: SUNY Press, 1985), 51.

21. George B. Hartzog Jr., *Battling for the National Parks* (Mt. Kisko, N.Y.: Moyer Bell, 1988), 205.

22. Foresta, *America's National Parks*, 118. For Nixon's new approach to environmental policy, see J. Brooks Flippen, *Nixon and the Environment* (Albuquerque: Univ. of New Mexico Press, 2000), 185–87, 189–219.

23. See, e.g., Loretta Neumann to JFS, June 4, 1973, JFS office files, A182.

24. JFS to John R. Daily, Feb. 16, 1971, JFS office files, A308.

25. Cockrell, "*Green Shrouded Miracle*," 58.

26. JFS to D. Bruce Mansfield, Aug. 9, 1973, JFS office files, A331; Cockrell, "*Green Shrouded Miracle*," 58–59.

27. Fairfax et al., *Buying Nature*, 147. Also see Amy Meyer, *New Guardians for the Golden Gate: How America Got a Great National Park* (Berkeley and Los Angeles: Univ. of California Press, 2006).

28. JFS to Frances Hoag, Aug. 2, 1971, JFS office files, A308.

29. Minutes, Membership Meeting, Cuyahoga Valley Association, Feb. 5, 1972, JFS Papers, Box 187.

30. JFS to William Nye, Mar. 27, 1971, JFS office files, A187.

31. JFS, "The Ohio Canal, Cuyahoga Valley Natl. Historical & Recreation Area," Apr. 22, 1971, JFS office files, A187.

32. Loretta Neumann to JFS, Oct. 8, 1973, JFS office files, A322.

33. "John F. Seiberling Talk with John Pike," July 16, 1971, JFS office files, A187.

34. R. M. Pierson to JFS et al., Nov. 8, 1971, JFS office files, A187.

35. "Talk with Tedd McCann," Nov. 16, 1971, JFS office files, A187.

36. John C. Whittaker to Director, NPS, et al., June 6, 1973, JFS office files, A182.

37. Cockrell, "*Green Shrouded Miracle*," 82–83.

38. *Cleveland Plain Dealer,* Apr. 12, 1972.

39. Barry Sugden to JFS, Mar. 9, 1972, JFS office files, A182.

40. *Cleveland Plain Dealer,* Apr. 6, 1972; also *Akron Beacon Journal,* Apr. 30, 1972.

41. "Meeting in Office, October 30, 1972," JFS office files, A182.

42. JFS to Robert Hunker, June 20, 1973, JFS office files, A331.

43. Interview with Cleve Pinnix, Mar. 28, 1998, Neumann Papers.

44. JFS to Roy Taylor, Sept. 12, 1973, JFS office files, A330; *ABJ,* Aug. 12, 1973.

45. Minutes, Aug. 30, 1973, Meeting, JFS office files, A182.

46. Ibid.

47. *ABJ,* Feb. 17, 1974.

48. *Sierra Club Newsletter,* September 1973, 1.

49. Loretta Neumann to JFS, Nov. 19, 1973, JFS office files, A182.

50. *Washington Post,* Dec. 1, 1974.

51. *Wall Street Journal,* May 10, 1974.

52. Hearing before the Subcommittee on National Parks and Recreation of the Committee on Interior and Insular Affairs, 93d Cong., Mar. 1, 1974 (Washington, D.C.: GPO, 1974), 42 [hereafter Hearing, 1974].

53. Ibid., 45.

54. *ABJ,* Sept. 13, 1973; Loretta Neumann to JFS, June 4, 1973, JFS office files, A182.

55. Jim Jackson to CVA Members, Sept. 5, 1973, JFS office files, A331.

56. Hearing, 1974, 53–60.

57. Ibid., 60.

58. Ibid., 45.

59. Ibid., 74–75.

60. Ibid., 90–92.

61. *ABJ,* Mar. 11, 1974.

62. *Voice of the C.V.A.,* May 1974, 2.

63. JFS, "To Make a Difference . . . Preserving the Cuyahoga Valley," 13.

64. Interview, Cleve Pinnix, Mar. 28, 1998, Neumann Papers.

65. Detailed information on planning for the hearing is in JFS office files, A187.

66. Hearing before the Subcommittee on National Parks and Recreation of the Committee on Interior and Insular Affairs, 93d Cong., June 8, 1974 (Washington, D.C.: GPO, 1975), 188.

67. *Cleveland Plain Dealer,* June 8, 1974.

68. JFS, "To Make a Difference . . . Preserving the Cuyahoga Valley," 13.

69. *ABJ,* Aug. 18, 1974.

70. *ABJ,* Sept. 8, 1974.

71. Richard C. Curry to Roy Taylor, Oct. 4, 1974, JFS office files, A347.

72. JFS to Richard C. Curry, Oct. 7, 1974, JFS office files, A347.

73. *ABJ,* Nov. 25, Dec. 4, 1974.

74. *Cleveland Plain Dealer,* Oct. 24, 1974.

75. *Cleveland Plain Dealer,* Dec. 28, 1974.

76. *ABJ,* Dec. 11, 1974.

77. *Cleveland Plain Dealer,* Dec. 28, 1974.

78. JFS, "To Make a Difference . . . Preserving the Cuyahoga Valley," 15; *Cleveland Plain Dealer,* Oct. 24, 1974.

79. *ABJ,* Dec. 19, 1974.

80. Loretta Neumann to JFS, Nov. 19, 1973, JFS office files, A182.

5. Transition Years, 1973–76

1. *ABJ,* Feb. 17, 1974.

2. *ABJ,* Apr. 4, 1976.

3. Ibid.

4. Ibid.

5. Paul R. Clancy, "All the Presidential Men," *Washington Monthly,* March 1975, 30.

6. *Cleveland Plain Dealer,* Oct. 23, 1973; *ABJ,* Feb. 21, 1974. Important secondary works include Stanley I. Kutler, *The Wars of Watergate: The Last Crisis of Richard Nixon* (New York: Knopf, 1990), and Howard Fields, *High Crimes and Misdemeanors: "Wherefore Richard M. Nixon . . . Warrants Impeachment"; The Dramatic Story of the Rodino Committee* (New York: W. W. Norton, 1978).

7. David E. Kyvig, *The Age of Impeachment: American Constitutional Culture since 1960* (Lawrence: Univ. Press of Kansas, 2008), 143.

8. Elizabeth Drew, *Washington Journal: The Events of 1973–1974* (New York: Random House, 1974), 174–75; James Cannon, *Time and Chance: Gerald Ford's Appointment with History* (New York: HarperCollins, 1994), 232–33, 271.

9. *Washington Post,* Jan. 18, 1973.

10. *ABJ,* Apr. 1, 1973.

11. *ABJ,* Aug. 17, 1973.

12. *ABJ,* Nov. 30, 1973.

13. Kyvig, *Age of Impeachment,* 148.

14. *ABJ,* Oct. 28, 1973.

15. JFS interview, Oct. 10, 1998, Neumann Papers.

16. *ABJ,* Mar. 17, 1974.

17. A. L. Harrison, "Impeachment: The Crucial Committee," *Progressive*, Mar. 28, 1974, 40; James Fallows, "The Fuse for Impeachment," *Rolling Stone*, Mar. 28, 1974, 43.

18. *ABJ*, May 30, 1974.

19. *ABJ*, July 28, 1974.

20. Ibid.

21. *Washington Post*, July 22, 1974.

22. *New York Times*, June 29, 1974; *ABJ*, June 28, 1974; *New York Daily News*, June 28, 1974; *Washington Post*, June 28, 1974.

23. *ABJ*, July 27, 1974.

24. *Cleveland Plain Dealer*, July 27, 1974.

25. *ABJ*, July 28, 1974.

26. *ABJ*, July 29, 1974.

27. *ABJ*, Aug. 9, 1974.

28. *New York Times*, Aug. 1, 1974.

29. *ABJ*, Aug. 16, 1974.

30. *ABJ*, Aug. 10, 1974.

31. *ABJ*, Aug. 13, 1975.

32. See Daniel Nelson, *Northern Landscapes: The Struggle for Wilderness Alaska* (Washington, D.C.: Resources for the Future, 2004), chaps. 1, 3–4; Donald Craig Mitchell examines the Native claims in *Sold American: The Story of Alaska Natives and Their Land, 1867–1959* (Hanover, N.H.: Univ. Press of New England, 1997), and in *Take My Land, Take My Life: The Story of Congress's Historic Settlement of Alaska Native Land Claims* (Fairbanks: Univ. of Alaska Press, 2001).

33. Nelson, *Northern Landscapes*, 108–17.

34. Ibid., 112–13.

35. Ibid., 117.

36. JFS to Karl L. Rothermund Jr., July 20, 1973, JFS office files, A330.

37. Allen R. Ferguson to JFS, July 23, 2973, JFS office files, A290.

38. JFS to Raymond R. Wernig, Aug. 9, 1973, JFS office files, A330.

39. *ABJ*, Mar. 1, 1976.

40. JFS interview, Apr. 27, 1997, Neumann Papers.

41. NPS, "Land Acquisition," Jan. 30, 1976, JFS office files, A2.

42. James Haley to Nathaniel Reed, Dec. 18, 1975, JFS office files, A228.

43. *ABJ*, Jan. 27, June 28, 1976.

44. *ABJ*, Apr. 6, 1976.

45. *ABJ*, Sept. 5, 1976.

46. *ABJ*, Feb. 11, 1976.

47. *ABJ*, Feb. 8, 1976.

48. R. Richard Fawcett to Tedd McCann, Feb. 10, 1975, Neumann Papers.

49. *Cleveland Plain Dealer*, Oct. 28, 1975.

50. *Cleveland Press*, Oct. 10, 1976.

51. *Northside Neighbor*, Oct. 8, 1975.

52. JFS interview, Apr. 26, 1997, Neumann Papers.

53. *Washington Star,* Sept. 19, 1975.

54. Cleve Pinnix interview, Mar. 28, 1998, Neumann Papers.

55. Nancy Lord to JFS, Nov. 15, 1976, JFS office files, A321.

56. Michael McCloskey to Peter Borelli, Nov. 30, 1971; Francis J. Walcott to Theodore A. Snyder, Jan. 4, 1972, Sierra Club National Legislative Office Papers, University of California, Berkeley, Box 133 [hereafter SCNLO Papers].

57. Peter Borelli to George Marshall, Dec. 20, 1972, SCNLO Papers, Box 133.

58. Dan Saylor to Citizens for Eastern Wilderness, June 4, 1974, SCNLO Papers, Box 133.

59. Dan Saylor to Citizens for Eastern Wilderness, Nov. 25, 1974, Feb. 14, 1975; Brad Evans to Dennis Shaffer, Nov. 26, 1974, SCNLO Papers, Box 133.

60. Chuck Clusen interview, Dec. 1, 1997, Neumann Papers.

61. James Alkire to JFS, Oct. 11, 1973, JFS office files, A357.

62. JFS to Charles Vanik, Nov. 7, 1973, JFS office files, A330.

63. *ABJ,* Mar. 19, 1974; also see *American Institute of Planners Newsletter,* July 1974, 1, JFS office files, A357. For Nixon's position, see J. Brooks Flippen, *Conservative Conservationist: Russell E. Train and the Emergence of American Environmentalism* (Baton Rouge: Louisiana State Univ. Press, 2006), 116–18, 152.

64. Loretta Neumann to JFS, May 1, 1975, JFS office files, A357.

65. *ABJ,* July 15, 1975.

66. JFS to various correspondents, September 1976, JFS office files, A321.

67. For the impact, see Samuel P. Hays, *Wars in the Woods: The Rise of Ecological Forestry in America* (Pittsburgh, Pa.: Univ. of Pittsburgh Press, 2007).

68. Harry Crandell interview, Sept. 9, 1997, Neumann Papers; Scott, *Enduring Wilderness,* 85.

69. "Major Amendments Needed . . ." JFS office files, A322.

70. "Legislative History of the Federal Land Policy and Management Act of 1976," 95th Cong., 2d sess. (Washington, D.C.: GPO, 1978), 658–59.

71. Ibid., 927–36; Chuck Clusen interview, Dec. 1, 1997, Neumann Papers.

72. See Montrie, *To Save the Land and People.*

73. *ABJ,* Jan. 21, 1973.

74. JFS to William J. Cox, May 31, 1973, JFS office files, A347.

75. Linda Billings to John H. Williams, Aug. 6, 1973, JFS office files, A347.

76. James A. Noone, "Energy Report," *National Journal Reports,* Jan. 26, 1974, 139.

77. Ibid., 141.

78. William E. Simon to JFS, Jan. 7, 1974, JFS office files, A352.

79. *ABJ,* Feb. 17, 1974.

80. James A. Noone, "Environmental Report," *National Journal Reports,* June 15, 1974, 890.

81. See Dear Colleague letter, Apr. 26, 1974, JFS office files, A287; Noone, "Environmental Report," 892.

82. JFS to Bill Deering, Oct. 3, 1974, JFS office files, A347.

83. JFS to C. Roy, Nov. 1, 1974, JFS office files, A347.

84. *ABJ*, Dec. 15, 1974.
85. "Special Alert," Environmental Study Conference, June 9, 1975, Neumann Papers; Flippen, *Conservative Conservationist*, 172.
86. *Washington Post*, June 10, 1975; "Special Alert," Environmental Study Conference, Neumann Papers.
87. *New York Times*, June 6, 1975; Morris Udall to Colleague, June 9, 1975, Neumann Papers.
88. *Washington Post*, Nov. 13, 1975.
89. Acting Secretary of the Interior to James A. Haley, June 22, 1976, JFS office files, A357.
90. *ABJ*, Aug. 19, 1976.

6. Wider Horizons, 1977–78

1. *ABJ*, June 22, 1980.
2. Ibid.
3. *ABJ*, Feb. 1, 1976.
4. *Vineyard Gazette*, June 22, 1976.
5. *ABJ*, Apr. 24, 1977.
6. *ABJ*, June 22, 1980.
7. *ABJ*, June 1, 1975. Also see *East Ohio Gay News*, Feb. 1, Mar. 1, 1975.
8. *ABJ*, June 6, 1976.
9. *Cleveland Plain Dealer*, June 11, 1975.
10. *ABJ*, June 2, 1976; Carson and Johnson, *MO*, 70–71.
11. *ABJ*, July 16, 1976.
12. *Cleveland Plain Dealer*, Oct. 24, 1976; *ABJ*, Oct. 18, 1976.
13. *ABJ*, Nov. 25, 1976.
14. *New York Times*, Dec. 12, 1976.
15. See *ABJ*, Dec. 12, 1976.
16. JFS notes, Dec. 5, 1976, JFS office files, A08.
17. *ABJ*, Dec. 26, 1976. Carter's environmental record is discussed in Jeffrey K. Stine, "Environmental Policy during the Carter Presidency," in *The Carter Presidency: Policy Choices in the Post–New Deal Era*, ed. Gary M. Fink and Hugh Davis Graham (Lawrence: Univ. Press of Kansas, 1998), 179–201.
18. See John Aloysius Farrell, *Tip O'Neill and the Democratic Century* (Boston: Little, Brown, 2001), 408–14.
19. Carson and Johnson, *MO*, 185.
20. Cleve Pinnix interview, Mar. 28, 1998, Neumann Papers.
21. Ibid.
22. John Jacobs, *A Rage for Justice: The Passion and Politics of Philip Burton* (Berkeley: Univ. of California Press, 1995), 233.
23. Pinnix interview, Mar. 28, 1998, Neumann Papers.
24. Ibid.
25. Dale Crane interview, Mar. 26, 1998, Neumann Papers.

26. JFS interview, Aug. 5, 1997, Neumann Papers.

27. Pinnix interview, Mar. 28, 1998, Neumann Papers.

28. *New York Times,* Apr, 20, 30, 1977.

29. *New York Times,* July 5, 1977.

30. *New York Times,* Aug. 4, 1977.

31. *The Signal,* July 5, 1977.

32. JFS interview, Apr. 26, 27, 1997, Neumann Papers.

33. JFS to Stan Sloss, Dec. 1, 1997, Neumann Papers.

34. Harry Crandell interview, Oct. 21, 1997, Neumann Papers.

35. Nelson, *Northern Landscapes,* 118–19.

36. Ken Ross, *Pioneering Conservation in Alaska* (Boulder: Univ. Press of Colorado, 2006), chaps. 6–8.

37. Ibid., chap. 17.

38. Nelson, *Northern Landscapes,* 122–29.

39. Ibid., 139.

40. Ibid., 152–64. Also see Roger Kaye, *Last Great Wilderness: The Campaign to Establish the Arctic National Wildlife Refuge* (Fairbanks: Univ. of Alaska Press, 2006).

41. Nelson, *Northern Landscapes,* 174.

42. Stanley Sloss interview, Mar. 21, 2007, author's files. Also JFS interview, Oct. 17, 1997, quoting Harry Crandell, Neumann Papers.

43. U.S. House of Representatives, Hearings before the Subcommittee on General Oversight and Alaska Lands of the Committee on Interior and Insular Affairs, 95th Cong., 1st sess., pt. 10 (Washington, D.C.: GPO, 1977), 83 [hereafter Hearings, 1977].

44. Ibid., pt. 5, 2.

45. Ibid., pt. 5, 99.

46. Ibid., pt. 7, 29–30.

47. Ibid., pt. 10, 2.

48. Nelson, *Northern Landscapes,* 195–96.

49. Hearings, 1977, pt. 5, 2.

50. Ibid., pt. 6, 157.

51. Ibid., pt. 8, 150.

52. Ibid., pt. 5, 37.

53. Ibid., pt. 6, 5.

54. Ibid., pt. 9, 4.

55. Ibid., pt. 9, 170.

56. Ibid., pt. 11, 239.

57. Ibid., pt. 12, 252.

58. Ibid., pt. 5, 82.

59. Ibid., pt. 9, 20.

60. Ibid., pt. 9, 94.

61. Ibid., pt. 4, 12.

62. Ibid., pt. 7, 144–45.

63. Ibid., pt. 7, 189–90.

64. Ibid., pt. 5, 130.
65. Ibid., pt. 7, 152.
66. Ibid., pt. 9, 15–16.
67. Ibid., pt. 9, 41.
68. Ibid., pt. 11, 240.
69. Ibid., pt. 11, 203.
70. Ibid., pt. 7, 130.
71. Ibid., pt. 9, 114.
72. Ibid., pt. 7, 119.
73. Ibid., pt. 10, 47.
74. Ibid., pt. 12, 60.
75. Ibid., pt. 13, 68.
76. Ibid., pt. 6, 178–79.
77. Nelson, *Northern Landscapes,* 197–207.
78. Harry Crandell interview, Oct. 21, 1997, Neumann Papers.
79. JFS interview, Apr. 26–27, 1997, Neumann Papers.
80. Nelson, *Northern Landscapes,* 225.
81. JFS interview, Apr. 26–27, 1997, Neumann Papers.
82. Ibid.
83. Quoted in Jacobs, *Rage for Justice,* 330.
84. Ibid.
85. Ibid., 333–46.
86. Ibid., 371.

7. New Challenges, 1978–80

1. See *ABJ,* Apr. 16, 1977. For the larger economy, see Allen J. Matusow, *Nixon's Economy: Booms, Busts, Dollars, Votes* (Lawrence: Univ. Press of Kansas, 1998).
2. Andrews, *Managing the Environment,* chap. 12; Flippen, *Nixon and the Environment.*
3. *ABJ,* Sept. 26, 1979.
4. "Update on Foundries," Jan. 11, 1979, JFS office files, A68.
5. See *ABJ,* June 24, Aug. 27, 1979.
6. *ABJ,* Feb. 10, 1979.
7. "Background on JFS Role in Akron Clean Air Controversy," [ca. 1980], JFS office files, A68.
8. Suzanne [Goulet] to JFS, July 31, 1979, JFS office files, A68.
9. *ABJ,* Aug. 1, 1979.
10. Suzanne [Goulet] to JFS, June 16, 1979, and notes, JFS office files, A173.
11. See W. Carl Bliven, *Jimmy Carter's Economy: Policy in an Age of Limits* (Chapel Hill: Univ. of North Carolina Press, 2002).
12. Gregory Pappas, *The Magic City: Unemployment in a Working Class Community* (Ithaca, N.Y.: Cornell Univ. Press, 1989).

13. "Special Cuyahoga Task Force to Director Whalen," Jan. 24, 1980, Neumann Papers.

14. Betsy Cuthbertson interview, Dec. 1, 1997, Neumann Papers.

15. JFS to David Cooper, June 21, 1982, JFS office files, A109.

16. M. J. Sweeney to Assistant Chief, Land Acquisition Division, Oct. 18, 1977, JFS office files, A109.

17. JFS to David Cooper, June 21, 1982, JFS office files, A137.

18. See *Brecksville Sun Courier,* Sept. 1, 1977.

19. See *ABJ,* Oct. 16, 1975; Oct. 12, 1978.

20. JFS interview, Dec. 1, 1997, Neumann Papers.

21. See, e.g., *Cleveland Plain Dealer,* Oct. 20, 1978.

22. *ABJ,* Oct. 27, 1978.

23. Cockrell, *"Green Shrouded Miracle,"* chap. 11, p. 5.

24. "Re: Leonard Stein-Sapir," JFS office files, X9.

25. See *ABJ,* Feb. 7, 1980.

26. "CVNRA Land Acquisition," 1979, p. 19, Neumann Papers.

27. See www.landrights.org/Mission.htm.

28. "CVNRA Land Acquisition," 1979, p. 22, Neumann Papers.

29. JFS to Paul Poorman, Jan. 2, 1980, JFS office files, A137.

30. Ibid.

31. Cockrell, *"Green Shrouded Miracle,"* chap. 11, pp. 5–6.

32. JFS to Walter Sheppe, Jan. 28, 1980, JFS office files, A137.

33. Karen Rikhoff and Janet B. Hutchinson to JFS, Jan. 21, 1980; Sue Klein to Cuyahoga Valley Park Federation, April 1980, JFS office files, A137.

34. *ABJ,* Jan. 5, 1980.

35. *ABJ,* Jan. 7, 1980.

36. "Press Release," Feb. 2, 1980, JFS office files, A137.

37. *ABJ,* Feb. 7, 1980.

38. JFS and Howard Metzenbaum to William Whalen, July 14, 1980, JFS office files, A109.

39. Cuyahoga Task Force, Confidential to Director Whalen, Jan. 24, 1980, Neumann Papers.

40. Meeting on CVNRA, May 22, 1980, JFS office files, A137.

41. JFS to William Birdsell, May 25, 1980, JFS office files, A137.

42. *ABJ,* Aug. 17, 19, 1980.

43. Lewis Albert to Regional Director, Dec. 11, 1980, JFS office files, X9.

44. JFS to Ralph Gillman, Mar. 6, 1981, JFS office files, A147.

45. Nelson, *Northern Landscapes,* 232–33.

46. Quoted in ibid., 230.

47. Quoted in ibid., 234.

48. Elizabeth A. Lyon and David L. S. Brook, "The States: The Backbone of Preservation," in *A Richer Heritage: Historic Preservation in the Twenty-First Century,* ed. Robert E. Stipe (Chapel Hill: Univ. of North Carolina Press, 2003), 84. Also see Philip A. Scarpino, "Planning for Preservation: A Look at the Federal-State Historic Preservation Program, 1966–1986," *Public*

Historian 14 (Spring 1992): 49–66; "House Interior Committee Meeting on H.R. 6504, March 18, 1980," Neumann Papers.

49. Quoted in Nelson, *Northern Landscapes,* 241.

50. JFS interview, May 5, 1998, Neumann Papers.

51. Nelson, *Northern Landscapes,* 256–61.

52. Ibid., 255–56; Sierra Club Legal Defense Fund, *In Brief,* November 1982, 3.

53. See Andy Wiessner, "Wilderness Legislation and Action, 1963–78," in Wiessner to JFS, Feb. 26, 1979; "Wilderness/Release History," JFS Papers, Box 230:15.

54. JFS interview, Apr. 26, 1997, Neumann Papers. Also Andy Wiessner to Loretta Neumann, Mar. 21, 2000, Neumann Papers.

55. Dennis M. Roth, *The Wilderness Movement and the National Forests, 1980–1984* (Washington, D.C.: USDA Forest Service History Series, n.d.), 52.

56. Laine Heiser, "RARE II, Forest Service New Mexico Workshops," Wilderness Society Papers, Box 3:12.

57. Clary, *Timber,* 176.

58. "Democratic Subcommittee Caucus," Mar. 21, 1979, Seiberling-Denver Papers, Box 20:10.

59. Roth, *Wilderness Movement, 1980–1984,* 52–53.

60. JFS interview, Apr. 26–27, 1997, Neumann Papers.

61. Andy Wiessner to Morris Udall, JFS, Sept. 18, 1979, Seiberling-Denver Papers, Box 20:10.

62. Ibid.

63. "Democratic Subcommittee Caucus," Mar. 21, 1979, Seiberling-Denver Papers, Box 20:10.

64. *Redding Record Searchlight,* July 3, 1979; *Trinity Journal,* July 5, 1979.

65. Jim Eaton statement, Nov. 13, 1979, JFS office files, C18.

66. See Peter Kirby to Bill Turnage, Apr. 18, 1980, Wilderness Society Papers, Box 4:63; Joe Fontaine and William M. Thomas to JFS, July 24, 1980, SCNLO Papers, Box 145.

67. Tim Mahoney to John McComb et al., July 18, 1979, SCNLO Papers, Box 145.

68. Mahoney to McComb et al., July 18, 1979; Sierra Club, *National News Report* 12 (Jan. 11, 1980): 1.

69. JFS interview, Apr. 26–27, 1997, Neumann Papers.

70. JFS to Don H. Clausen, Aug. 1, 1980, JFS office files, A138.

71. *Sierra Club Newsletter,* Aug. 7, 1980; Doug Scott, Tim Mahoney et al. to John Hooper and Carl Pope, Aug. 18, 1980, SCNLO Papers, Box 145.

72. Text of HR 7702, JFS office files, C18.

73. Russ Shay to California Wilderness Leaders, Sept. 6, 1980, SCNLO Papers, Box 145.

74. Russ Shay to Friends, Dec. 19, 1980, SCNLO Papers, Box 145.

75. See Rupert Cutler to JFS, May 12, 1980; JFS to Gary Hart, May 13, 1980, Seiberling-Denver Papers, Box 20:10; Harry Crandell to JFS, Apr. 17, 1980, Seiberling-Denver Papers, Box 20:11.

76. Craig W. Allin, "Wilderness Policy," in *Western Public Lands and Environmental Politics*, ed. Charles Davis (Boulder, Colo.: Westview, 2001), 213.

77. *Idaho Statesman*, Feb. 6, 1980; "Environmental Study Committee Floor Brief, March 31, 1980," Seiberling-Denver Papers, Box 23:4; Dave Foreman and Howie Wolke, *The Big Outside: A Descriptive Inventory of the Big Wilderness Areas of the U.S.* (New York: Harmony Books, 1992), 89.

78. Itinerary, May 18–19, 1979, JFS office files, A222.

79. Itineraries, June 29–July 6, Aug. 3–21, 1979, JFS office files, A22.

80. Wiessner to JFS, Sept. 19, 1980, JFS office files, C19.

81. JFS interview, Apr. 26, 1997, Neumann Papers.

82. JFS to Lee Hamilton, Apr. 18, 1980; Paul Simon to M. K. Udall, May 21, 1999, JFS office files, C19.

83. Wiessner to JFS, Dec. 24, 1980, Seiberling-Denver Papers, Box 20:11.

8. Confronting Adversity, 1981–84

1. *ABJ*, Dec. 8, 1981.

2. See, e.g., Lou Cannon, *President Reagan: The Role of a Lifetime* (New York: Simon and Schuster, 1991), 85–86; Jeffrey K. Stine, "Natural Resources and Environmental Policy," in *The Reagan Presidency: Pragmatic Conservatism and Its Legacies*, ed. W. Elliot Brownlee and Hugh Graham Davis (Lawrence: Univ. Press of Kansas, 2003), 233–56; Ronnie Dugger, *On Reagan: The Man and His Presidency* (New York: McGraw-Hill, 1983), chap. 4; Robert F. Durant, *The Administrative Presidency Revisited: Public Lands, the BLM, and the Reagan Revolution* (Albany: SUNY Press, 1992), chap. 3. Watt defended his actions in James Watt with Doug Wead, *The Courage of a Conservative* (New York: Simon and Schuster, 1985).

3. JFS interview, Apr. 26–27, 1997, Neumann Papers.

4. Ron Wolf, "New Voice in the Wilderness," *Rocky Mountain Magazine*, [1981], 29–34, Seiberling-Denver Papers, Box 26:27.

5. Ron Arnold, *At the Eye of the Storm: James Watt and the Environmentalists* (Chicago: Regnery Gateway, 1982), 55. Also see Benjamin Ginsberg and Martin Shefter, *Politics by Other Means: Politicians, Prosecutors, and the Press from Watergate to Whitewater* (New York: W. W. Norton, 1999), 104–8.

6. Cleve Pinnix interview, Mar. 28, 1998, Neumann Papers.

7. Wolf, "New Voice," 32; "Supplementary Fact Sheet on James G. Watt," [ca. 1981], JFS office files, C5.

8. See William L. Graf, *Wilderness Preservation and the Sagebrush Rebellions* (Savage, Md.: Rowman and Littlefield, 1990), 225–31. Also see Robert H. Nelson, *Public Lands and Private Rights: The Failure of Scientific Management* (Lanham, Md.: Rowman and Littlefield, 1995), 170–85.

9. Wolf, "New Voice," 33.

10. Cannon, *President Reagan*, 330.

11. "Supplementary Fact Sheet on James G. Watt," JFS office files, C5.

12. JFS to William D. Ford, Mar. 4, 1982, Seiberling-Denver Papers, Box 20:14.

13. Loretta Neumann Note, Interior Department Press Release, Dec. 1, 1981, JFS office files, C5.

14. *New York Times,* Aug. 20, 1981.

15. *Washington Post,* May 20, 1982.

16. James G. Watt to Ronald Reagan, Jan. 20, 1983, Seiberling-Denver Papers, Box 26.

17. *New York Times,* Nov. 13, 1981.

18. *Washington Post,* Feb. 24, 1982.

19. *San Jose Mercury,* Feb. 23, 1982.

20. *Washington Post,* Mar. 19, 1982.

21. Andrew Wiessner to JFS, Mar. 27, 1981, Seiberling-Denver Papers, Box 20:13.

22. Arnold, *Eye of the Storm,* 159; Stine, "Natural Resources," 233–36.

23. James Watt to JFS, Apr. 20, 1981, JFS office files, C5; Arnold, *Eye of the Storm,* 104.

24. Ray Arnett to Russell Dickenson, Apr. 23, 1981, JFS office files, A109.

25. *ABJ,* May 15, 1981.

26. Subcommittee Staff, "Brief Chronology of the NPS Land Acquisition Program," July 25, 1983, Neumann Papers.

27. JFS interview, Apr. 26–27, 1997, Neumann Papers.

28. Loretta Neumann to JFS, May 15, 1981, JFS office files, C5.

29. Associated Press Release, May 13, 1981, JFS office files, A109.

30. JFS interview, Dec. 1, 1997, Neumann Papers.

31. *ABJ,* Apr. 7, 1982.

32. *ABJ,* Apr. 2, 1982.

33. *ABJ,* June 7, 1982.

34. Andy [Wiessner] to JFS, May 14, 1981, Neumann Papers.

35. Harry Crandell to JFS, Mar. 31, 1981, Seiberling-Denver Papers, Box 20:13.

36. JFS to James J. Blanchard, May 29, 1981, JFS office files, A148.

37. *Washington Post,* May 21, 1981.

38. Christopher J. Bosso, *Environment, Inc.: From Grassroots to Beltway* (Lawrence: Univ. Press of Kansas, 2005), 56–57.

39. Ronald Reagan, *The Reagan Diaries,* ed. Douglas Brinkley (New York: HarperCollins, 2007), 85.

40. John F. Seiberling, "To Make a Difference . . . Reagan Administration and Interior Department," 4.

41. Subcommittee Staff, "Land Acquisition Policy and Program of the National Park Service," June 1984, 12, 16, Neumann Papers.

42. Uday Desai, *Moving the Earth: Cooperative Federalism and Implementation of the Surface Mining Act* (Westport, Conn.: Greenwood Press, 1993), 21.

43. "Let's Make an Election Year Deal," *National Journal* (Feb. 24, 1979): 317.

44. Oversight Hearings before the Subcommittee on Energy and the Environment, 96th Cong., 1st sess., March 5–6, 1979, 65.

45. "Statement of James C. Watt, March 6, 1981," JFS office files, A148; James M. McElfish Jr., "The Surface Mining Control and Reclamation Act and Environmental Groups," in Desai, *Moving the Earth*, 69.
46. Donal C. Menzel, "Creating a Regulatory Agency: Profile of the Office of Surface Mining," in Desai, *Moving the Earth*, 36.
47. Ibid., 38.
48. McElfish, "Surface Mining," 71.
49. Oversight Hearings before the Subcommittee on Energy and the Environment, 97th Cong., 1st sess., July 16, 1981, 6.
50. Ibid., 18.
51. Ibid., 28.
52. Ibid., 88.
53. Ibid., 19.
54. Ibid., 28.
55. David Howard Davis, "Energy on Federal Lands," in *Western Public Lands and Environmental Politics*, ed. Charles Davis (Boulder, Colo.: Westview, 2001), 157.
56. Wiessner to JFS, Apr. 8, 1981, Seiberling-Denver Papers, Box 20:14.
57. Tim Mahoney to various, Aug. 18, 1981, Wilderness Society Papers, Box 4:6.
58. "Press Release, House Committee on the Interior," *Los Angeles Times*, Feb. 10, 1983.
59. *Los Angeles Times*, Feb. 10, 1983.
60. See Russ Shay to various, Jan. 22, 1983, SCNLO Papers, Box 145.
61. Tim Mahoney, John Hoopes to various, Feb. 11, 1983, SCNLO Papers, Box 145.
62. Wiessner to JFS, May 3, 1982, Seiberling-Denver Papers, Box 20:14.
63. Roth, *Wilderness Movement*, 62–63.
64. Tim Mahoney to Joe Fontaine et al., Aug. 18, 1981, Wilderness Society Papers, Box 4:6.
65. *Trinity Journal*, May 22, 1981.
66. *Trinity Journal*, May 28, 1981.
67. Russ Shay to Wilderness Leaders, May 27, 1981, SCNLO Papers, Box 145.
68. Richard G. Reid to Eugene Chappie, May 26, 1981; JFS to Eugene Chappie, June 8, 1981, JFS office files, C18.
69. See Russ Shay to Wilderness Leaders, May 27, 1981, SCNLO Papers, Box 145.
70. Northwest letter, July 27, 1981, SCNLO Papers, Box 145.
71. Tim Mahoney to Joe Fontaine et al., Aug. 18, 1981, Wilderness Society Papers, Box 4:6.
72. Mark J. Palmer to Interested Parties, Apr. 8, 1983, SCNLO Papers, Box 145.
73. Richard G. Reid to California Industry Land Withdrawal Committee, Mar. 7, 1983, JFS office files, C18.
74. JFS interview, Apr. 26–27, 1997, Neumann Papers; Russ Shay to Friends, Apr. 19, 1983, SCNLO Papers, Box 145.
75. Shay to Friends, Apr. 19, 1983, SCNLO Papers, Box 145.

76. *San Francisco Examiner,* Feb. 10, 1984.
77. Shay to Edgar Wayburn, Mar. 8, 1984, SCNLO Papers, Box 146.
78. *New York Times,* Feb. 12, 1984.
79. JFS interview, Apr. 27, 1997, Neumann Papers.
80. Shay to Wilderness Activists, May 5, 1984, SCNLO Papers, Box 146.
81. Ibid.; JFS to Ansel Adams, Apr. 6, 1984, Seiberling-Denver Papers, Box 21:19.
82. Shay to Activists, June 1984, SCNLO Papers, Box 146.
83. *Los Angeles Times,* Sept. 13, 1984.
84. Ibid.
85. *Sacramento Bee,* Sept. 13, 1984.
86. *San Francisco Chronicle,* Sept. 13, 1984.
87. JFS interview, Oct. 11, 1998, Neumann Papers.
88. See "Confidential Working Draft," Nov. 3, 1983, Seiberling-Denver Papers, Box 26:12.
89. Peter Kirby and Mark Anderson, "Report on Interim Protection of Non-Wilderness RARE II Areas," June 18, 1983, Wilderness Society Papers, Box 4:6.
90. Shay to Wilderness Activists, May 5, 1984, SCNLO Papers, Box 146.
91. JFS interview, Oct. 18, 1997, Neumann Papers.
92. Wiessner to JFS, Oct. 3, 1983, JFS office files, C17.
93. *Deseret News,* May 29, 1984.
94. JFS interview, Oct. 17, 1997, Neumann Papers.
95. Ron Tipton to Bill Turnage et al., Mar. 4, 1981, Wilderness Society Papers, Box 4:75.
96. Philip Hocker to Wiessner, Aug. 15, 1979, JFS office files, C17.
97. Hocker to Loretta Neumann, Sept. 17, 2006, Neumann Papers.
98. JFS to Malcolm Wallop, Aug. 26, 1981, Seiberling-Denver Papers, Box 20.
99. *Caspar Star Tribune,* Apr. 16, 1983.
100. *Lander (WY) High Country News,* July 22, 1983.
101. Wiessner to JFS, Sept. 21, 1983, JFS office files, C17.
102. Harry Crandell memo, Sept. 22, 1983, Seiberling-Denver Papers, Box 26:12.
103. "Confidential Working Draft," Nov. 3, 1983, Seiberling-Denver Papers Box 26:12; *Caspar Star Tribune,* Dec. 5, 1985.
104. JFS to Richard Cheney, Feb. 8, 1984, JFS office files, C17.
105. *Caspar Star Tribune,* Feb. 10, 1984.
106. JFS to Philip Hocker, Apr. 12, 1984, JFS office files, A55.
107. John R. Barlow, Stuart C. Thompson to JFS, Mar. 1, 1984, JFS office files, C17.
108. See Ted Kerasote, "Landed People: The Creation of the Wyoming Wilderness Association," in *Ahead of Their Time: Wyoming Voices for Wilderness,* ed. Broughton Coburn and Leila Bruno (n.p., Wyoming Wilderness Association, 2004), 183.

109. JFS to Loring Woodman, Dec. 21, 1984, JFS office files, A55.
110. JFS interview, Feb. 1, 2002, Neumann Papers.
111. Fairfax et al., *Buying Nature,* chap. 7.

9. Retirement

1. JFS to Phil Hocker, Apr. 12, 1984, JFS office files, A55.
2. John Hamilton, "Fare Thee Well John Seiberling," *Sierra* (November–December 1986): 54.
3. Tom Diemer, "Coming Home," *Plain Dealer Magazine,* Nov. 2, 1986, 8.
4. Hamilton, "Fare Thee Well," 54.
5. *ABJ,* July 20, 1973.
6. Ibid.
7. Andy Wiessner to JFS, June 28, 1985, JFS office files, C19.
8. Shay to JFS, July 21, 1986, JFS office files, C19.
9. JFS interview, Oct. 17, 1997, Neumann Papers.
10. Ibid.
11. Diemer, "Coming Home," 8.
12. JFS, "To Make a Difference . . . U.S. European Parliamentary Exchange," 16–17.
13. Ibid., 9.
14. Diemer, "Coming Home," 8.
15. Ibid.
16. JFS, "To Make a Difference . . . Post-ANILCA Alaska," 6.
17. *Anchorage Times,* Aug. 16, 1983.
18. JFS interview, Apr. 26, 1997, Neumann Papers.
19. JFS, "To Make a Difference . . . 1985 Committee Trip to Siberia and Russia," 3, 12.
20. William Hershey, "From Lawmaker to Peacemaker," *Beacon Magazine,* Feb. 27, 1994, 8.
21. Diemer, "Coming Home," 8.
22. Donald N. Stull, "The Dynamics of Standing Still: Firestone Tire and Rubber and the Radial Revolution," *Business History Review* 73 (Autumn 1999): 430–64.
23. *ABJ,* Nov. 18–20, 1986. Also Steve Love and David Giffels, *Wheels of Fortune: The Story of Rubber in Akron* (Akron, Ohio: Univ. of Akron Press, 1999), 251.
24. JFS interview, Apr. 28, 1997, Neumann Papers.
25. Loretta to JFS, Sept. 16, 1986, Neumann Papers.
26. "Farewell Party, 1986, Song from 'Gigi,'" Neumann Papers.
27. JFS, "To Make a Difference . . . Retirement," 7–8.
28. Ibid., 11.
29. Ibid., 10–11.

30. Diemer, "Coming Home," 8.
31. Jeanne Nienaber Clarke and Kurt Angersbach, "The Federal Four," in *Western Public Lands and Environmental Politics,* ed. Charles Davis (Boulder, Colo.: Westview, 2001), 39. For the subsequent years and the legacy of the 1960s–1980s, see Christopher McGrory Klyza and David J. Sousa, *American Environmental Policy, 1990–2006: Beyond Gridlock* (Cambridge, Mass.: MIT Press, 2008), esp. chap. 8, and Robert B. Keiter, *Keeping Faith with Nature: Ecosystems, Democracy, and America's Public Lands* (New Haven, Ct.: Yale Univ. Press, 2003).
32. JFS to Ron Hoppe, Mar. 28, 1980, JFS office files, C18.
33. JFS, "To Make a Difference . . . Postscript," 1.

Bibliographical Note

John Seiberling has received remarkably little attention in the many books on late twentieth-century American politics and public policy that have appeared in the last quarter century. This is due partly to the remarkable variety of the subject matter and partly, perhaps mostly, to Seiberling's personal reticence and distaste for the contrived publicity that is the contemporary politician's stock-in-trade. In any case, his relative invisibility has meant that virtually all of the information in this work has come from unpublished sources or contemporary newspaper accounts.

There are a number of important manuscript sources that document Seiberling's activities—so many, in fact, that they require some explanation. The largest, in terms of volume and significance, is the Seiberling collection at the University of Akron Archives. I have labeled this collection the Seiberling office files (or JFS office files, in Notes). It consists of more than three hundred boxes, provides information on most aspects of Seiberling's congressional career, and is an indispensable source on environmental policy during the years of his service. A recently completed finding aid has greatly simplified its use.

Harry Crandell, who headed the staff when Seiberling chaired the House interior subcommittee on public lands, donated his office files to the Denver Public Library and created a second John F. Seiberling collection. Predictably, there is some overlap with the Akron papers; many of Andy Wiessner's long memos on wilderness bills appear in both collections, for example. I have called the Denver materials the Seiberling-Denver Papers to distinguish them from the Akron Seiberling papers.

There is a third Seiberling collection, a small group of personal papers and letters, including letters to and from Seiberling's mother, Henrietta. This material is privately held at the Seiberlings' home. I have called these materials simply the John F. Seiberling Papers.

Also, there are two major collections of Seiberling family papers, the Frank A. and J. Penfield collections, both at the Ohio Historical Society in Columbus.

Both are voluminous and both provide rare insight into the activities of a large and remarkable family.

Apart from the various Seiberling collections, the best sources on Seiberling's congressional career are the records of the environmental groups that promoted national park and wilderness initiatives. The Wilderness Society and the Sierra Club archives, at the Denver Public Library and the Bancroft Library, University of California, Berkeley, respectively, contain enormous quantities of material on virtually everything that interested Seiberling and are indispensable sources on environmental politics in the late twentieth century.

The other major unpublished resource for this study was the large collection of transcribed interviews and correspondence that Loretta Neumann collected, with the support of the American Conservation Association and the George Gund Foundation, and recently donated to the University of Akron Archives. In the 1990s she conducted numerous interviews with Seiberling and many former members of his personal and subcommittee staffs. The collection also includes the materials that her husband, Tedd McCann, preserved from his associations with the CVNRA.

The Robert L. Hunker Papers, at Hunker's foundation in Peninsula, Ohio, and the James Jackson Papers, at the University of Akron, contain additional information on the formative years of the CVNRA.

Seiberling's career can also be traced in the work of the congressional committees on which he served. The special Alaska subcommittee of 1977 was especially notable, and the multivolume record of its hearings is one of the most significant snapshots of grassroots reform activity in the twentieth-century American experience. The hearings also afforded Seiberling a rare opportunity to express his own views on a variety of subjects related to the Alaskan lands issue. Together with his comments in the many hearings on strip-mining and wilderness that preceded and followed the Alaska legislation, they document a perspective that reflected his personal background, long-held views on preserving the natural world, and concerns about the future.

Index